FROM BOER WAR TO WORLD WAR

CAMPAIGNS & COMMANDERS

GREGORY J. W. URWIN, SERIES EDITOR

FROM BOER WAR TO WORLD WAR

Tactical Reform of the British Army, 1902–1914

Spencer Jones

University of Oklahoma Press : Norman

This book is published with the generous assistance
of The Kerr Foundation, Inc.

Library of Congress Cataloging-in-Publication Data

Jones, Spencer, 1981–
  From Boer War to World War : tactical reform of the British Army,
1902–1914 / Spencer Jones.
    p. cm.
  ISBN 978-08061-4289-0 (cloth)
  ISBN 978-08061-4415-3 (paper)
  Includes bibliographical references and index.
1. Great Britain. Army—History—20th century. 2. Great Britain. Army—
Drill and tactics—History—20th century. 3. Tactics—History—20th
century. I. Title.
  UA649.J66 2012
  355.4'2094109041—dc23

                                                            2012013996

*From Boer War to World War: Tactical Reform of the British Army,
1902–1914* is Volume 35 in the Campaigns and Commanders series.

The paper in this book meets the guidelines for permanence and durability
of the Committee on Production Guidelines for Book Longevity of the
Council on Library Resources, Inc. ∞

Copyright © 2012 by the University of Oklahoma Press, Norman,
Publishing Division of the University. Paperback published 2013.
Manufactured in the U.S.A.

To my parents

Contents

ILLUSTRATIONS

MAPS

FIGURES

All figures are from H. W. Wilson, *With the Flag to Pretoria: A History of the Boer War of 1899–1900* (London: Harmsworth Brothers Limited, 1900). For certain illustrations Wilson provided a specific credit, which has been included in the caption.

ACKNOWLEDGMENTS

The genesis of this work can be traced back to a casual conversation with John Buckley over a cafeteria lunch. John suggested a new study of the influence of the Boer War on the British Army would be an interesting topic to tackle. The seed of this idea developed a life of its own and ultimately produced the book that you now hold before you.

The completion of the work owes a great deal to the encouragement of John Buckley and Stephen Badsey. Each read innumerable drafts of the manuscript, discussed ideas, and shared his own research. Furthermore, their support of my fledging academic career during a time of great economic uncertainty ensured that I did not abandon the subject of history entirely. I also owe particular thanks to Stephen for his generosity in offering indefinite loans of hard-to-acquire books from his private collection.

A wide variety of people contributed to the development of the work, providing advice, assistance, or encouragement. Particular thanks are owed to the late Paddy Griffith, Mark Connelly, Fransjohan Pretorius, Gary Sheffield, John Bourne, Nicholas Evans, Howard Fuller, Jim Beach, Matthew Ford, and Ken Gillings. I would also like to record my gratitude to Kimberly Kinne, my copyeditor at the

University of Oklahoma Press, who added polish to the manuscript and demonstrated great patience with my endless queries.

My research would not have been possible without the help of the staff of numerous libraries and archives, including the University of Wolverhampton Learning Centre, Birmingham Central Library, University of Cambridge Library, the British Library, the National Archives, the National Army Museum, the Royal Artillery Museum, the Imperial War Museum, the Liddell Hart Centre for Military Archives, and the Royal United Services Institute.

I owe thanks to the University of Wolverhampton Learning Centre for providing copyright advice and support regarding the pictures used in this book. A special thank you is also reserved for Jon Burrage, who spent countless hours carefully scanning and digitizing the original pictures.

On a more personal note, I would like to thank my friends, who have been rocks of support throughout the creation of this work. While there are too many names to list in full, I would like to offer particular thanks to Andy, Jon, Richard, and Leeann (and Alexander) for always being ready to listen, sympathize, and, above all, encourage. I also owe special thanks to my former English teacher, Mary Hawthorne, for providing me with the "tools" to write this book!

Last but by no means least, I would like to express my gratitude to my family and parents, for offering timely financial assistance and endless moral encouragement. During the most difficult periods of my research, their love and support ensured that I did not abandon my studies. I have dedicated the work to my parents as a small token of thanks for their selfless support, for without it the book would never have been started, let alone completed.

MAPS

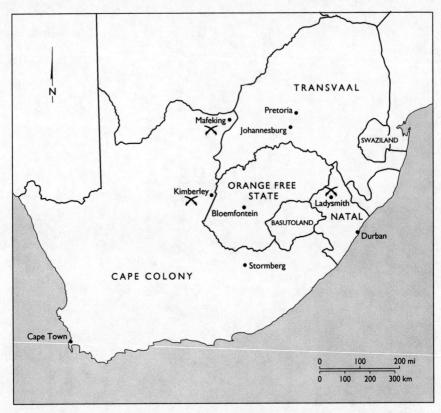

South Africa and bordering states, including British towns besieged by the Boers in 1899.

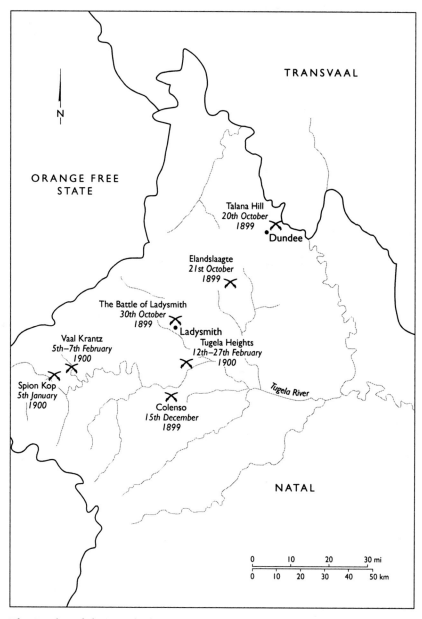

TRANSVAAL

ORANGE FREE
STATE

Talana Hill
20th October
1899
●Dundee

Elandslaagte
21st October
1899

The Battle of Ladysmith
30th October
1899
●Ladysmith

Vaal Krantz
5th–7th February
1900

Tugela Heights
12th–27th February
1900

Spion Kop
5th January
1900

Tugela River

Colenso
15th December
1899

NATAL

| 0 | 10 | 20 | 30 mi |
| 0 | 10 | 20 | 30 | 40 | 50 km |

The Battles of the Natal Theater, 1899–1900.

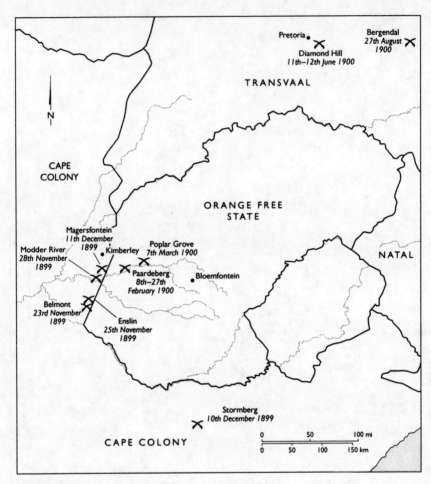

The Battles of the Western Theater, 1899–1900.

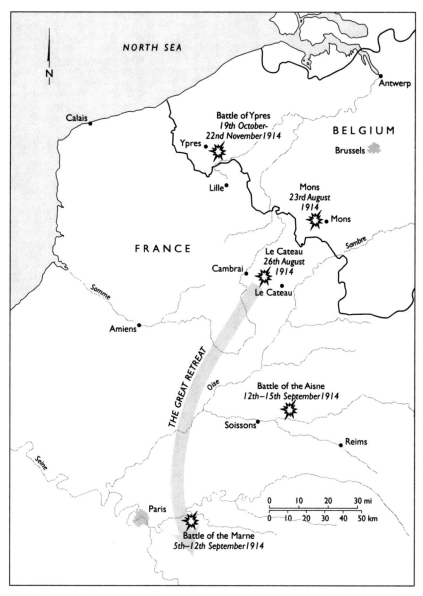

The Battles of the British Expeditionary Force in Belgium and France, 1914.

From Boer War to World War

INTRODUCTION

On 4 August 1914, Great Britain declared war on Germany as a response to the German invasion of neutral Belgium. In doing so, Britain joined the conflict that would swell into the First World War and committed its small, professional army to a continental struggle for the first time since the defeat of Napoleon, almost a century earlier.

The British Expeditionary Force (BEF) deployed to France was tiny by the standards of the armies fielded by the other belligerent powers. Its peacetime paper strength consisted of six infantry divisions and a single cavalry division, with a fighting establishment of approximately 120,000 men.[1] Furthermore, the BEF deployed to France was not initially at full strength—it consisted of four infantry divisions and an independent infantry brigade, supported by the cavalry division and an independent cavalry brigade. The remaining two divisions were held in reserve in England, although both were soon deployed as reinforcements.[2]

The senior commanders of the BEF had learned their craft in the colonial wars of the previous century. In particular, the army commander Field Marshal Sir John French; his two corps commanders,

Lieutenant-General Sir Douglas Haig and General Sir Horace Smith-Dorrien;[3] and leader of the cavalry division, Major-General Edmund Allenby, had all served with varying degrees of success in the Boer War of 1899–1902. However, only a small handful of their men had any combat experience, and almost a third of their troops had been with the army for two years or less.[4]

The British Army appeared a fragile instrument when compared with the armies of France, Russia, and Germany, whose manpower numbered in the millions. However, its one great advantage lay in its professional roots, which allowed it to achieve a considerably higher standard of individual training than the mass conscript forces deployed by the continental powers. Basil Liddell Hart aptly described the BEF as "a rapier among scythes"—small, flexible, and deadly if handled with skill but vulnerable to destruction from the sheer weight of its opponent's blows.

The BEF concentrated between Maubeuge and Le Cateau near the Franco-Belgian border between 12–19 August 1914.[5] Conscious of the need to remain close to the Channel ports and supplies from England, the British were to operate on the left flank of the front, with the intention of advancing into Belgium to support the Belgians in their fight against the German invaders. A scattering of French territorial forces covered the British left flank, while the French Fifth Army[6] was operating to its right. The main French effort was to be made farther to the south, where a major offensive was underway into the territories of Alsace-Lorraine. It was assumed that it was here that the war would be decided.

However, the small British force had been unwittingly placed directly in the path of an oncoming German juggernaut. Allied intelligence had failed to identify that the main German effort, commonly known as the "Schlieffen Plan," involved a massive offensive through Belgium that would aim to outflank and surround the concentration of French armies opposite Alsace-Lorraine, thus destroying France's military power in one sweeping blow. Largely unaware of the dangers that faced them, the BEF advanced into Belgium with the intention of conducting offensive action against the Germans. Cavalry and aerial reconnaissance soon began to bring reports of an ominous concentration of enemy strength in Belgium, but such reports were initially disregarded by John French and his overoptimistic staff.[7]

The advancing Germans consisted of First Army under the leadership of Alexander von Kluck supported by elements of Second Army under Karl von Bülow. The Germans were almost equally ignorant of the presence of the British. German cavalry struggled to break through the British cavalry screen, and the handful of accurate reports that were made were apparently ignored by von Kluck's headquarters. It seems that little importance was attached to the presence of the BEF in the theater of operations. Its small size and supposedly limited fighting qualities apparently inspired Kaiser Wilhelm II to issue a notorious army order dated 19 August 1914, in which he urged his troops to "exterminate first the treacherous English and walk over General [John] French's contemptible little army."[8] It was from this reference that the BEF drew the nickname "The Old Contemptibles."

Somewhat ignorant of their opponent's strength and intentions, both armies advanced, which led to a collision at the Battle of Mons on 23 August 1914. A confused encounter battle followed. The smaller British force defended an awkward position among small mining villages and slag heaps, using the line of the Mons canal as a natural obstacle. The British official history described it as "close and blind country."[9] The full force of the German attack fell on Smith-Dorrien's II Corps, with Haig's I Corps essentially unengaged throughout the battle. Clumsy German attacks were initially beaten back, but renewed assaults were gradually able to gain a foothold over the canal.[10] The British position was soon untenable. With mounting pressure to the front and with news that French forces were retreating on the flanks, the BEF found itself in danger of encirclement. The decision was made to fall back to the southwest, but the proximity of German forces made this a perilous exercise. Fierce and sometimes costly rearguard actions were fought throughout the 24th and 25th of August as the BEF began what would become known as the "Great Retreat."

Although it was envisaged as a temporary expedient by several senior officers, the retreat from Mons would become one of the great epics of British military history. Dogged by German pursuit and concerned about the reliability of French allies on the flanks, the retreat was soon in danger of losing cohesion. John French and his staff failed to coordinate the retreat effectively, causing I and II Corps to lose touch with one another. This problem became critical as the two formations passed either side of the Forest of Mormal on the 25th of August. Harried by pursuing German forces, II Corps found itself in a potentially disastrous position. Informed by Allenby that the disordered cavalry would not be able to screen his retreating infantry on 26 August, Smith-Dorrien took a calculated gamble. German pursuit was closing in, and the risk of being caught in marching order was too great to allow the retreat to continue; instead, Smith-Dorrien resolved to turn and fight in an attempt to deal the enemy a "stopping blow" and thus buy time for a continued withdrawal.[11]

The result of this decision was the Battle of Le Cateau on 26 August 1914. In contrast to the built-up environment of Mons, the battlefield was described by one participant as "Salisbury Plain without the trees."[12] The British position was far from ideal. The fighting of the previous three days had caused severe dislocation of the chain of command, with companies becoming separated from their parent battalions. A number of units were still arriving on the field during the early hours of the morning and were forced to prepare for battle without rest. There was little time to dig earthworks for the coming action, an endeavor further complicated by the relentless August heat and the exhaustion of many of the soldiers.[13] Most seriously, both of II Corps's flanks were vulnerable, particularly on the right, where it was erroneously assumed I Corps would provide support.

The Battle of Le Cateau was a bloody encounter. Numerically superior German artillery and machine guns pounded the British positions throughout the day, while rapid British rifle fire broke up German infantry and cavalry attacks. By mid-afternoon, German forces were exerting great pressure to the front and lapping around the open right flank of the British position; it was clear to Smith-Dorrien that now was the time to withdraw. Although the bulk of II Corps was able to fall back, British casualties were heavier than at Mons, including thirty-eight artillery pieces abandoned on the field.

However, the stand had achieved its desired objective. It had delayed the German advance and given II Corps crucial breathing space. German cavalry continued the pursuit, and there were sharp rearguard actions throughout August and early September, but the movements of the main body of the BEF were not seriously threatened for the remainder of the retreat. Despite the easing of enemy pressure, the movement remained an exhausting undertaking for the troops involved. As one soldier grumbled, "After the first couple of days at Mons, we seem to have spent our time just marching and crossing rivers. . . . It had been very hot and very tiring. . . . Some of our battalion were certainly in a bad way with their feet worn raw."[14]

It was not until 4 September that the retreat finally came to an end and the BEF enjoyed a well-earned rest day. This was to prove a short respite, as the wider struggle between France and Germany was approaching a decisive point. In a continuation of the principles of the Schlieffen Plan, the main German offensive had wheeled south, intending to pass to the east of Paris and trap French armies against the Franco-German border. However, a dangerous gap had opened up between von Kluck's First Army and von Bulow's Second Army. Joseph Joffre, French supreme commander, identified this gap as offering an opportunity to deliver a devastating Allied riposte.

The result was the Battle of the Marne (5–12 September 1914). A full examination of this complex and important struggle is beyond the scope of this work.[15] The BEF played a small but important part, with larger French forces bearing the brunt of the fighting. Through a combination of luck and skill, the German armies were able to avoid being encircled or defeated in detail but were forced to retreat approximately sixty miles to the north to the line of the river Aisne. The bold attempt to crush France in a single great offensive was defeated at the Marne. Although the German armies had escaped destruction, for the German war effort the battle represented a decisive strategic defeat.

British involvement in the combat of early September was characterized by a series of fighting advances against a withdrawing enemy. Casualties during four days of fighting (6–10 September) were lower than those suffered during a single day at the Battle of Mons.[16] However, the situation changed dramatically as the BEF reached the Aisne. German forces had taken up strong defensive positions and had benefitted from reinforcement with heavy artillery, freshly available as siege operations in Belgium came to a close. In the Battle of the Aisne (12–15 September), an initial British offensive secured bridgeheads across the river, but attempts to expand these and drive the Germans from their positions proved costly and were ultimately unsuccessful. It was clear that the pursuit that had begun on the Marne was over.

However, the rapid movements that had characterized the German drive south during August and September 1914 had left the northern flank largely unoccupied. Both sides now sought to exploit this area of open space to turn the flanks of their opponent. The area was particularly crucial to the British, as control of the coast and Channel ports was essential for continued supply.[17] From 8 to 19 October, the BEF redeployed to the Franco-Belgian frontier. The army was now strengthened to a total of five corps of two divisions each, for a total of seven infantry and three cavalry divisions.[18] There was also additional support from the recently arrived Indian Corps.[19] The British forces were to be a single component of a much larger Allied effort in this area, with support from Belgian troops and redeployed French armies.

The result of this redeployment was the epic series of battles commonly known as the First Battle of Ypres, fought between 19 October and 22 November 1914.[20] A full account of this vast struggle is beyond the scope of this work; only a brief outline can be given here.[21] The town of Ypres was to form the focal point of the campaign. By early October, Ypres was the only major Belgian town still in the hands of its own people, lending it unique emotional and political significance. It was also a vital center of communications and transportation, and whoever controlled it held the key to the north coast of France. The intention of the German offensives in this area was to break through the Allied lines and capture Calais.[22] In doing so, they would turn the left flank of the Allied armies and choke the line of the supply for the BEF. The Allies initially held hopes for an offensive into Belgium to liberate Brussels, but their aggressive posture was gradually abandoned in the face of greater weight of German men and material. From 19 October onward, the Allies, and particularly the British, were forced to withstand a series of sustained German offensives.

The German offensives were supported by a great weight of artillery that the British were unable to match. This disparity was exacerbated by a serious shortage of ammunition among British batteries, with shells being rationed on a daily basis.[23] Yet, although outnumbered and outgunned, the British line somehow withstood the repeated hammer blows. On several occasions the front line was partially broken, and desperate measures were used to fill the gaps. Troops from broken or disorganized units formed improvised groups under local leaders, while rear area troops such as engineers, drivers, and even mess servants were drafted into the front line.[24] The cost of this tenacious defense was immense. Casualties were severe on both sides, with several British regiments losing their entire compliment of officers and others being reduced to less than a third of their paper strength.[25] On several occasions, the result of the battle hung in the balance, and only the grim resolve of the defenders prevented a collapse. One British officer recorded in his diary during a critical period of fighting, "We were only clinging to the ground by our eyelids."[26]

The First Battle of Ypres highlighted many of the strengths of the BEF. It was a soldier's battle, in which the intentions of higher command were often rendered irrelevant by the tactical realities of the front line. In such circumstances, a great deal of responsibility fell on the junior and noncommissioned officers of the army. Fortunately for the British, the training and professionalism of the force meant that even in the face of severe casualties, units were able to retain a degree of coherence and continue to defend key positions.[27] Although short of artillery and machine guns, British infantry and cavalry had been trained in peacetime to deliver fifteen aimed shots in sixty seconds, in an exercise known as the "mad minute." At Ypres, this rapid rifle fire proved devastating against densely packed German assault columns.[28] For example, during fierce fighting on 31 October 1914, British troops produced such a volume of fire that an official German account refers to large quantities of machine guns being used.[29] Indeed, the same official history of the battle makes repeated reference to the British numerical advantage in machine guns, but in fact the exact opposite was true. Instead, it seems that rapid, sustained rifle fire was mistaken for machine guns by inexperienced troops.[30] One German veteran of Ypres recalled the difficultly of assaulting the Old Contemptibles, noting, "Unthinking, section after section ran into the well-directed fire of experienced troops. Every effort had been put into our training, but it was completely inadequate preparation for such a serious assault on battle-hardened, long service colonial soldiers."[31]

Yet, despite the BEF's tactical advantages, the sheer weight of German pressure extracted a dreadful toll on the BEF. From its first deployment in August to the end of major operations in late November, the BEF suffered 89,864 casualties.[32] More than 58,000 of these occurred during the First Battle of Ypres.[33] Of the British battalions that fought from Mons to Ypres, an average of just one officer and thirty men remained.[34] Although the Battle of Ypres ended in an

Allied victory, the old regular army had effectively been destroyed in the process. By the end of the fighting, as one surviving noncommissioned officer noted sadly, "The old army was finished."[35] Its place would be taken by the new citizen armies that would endure their own epic struggles from 1915 to 1918.

Although it had paid a high price for its success, the skill, professionalism, and sheer tenacity of the BEF had played a vital role in stemming the German offensives of 1914. The German attempt to defeat France in one great stroke had been thwarted at the Battle of the Marne, while the attempt to turn the Allied flank and seize the crucial Channel ports had been stopped at Ypres. Arguably, Germany never had the same opportunity to win decisive victory in the west as it had possessed in 1914. It would take a further four years of fighting before Germany was defeated, but the strategic balance now favored the Allies. Although the fortunes of war fluctuated over the years that followed, growing Allied economic strength, the entry of America into the war, and the deleterious effect of the British naval blockade steadily eroded Germany's strategic position. It was these strategic realities that prompted Germany to launch her desperate offensives in 1918. Initial success in these operations proved chimerical, as concerted Allied counteroffensives led directly to Germany's defeat.[36]

By the end of the 1914 campaign, the Old Contemptibles had achieved lasting fame. The professional and tactical skill of the BEF, which proved so important in 1914, had been developed through a difficult process of reform and rearmament that had taken place in the years 1902 to 1914. It is the purpose of this work to examine how the tactical foundations for the victories of 1914 were laid down by the bitter experience of the Boer War (1899–1902) and subsequent reforms.

INFLUENCE OF THE BOER WAR

The 1902–1914 period was one of the most critical in the history of the British Army's development. In the twelve years between the end of the Boer War and the outbreak of the First World War, the army underwent vast and important organizational and tactical reforms that ultimately produced, in the words of official historian John Edmonds, "incomparably the best trained, best organised, and best equipped British Army which ever went forth to war."[37] The Boer War (1899–1902) played an important part in creating this elite force. The shock of battlefield defeats in this conflict dispelled the aura of complacency that had settled over the British Army after years of easy victories against crudely armed foes during the Victorian era. Although the army was ultimately able to adapt and overcome the Boers, the duration and cost of the war led to public outcry and searching introspection within the military. Furthermore, the hostile attitude of continental powers such as France, Germany, and Russia during the war left Britain feeling especially vulnerable. In this respect, the struggle in South Africa provided the key impetus to undertake a thorough overhaul of the British Army in the years following the end of the conflict. In the words of Rudyard Kipling's famous poem, it was clear the nation and the army had been taught "no end of a lesson."[38]

However, although many historians have identified the Boer War as a catalyst for change and reform in the British Army, their focus has tended to be on organizational-level reform, particularly the creation of the Territorial Army and the General Staff.[39] Other writers have commented on the tactical skill demonstrated by the British in 1914 but have neglected or referred only in passing to the role of the Boer War in developing the army to this level.[40] Some historians have even seen the South Africa experience as a negative influence.[41] The comparative lack of detailed study of the Boer War's influence on tactics in the period of 1902 to 1914 represents a gap in the historiography. This gap, in turn, has led to recent studies of the BEF of 1914 that only vaguely assert that the Boer War played a role in tactical reform.[42] Therefore, it is my aim in this work to analyze the extent to which the bitter conflict in South Africa shaped the tactical and operational development of the British Army from 1902 to 1914.

The terms doctrine, strategy, operations, and tactics are used throughout this work, and it is important to define their meaning. The meaning of these phrases has altered subtly since they were first introduced; thus, modern definitions are used to avoid confusion. "Military doctrine," in the words of Stephen Badsey, "means the prescriptive setting out of the courses of action the armed forces should follow."[43] In the twenty-first century the definition of military doctrine has come to mean centralized, written guidelines for

the conduct of military operations and tactics, and it is this definition that is used throughout this work. "Military strategy" is the
question of how to fight wars and achieve desired political objectives using available national resources. The term "operations" has
been defined as "the employment of military forces to attain strategic goals in a theatre of war . . . through the design, organization,
and conduct of campaigns," and thus it relates to the handling of
armies and larger formations, such as corps, during campaigns and
in battle.[44] "Tactics" refers to the employment of weapons and units
in combination to defeat an enemy in combat. Smaller formations,
typically brigade level and below, use tactics against the enemy to
achieve local objectives in combat.[45] Unless otherwise stated, these
definitions are used throughout this work.

Although the Boer War was a key element in the development
of tactics in the 1902–1914 period, there were additional factors that
shaped the reform of the British Army. These outside influences
served to add a layer of complexity to the tactical debates that had
emerged from the South African conflict.

The Russo-Japanese War (1904–1905) was a conflict fought between two modern armies equipped to European standards, and as
such it distracted attention away from the South African experience.
Observers from Europe's armies flocked to study the war in Manchuria, their reports and observations sparking considerable debate.
Both the reformists and the more traditionally minded within the
British Army used the conflict in the Far East to provide evidence to
support their respective cases. However, the apparent lessons from
the Russo-Japanese War were not as clear-cut as some writers at first
believed; thus, the debate on tactics continued.[46] Historians of the
Russo-Japanese War have argued that continental European militaries tended to use the example of the war in the Far East to confirm
existing lines of thought.[47] This confirmation bias was largely true
of the British Army, which drew on Manchurian observations to
contribute to ongoing debates on the value of ideas developed from
the Boer War but did not use them to create entirely new tactics.
Therefore, although the Manchurian conflict had relatively little
lasting impact on British tactics, it served as a prism through which
many of the earlier Boer War lessons were viewed.

Furthermore, as the period drew on and Britain became more
closely allied with France, a third influence on the army—particularly

the artillery—began to emerge as French thinking filtered through into the British military. As war with Germany became ever more likely, the example of the French, also preparing for a war with the Germans, drew increased attention from sections of the British Army, who began to wonder whether their own tactical and operational ideas were suitable for continental warfare or if the examples from France provided a better model to follow. French infatuation with the offensive also filtered into elements of the British Army, lending credence to arguments from traditional thinkers who rejected the arguments of the revisionist firepower school. However, although French tactics were admired by sections of the British Army, the fundamentally different composition and anticipated roles of the French and British militaries made direct emulation difficult.

The tactical development of the British Army from 1902 to 1914 was thus an on-going and complex process. It is the central aim of this work to analyze the extent to which deductions derived from the Boer War became the cornerstones of tactics and training in the British Army during the period of 1902 to 1914. In analyzing this issue, I address several key questions. First, what were the key tactical lessons derived from the Boer War; second, how were these ideas implemented into tactical and training reforms; and finally, to what extent was the BEF of 1914 ultimately shaped by the tactical and operational lessons derived from the Boer War? The focus of this study is thus on the tactical ideas, resulting reforms, and the attendant changes in training that made improvement possible.

To address the first question, I analyze the development of key tactical ideas that emerged during combat in the Boer War itself. As will be discussed subsequently, the conflict in South Africa was unusual for a variety of reasons and posed a serious challenge to preconceived ideas in the British Army. Facing unanticipated tactical problems, such as smokeless powder, heavy artillery, and a supremely mobile opponent, the British were forced to adapt in the field, suffering several stinging defeats before finally devising battle-winning tactics that brought the conventional stage of the war to a close. British tactics in South Africa varied by commander and by region, with the geography of the country imposing its own limitations. For example, the campaign in Natal revolved around attritional struggles for control of important positions, whereas the

more open terrain of the Orange Free State produced a mobile campaign in which large numbers of cavalry and mounted infantry were
the key to victory. Faced with diverse experiences, the problem that
confronted the British military following the end of hostilities was
determining which of these ideas had enduring value and which
were theater-specific. In this work I argue that several crucial ideas
emerged in each of the three main services as a result of South African experience, providing a foundation for the tactical development
of the British Army throughout the 1902–1914 period.

How these ideas were adopted into training and tactics forms
the focus of the second research question. The embarrassments
of the Boer War provided a great impetus toward military reform,
and the experience of the conflict provided an initial direction.
In the immediate aftermath of the war, ideas drawn from combat
against the Boers were dominant in informing training and tactics,
but some officers felt that the unique aspects of the struggle made
drawing specific tactical lessons difficult and potentially dangerous.
Furthermore, the need for the British Army to remain flexible to
fight a wide range of opponents further complicated developments.
In this environment, tactical concepts drawn from South Africa
were subjected to considerable debate, with some officers lauding
their value while others dismissed them as irrelevant. In this work
I analyze how ideas drawn from the Boer War were modified and
adapted during the 1902–1914 era, demonstrating to what extent
they were integrated into training and tactics over time.

The relative absence of formal, codified doctrine within the British Army of this period poses problems for identifying how diverse
ideas became firm tactical concepts. Previous studies have made
substantial use of the minutes of General Staff meetings to build
a picture of British tactics. However, such minutes demonstrate
thinking at only the highest strata of the army; they do not reflect
the reality of training at lower levels. Instead, by consulting sources
such as Army Council minutes, inspector general of forces reports,
and training memorandums from various commands—particularly
Aldershot—this work attempts to determine to what extent the tactical ideas of the Boer War prevailed at brigade level and below.

The final issue to be addressed in this work is the extent to which
the BEF of 1914 was shaped by the lessons of the Boer War and how
relevant those lessons proved in combat during the opening months

of the First World War. The outbreak of war in 1914 placed the small, colonial-orientated British Army directly in the path of the German offensive through Belgium and France. Vastly outnumbered and outgunned, the BEF was forced to fight pitched battles against an enemy regarded as the finest army on the continent. The experience of the Boer War provided few operational lessons, and the need to handle multiple divisions in the field had been neglected in prewar training in favor of developing skill at brigade level and below. The unique nature of the British Army and its focus on small-scale deployments meant that it was not ideally suited to a vast continental struggle, and a number of operational flaws became apparent in these early battles, with higher command struggling to cope with the pressure of campaigning.[48] However, despite these problems, the BEF acquitted itself commendably in combat, where its high-quality tactical expertise meant that it was able to perform a crucial role, particularly at the First Battle of Ypres. The tactical performance of the BEF has drawn praise. In this study I analyze the extent to which tactics drawn from the Boer War proved useful in 1914, and I demonstrate that, although specific ideas were not always appropriate, the fundamental principles developed in the 1902–1914 period remained valuable and relevant in the opening months of the First World War.

In this work I use various official and semi-official sources to trace the development of the British Army. Reports from the front and the evidence presented to the post–Boer War Elgin Commission—a royal commission assembled to investigate the military's preparations, organization, and conduct of the war[49]—identified a number of key tactical problems that had emerged in South Africa. From this point, solutions and responses were widely debated in the service journals and also in various training papers produced for individual commands, such as Aldershot. Ultimately, some of the proposed solutions were accepted, with evidence of their usage in training appearing in the reports of the inspector general of forces and in annual training memorandums issued by local commands. Therefore, by using this range of sources, it is possible to triangulate evidence from the era to trace the progression of tactical ideas from their roots in the Boer War to the point of official acceptance. The private papers of various high-ranking officers who fought in the Boer War and First World War are referred to only sparingly. Because of the high rank of many of the officers in question, much of the material within the private paper collections refers to strategic and organizational thought, rather than tactical development, and are thus of less immediate use in addressing the key research questions.

Throughout this work, the focus is on tactics and training, principally at brigade level and below. Therefore, the wider organizational changes underway in this period, such as the reforms initiated by Secretary of State for War Richard Haldane, the creation of the Territorial Army, and the implementation of the General Staff, are referred to only in passing. As the focus is on tactics, large-scale strategic issues, such as plans to deploy the BEF to the continent, are not discussed. In addition, although British auxiliary forces such as the volunteers, militia, yeomanry, and colonial contingents played a vital role in the Boer War, the focus of this study remains on the development of the regular BEF; thus, the experiences of second-line forces are not specifically detailed. The regular army was the driving force in developing training and tactics, and the second-line forces tended to follow its lead rather than contribute fresh ideas. As such, the influence of the auxiliary forces in the ongoing tactical debates of the 1902–1914 period was negligible.

This work is divided into five separate chapters. The first offers a brief account of the origins and course of the Boer War itself, and the remaining chapters examine the process of reform in the aftermath of the conflict. These chapters comprise doctrine and ethos, infantry, artillery, and cavalry. Although the British aspired toward close cooperation in battle, individual arms tended to absorb and assess the tactical lessons of the Boer War in isolation. Therefore, an arm-by-arm structure facilitates closer analysis of the tactical questions that drove reform in the 1902–1914 period. Taken as a whole, the chapters argue that although not all the lessons of the Boer War endured, key ideas in each service arm remained in place, encouraged by an overall ethos that emphasized skill in minor tactics. Although the British Army of 1914 possessed certain flaws, the reforms that were developed from the Boer War created an army that performed well in the fierce battles that marked the opening months of the First World War.

1

THE BOER WAR,
1899–1902

Although a detailed discussion of the origins of the Boer War is beyond the scope of this work, it is necessary to offer a brief background on the conflict. The Boers were descendents of the original Dutch settlers who had first arrived on the coast of South Africa in 1652.[1] The area struggled to attract immigration from the Netherlands, and the settler population only numbered around 40,000 by 1800. During the Napoleonic Wars (1803–1815), the position of Cape Colony gave it great strategic value, as it sat astride the shipping lanes to India. Concerned about French ambitions in the region, the British seized Cape Town[2] in January 1806, defeating the small Dutch garrison at the Battle of Blaauwberg. The colony was formally ceded to Britain at the end of the conflict, but the fiercely independent Afrikaners immediately resented British rule. By the 1830s, growing frustration with British policies caused a number of Boers to undertake the "Great Trek," an overland migration that took them in search of an area where they could establish their own republics. The first of these was the Natalia Republic, but by 1843 it had been annexed by the British to secure access to the deep-water port of Durban. However, two inland nations founded subsequently, Transvaal and Orange Free State, were recognized as independent.

Relations between these nations and the British remained frosty until the discovery of diamonds in Transvaal prompted a British annexation in 1877. Simmering Boer resentment against the British ultimately erupted in open rebellion during the First Boer War of 1880–1881. In the decisive engagement of this conflict, a British force under General George Pommery Colley was humiliatingly defeated at the Battle of Majuba Hill on 27 February 1881. After this defeat, the British chose to make peace, and the Boers were once again granted their independence.

Relations between the two nations became increasingly strained during the coming years, as there were further discoveries of gold and diamond fields in Boer territory. Foreign settlers and workers, known as *uitlanders* by the Boers, flocked to South Africa. This sudden surge in immigration meant that the relatively small Afrikaner population was in danger of being outnumbered by these new white immigrants. Suspicious of the outsiders, the Boers refused immigrants many political rights and denied them the franchise. The growing imbalance between the Boers and the disenfranchised uitlanders offered an opportunity for the British to pursue their territorial ambitions.

The tensions between Boers and uitlanders led to the so-called Jameson Raid in December 1895. This incursion was a haphazard and foolhardy scheme designed to incite the uitlanders into a rebellion against the Boer government. Masterminded by the ambitious imperialist Cecil Rhodes, the raid consisted of an invasion of Boer territory and a march on Johannesburg by six hundred mounted men led by Dr. Leander Starr Jameson. It was hoped that the uitlanders would spontaneously rise in support of this invasion and thus overthrow Boer rule. Unfortunately for Jameson, the raid turned into a fiasco. There was no rising, and Jameson and his force were soon rounded up by the Boers. Although the British government stringently denied any involvement, the raid convinced the Boers that full-scale war was now only a matter of time. Recalling the issue in 1906, Boer leader Jan Smuts commented, "The Jameson Raid was the real declaration in the Anglo-Boer conflict, which dated from the 31st December, 1895, and not the 11th October, 1899."[3]

Over the following years, the British continued to exert political pressure on the Boers to offer uitlanders the franchise. The Boers resisted, recognizing that the large numbers of English-speaking uitlanders would dominate the electorate and possibly extinguish Afrikaner independence. Ultimately, British pressure on this issue forced the Boers into a corner.[4] Feeling that the only way to resist inevitable annexation was war, Transvaal president Paul Kruger issued the British an ultimatum to withdraw all troops from his nation's border within forty-eight hours. When this ultimatum was rejected, the Boers declared war on 11 October 1899.

THE OPPOSING ARMIES

Although the war ultimately provided a huge shock for the British Army, at the outset there appeared to be little cause for concern. On paper, the conflict appeared to be a mismatched struggle. On one side stood the two small Boer republics of Transvaal and Orange Free State, principally agrarian nations, with armies composed almost entirely of irregular militia called out by the government in times of crisis. Opposing them was the might of imperial Britain, commanding the greatest empire on earth, able to deploy regular troops from stations around the globe as well as to draw on volunteers from her dominions of Canada, Australia, and New Zealand.[5] Yet the war would prove to be by far the largest and costliest of all the colonial campaigns fought by Victorian Britain. Victory over the two Boer Republics came only after a long and bitter struggle that left substantial parts of South Africa devastated. In a conflict that lasted almost three years, the forces of the British Empire lost more than twenty thousand men suppressing the resistance of the Boers.[6]

The cost and duration of the war were all the more shocking given the string of virtually unbroken successes that the British Army had hitherto enjoyed in earlier colonial wars. The Victorian era was marked by a staggering number of these "small wars." For example, from 1838 to 1868, Britain was involved in at least one war every year except in 1862, when it came close to hostilities with the United States over the *Trent* affair.[7] In fact, the Boer War of 1899–1902 marked the 226th out of 230 imperial conflicts that would be fought during Victoria's reign.[8] These wars were fought in an enormous variety of geographical and climatic conditions, from the deserts of Egypt and the Sudan to the jungles of Burma or the forests of New Zealand. The variety of terrain was matched by the varied nature of Britain's enemies, from the Egyptian and Sikh armies, trained and organized on European lines, to the primitively armed but highly disciplined Zulus, to the fanatical and reckless Mahdists. However, in general, the quality of military opposition faced in these campaigns was not up to the standard of the British Army, although its opponents were capable of forcing hard fighting and even inflicting the occasional defeat. The technological and organizational advantage possessed by the British typically proved decisive, and in wars from 1857 onward, British forces only lost one hundred men killed in a single action twice prior to the Boer War, whereas their foes often suffered severe casualties.[9]

The wide variety of colonial experience was well illustrated by two campaigns that took place in different corners of the empire in 1898, a year before the outbreak of the Boer War. In the Sudan, a British force aiming to re-establish control of the volatile region fought the Battle of Omdurman, in which an Anglo-Egyptian army of around 25,000 men faced a Mahdist army of more than 40,000 troops. The Mahdists attacked in close formation across open ground and were met by a well-formed British line, which initially fired by volley. Despite their courage and fanaticism, the Mahdists were simply annihilated by superior firepower. By the end of the battle, the Mahdist army had suffered more than 20,000 casualties, with almost 10,000 killed, whereas the British had suffered less than 500 total casualties.[10] Conversely, from 1897 to 1898, thousands of miles away on the notorious North-West Frontier of India (present-day Pakistan), British and Indian troops conducted the Tirah campaign.[11] Fought in difficult, mountainous terrain, this campaign posed many tactical problems for the British. As in the Sudan, tribal attacks in the open were devastated by rifle fire, but the Afridi tribesmen soon began to employ skirmishing tactics using modern, breech-loading weapons. Making use of the plentiful cover available, the Afridi were able to inflict a number of casualties at long range, while suffering few in return.[12] Volley fire, devastating in the Sudan, was of little use against fleeting targets, and close-order formations were dangerous and impractical. Instead, one officer who fought in the campaign stated, "In hill-fighting, cover *must* be taken advantage of."[13] The local difficulties of the fighting necessitated a rough guide to tactics being circulated to troops in the field while the operations continued.[14] Ultimately, although both campaigns ended in British victory, the methods necessary to achieve success were strikingly different and illustrate the tremendous difficulties of formulating a doctrine that would be appropriate for all possible eventualities.

The Sudan and Tirah campaigns were particularly significant for the British as they demonstrated the potential problems posed by the latest improvements in firepower. Omdurman demonstrated the risks entailed in attack across open ground against a foe armed with modern weaponry, and Tirah showed the difficulty of engaging a well-armed foe who refused to fight in the open. The experiences of Tirah led to a considerable degree of introspection and the emergence of some useful lessons, with a number of veteran officers finding opportunity to put them into practice in South Africa.[15] However, the short space of time between the end of the Tirah campaign and the outbreak of the Boer War inevitably limited the degree to which combat experience could filter into peacetime thinking. Indeed, a considerable proportion of the army remained ignorant of tactical developments gained in colonial wars. Despite the British being involved in more combat than any other European army throughout the 1880s and 1890s, the variety of campaigns and their small scale meant that unless a disaster occurred they tended to leave little mark on the army as a whole. In addition, lack of a General Staff or any real doctrinal guidance from the top down meant that any learning from these experiences was limited. Although faced with a profusion of wars from which to draw examples, there was no formal system for disseminating tactical lessons drawn from combat to the wider army. Although prior combat experience could have a positive effect on individual units, it generally had little influence outside the regiments and officers who had fought in the action.

With no real system of disseminating tactical knowledge outside of unit and theater, the majority of the army was forced to rely on drill books and standard training to prepare for war. Unfortunately, training throughout this period varied greatly in quality and practicality. Despite the profusion of wars that the army had been called upon to fight during the Victorian period, attitudes toward field training were slow to catch up. An 1883 official work, *Life in the Ranks of the English Army*, described drilling and guard work as "by far the most important [duties] that the private soldier has to do," while including no mention whatsoever of shooting or field craft.[16] Victorian drill manuals varied in quality and provided little overall guidance for regimental officers, and indeed they frequently contradicted one another on fundamental principles.[17]

Training and tactics were further limited by a lack of ground over which to conduct maneuvers and the constant need to supply drafts for the garrison of India, reducing the number of men available for company training. Under such circumstances, individual training of the men focused on gymnastics to improve the soldier physically and drill to inculcate obedience to orders.[18] This training program produced sturdy soldiers who were noted for their endurance of hardship and courage in the face of adversity, but it left serious gaps, particularly with regard to field-craft and musketry. Marksmanship was a notable problem, with miserly allowances of practice ammunition preventing the development of individual accuracy in most regiments. Instead, rigid fire-control tactics were endorsed and volley fire was used in most circumstances, despite the fact that these methods had proved inadequate in Tirah and in earlier conflicts against the Boers.

Although the British Army was forced to prepare to fight a variety of opponents, it found itself ill-equipped for the unusual style of combat thrust upon it in the Boer War. However, years of North-West Frontier fighting and the recent Tirah campaign had highlighted a number of the problems that would be faced in South Africa, particularly regarding the inadequacy of volley fire and the need for greater field-craft and individual skill. Although the unusual conditions found in South Africa undoubtedly contributed to the early defeats suffered by the British Army during the Boer War, those defeats were also due to faulty tactics, the inadequate training of much of the army, and the inability to disseminate useful tactical lessons drawn from colonial experience.[19]

In contrast to the British, the Boers did not possess a standing army, instead relying on a citizen militia system.[20] Under this organization, the citizens of a district, known as "burghers," would form a military unit known as a "commando." There was no fixed size for a commando, with their numerical strength varying depending on the numbers of white citizens in the district from which it was drawn. Officers for the commando were decided by election. Each man was expected to bring a firearm, horse, and rations, with rifles being provided by the government for those who could not afford their own. The commandos were supported by a handful of artillery pieces, manned by professional gunners who constituted the only formal military organization of the two republics.[21] Thus, unlike the majority of the enemies around the empire, the Boers were armed to a near-European standard, equipped with magazine rifles and a small quantity of field and heavy artillery guns, which in some cases outclassed those of the British. The quality of Boer armament would prove particularly significant. Not only were both sides armed with long-range, flat-trajectory magazine rifles that created deadly fire-swept zones, but this was also a war in which the use of smokeless powder, for both small arms and artillery, created a disturbingly empty battlefield in which the source of enemy fire was often invisible.

Furthermore, the Boers possessed unusual military characteristics, notably a unique military heritage born of wars against regional natives that emphasized mobility and firepower. Experienced in fighting against superior numbers of tribal opposition, the Boers preferred to fight on the tactical defensive, using their modern weaponry to shoot down advancing opponents. If the fire of the Boers failed to stop the attack, then the position would simply be abandoned and a new one taken up some distance behind; the Boers attached little importance to holding geographical positions in the face of enemy assaults.[22] The fact that virtually every Boer was mounted gave them an unparalleled ability to maneuver and redeploy as necessary, and the vast geography of South Africa allowed them to trade space for time. In addition, when it was deemed prudent to strengthen a position, the use of labor drawn from the black population allowed the construction of formidable defensive works without exhausting the burghers themselves.[23]

The famous mobility of the Boers was matched by a reputation for excellent marksmanship. Writing after the war, Frederick Maurice commented, "A rifle had at all times an irresistible fascination for a Boer."[24] A key reason for Boer skill with firearms was related to the local climate. The atmosphere of much of South Africa is exceptionally clear and allows observation at enormous ranges. For those new to these conditions, it can be difficult to judge distances correctly. However, the Boers were well accustomed to their environment and thus were known for their long-range accuracy with their firearms. Developed through the regular hunting of game, the marksmanship of the Boers had been recognized as early as the 1840s and had been seen as a crucial factor in their victory over the British in 1881. Although hunting was declining in the years prior to the Boer War, the governments of the Transvaal and Orange Free State had attempted to offset the effects of this decline by encouraging the development of shooting clubs, using state funds to provide ammunition and prizes.[25]

The principles of maneuverability and firepower were ideally suited to South African conditions. The sheer scale of the South African terrain was daunting, with the grass veldt in the east and scrub deserts in the west providing relatively little cover, whereas high kopjes (hills) proved to be formidable defensive positions, granting dominating views over the surrounding country to those who occupied them. The depressingly flat nature of much of the terrain, the lack of cover, and the crystal-clear atmosphere all favored the use of defensive firepower. Forced into attacks against Boer positions, the British experienced numerous tactical difficulties that will be discussed in detail in subsequent chapters.

Although the Boer military system had a number of unique advantages, it also suffered from several drawbacks. The informal nature of the military contract between state and citizen meant that burghers often drifted away from the army to tend to their own business, returning at their own discretion.[26] The lack of military discipline also meant that the Boers were highly dependent on the presence of charismatic and talented leaders to ensure the burghers carried out their orders, much to the frustration of commanding officers. Christiaan De Wet, one of the most successful Boer commanders, was notorious for beating his men with his *sjambok*[27] when they refused to stand their ground.[28] Nevertheless, although Boer discipline was sometimes wayward, British hopes that their morale would be equally fragile proved overly optimistic. Although the Boer mood rose and fell with the fortunes of the war, the persistence and endurance of the *bittereinders*[29] came as a surprise to the British.

The British had fought a number of earlier conflicts against the Boers, and their military characteristics were well known. Yet, despite previous evidence of the formidable military capabilities of the Boers, initial assessments of them were often contemptuous. On the eve of the war, pro-imperialists in the *Economist* and the *Spectator* dismissed the Boers as "stock breeders of the lowest type," no

more than "a rough mob of good marksmen."[30] The British Military
Intelligence Department largely agreed in its secret report, "Military Notes on the Dutch Republics of South Africa." It was felt that
the decline of game on the veldt had reduced their once-famous accuracy with the rifle, and overall they were assessed to be inferior
to the men who had achieved victory at Majuba in 1881. The report expected the Boers to deploy little more than a raiding strategy
against British possessions in South Africa and offered the opinion,
"It appears certain that, after [one] serious defeat, they would be
too deficient in discipline and organization to make any further real
stand."[31] Events were soon to prove these early assessments wrong.

THE WAR

The opening moves of the conflict were to have lasting consequences for both sides. The Boers were conscious of the need to
win quick victories to demoralize the British to such an extent that
their government would seek peace, as had happened in 1881.[32] At
the outbreak of hostilities, the Boer forces outnumbered the British garrison in South Africa, but with reinforcements en-route from
Britain, this advantage would be fleeting.[33] Aware of this time pressure, the Boers assumed an immediate offensive. Commandos in-
vaded British territory, laying siege to the railway junction town of
Mafeking and the diamond mining center of Kimberley in the west,
and advancing into Natal in the east. The majority of British regular
troops were stationed in Natal at the outbreak of the war, using the
rail junction at Ladysmith as a base of operations.[34] Facing the Boer
advance were around 12,000 British troops under the command of
Lieutenant-General Sir George White, an experienced veteran of Afghanistan and the North-West Frontier.[35] Initially, the British plan
was to stall the Boer advance and await the arrival of an expeditionary army corps under the leadership of General Sir Redvers Buller, at
which point a major counteroffensive would begin.[36]

However, this relatively sound plan soon came undone. White's
predecessor in Natal, Lieutenant-General William Penn Symons,
had decided to take 4,000 men to the coal mining town of Dundee,
approximately seventy miles north of Ladysmith and close to the
Transvaal border. Overconfidence and contempt for the Boers played
a part in this decision, as did the political pressure to be seen to be

defending the northern part of the colony.[37] This was a serious strategic error. Symons's force was not strong enough to be certain of defeating a Boer attack and was too far away from White's troops to be able to receive timely reinforcement. White was deeply concerned about Symons's position, but Symons was determined to hold it regardless of risks.[38] Despite his misgivings, White allowed Symons to remain in place, conscious of the logistical problems involved in a rapid evacuation and feeling that the political damage that would be caused by abandoning northern Natal outweighed the military risks involved in holding the position.[39] This decision was to have serious consequences.

In the first major engagement of the war, approximately 3,500 Boers seized a position overlooking Symon's camp and began shelling it, forcing an immediate British attack.[40] This action would become known as the Battle of Talana Hill, which occurred on 20 October 1899. Although a tactical British victory, Symons was mortally wounded and his force left strategically isolated because the rail lines to Ladysmith were cut. The force was only able to rejoin the main British army after a grueling four-day march over rugged terrain. George White attempted to clear their route, ordering a sortie against Boers operating against the railway lines, which led to the Battle of Elandslaagte (21 October 1899). The Boers were caught in a relatively vulnerable, open position and were comprehensively defeated through a combination of skillful infantry tactics and cavalry pursuit. Although this was a striking tactical victory for the British and helped ease the retreat from Dundee, the Elandslaagte position could not be held. The maneuverability of fresh Boer forces threatened to outflank the British and caused White to order a retreat back to Ladysmith.[41]

White now faced a critical strategic decision that would define the future of the campaign. He could abandon Ladysmith, retreat south, and use the Tugela River as a defensive line until reinforcements from Britain arrived, or he could maintain his position and attempt to decisively defeat the Boers in battle before they surrounded the town. Unwilling to surrender the accumulated supplies at Ladysmith and fearing the tactical difficulties and political consequences of a retreat, White made the fateful decision to stand and fight. On the 30th of October, he launched his forces against the Boers, who were beginning to emplace heavy artillery to the north of the town. In the confused action that followed, the main British assault against Lombard's Kopje was bloodily repulsed by the Boers, while a force moving on an ambitious flanking march through the high kopjes to the northwest became surrounded at Nicholson's Nek and was forced to surrender, with eight hundred soldiers becoming Boer prisoners as a result. The dispiriting defeat, officially the Battle of Ladysmith, became known as "Mournful Monday." Unable to break the advancing Boer forces and unwilling to retreat, George White's force was surrounded and besieged in Ladysmith.

White's decision to defend Ladysmith and submit his forces to a siege placed the initiative firmly in the hands of the Boers. The main British army in South Africa was now trapped, and across the rest of the country only a handful of British regular forces remained operational. There was no prospect of a counteroffensive until the arrival of seaborne reinforcements, and surviving troops were limited to a largely defensive role. Sensing opportunity, some of the younger Boer leaders urged that their own offensive continue. The dynamic Louis Botha was a particular advocate of this course of action, suggesting that Boer forces should advance deeper into Natal, possibly attempting to seize or disrupt the port of Durban where British reinforcements were likely to disembark.[42] However, elderly Boer Commandant-General Piet Joubert was cautious about the strategy. Although he authorized a raid into Natal, his nerve was shaken after sustaining a serious injury in a fall from his horse, and he chose to call off the operation despite its promising start.[43] With the offensive halted, the Boers turned their attentions to the ongoing sieges and prepared to stem the inevitable British relief operations.

Although the Boers had allowed the initiative to slip from their grasp, the British still faced a difficult strategic situation. It had originally been intended that General Redvers Buller's 47,000-strong Army Corps would operate as a single army that would undertake an invasion of Boer territory.[44] However, as the reinforcements began to arrive in mid-November, the need to relieve the beleaguered towns was considered paramount, and any plans of a unified offensive were impossible. Faced with this strategic predicament, Buller split his force into three parts. Lord Methuen would advance against the Boers to the relief of Kimberley; Lieutenant-General William

Gatacre would take a force to secure the Cape Midlands area; and Buller, himself, would lead the army that would break through to Ladysmith.

Unfortunately for the British, all three relief forces suffered from a fundamental lack of mobility. The most immediate cause of this problem was a lack of mounted troops. Most of the regular cavalry available in South Africa had become trapped in Ladysmith, leaving the relief forces short.[45] Buller's column was supported by just two regiments of cavalry and Methuen's by one, whereas Gatacre's force had to make do without any regular cavalry whatsoever.[46] Although the relief forces could draw on the support of mounted infantry and irregular cavalry, even these troops were in short supply. Deficient in horsemen, the columns were hampered by poor reconnaissance, limited tactical mobility, and an inability to exploit local victories through effective pursuit. Further hampering mobility was the need to remain on relatively fixed axes of advance as dictated by rail lines, which were considered essential to maintaining supply, particularly in the arid territory around Kimberley. Lack of operational mobility meant that the Boers were able to position themselves to block the British advance, leaving the relief columns with no choice but to fight their way through preselected defensive positions. The battles that followed ideally suited the Boer military ethos and posed serious tactical problems for the British, as will be discussed in depth in subsequent chapters.

Ultimately, all three divisions suffered defeats within the space of a single week in December 1899. On 10 December 1899, Gatacre's force was defeated at Stormberg following a confused night march that inadvertently blundered into Boer positions. Lord Methuen's troops had initially experienced some success in pushing the Boers back at Belmont, Enslin, and Modder River. However, Methuen's force was unable to exploit local victories and was ultimately stopped at the Battle of Magersfontein on 11 December 1899 after a miscarried night march was caught in the open at dawn. Finally, at the Battle of Colenso on 15 December, Buller's army launched a clumsy frontal attack without having properly identified the location of the main Boer position, suffering a humiliating defeat as a result. The triple defeats became known as "Black Week."

Ironically, the very success of the Boers may have doomed their efforts. The British government, faced with military setbacks, imperial humiliation, and a wave of *schadenfreude* emanating from the continent, reacted not by seeking to make peace with the Boers, but by redoubling their efforts to win the war. A call for volunteers across Britain and her empire was met with a great response, and the war began to assume a national character.[47] The humiliating setbacks of Black Week also prompted a reshuffle of command. Although the defeated generals remained in control of the forces under their immediate command, overall leadership of British forces in South Africa was stripped from Buller and passed to the venerable but highly respected Lord Frederick Roberts. Roberts set sail for Africa on 17 December, still mourning the death of his only son, Freddy, who had been mortally wounded at the Battle of Colenso.

Although the Boers had defeated the initial British relief efforts, they gained little strategic advantage from these victories. The British forces had been stopped but had not been routed, and various proposals to drive them back with counterattacks were considered impractical.[48] The besieged towns continued to hold out, and the Boers were reluctant to attempt a direct assault for fear of the casualties that such action would entail. An effort to storm the southern ridgeline at Ladysmith was made on 6 January 1900, but despite some initial success, the Boers were halted and ultimately forced to withdraw.[49] Almost three weeks later, a fresh attempt by Buller to break through to Ladysmith was bloodily defeated at the Battle of Spion Kop (24 January 1900), but once again the Boers failed to gain any long-term benefit from their victory. Around Kimberley and Mafeking, inertia reigned on both sides.

This pause in operational tempo gave Lord Roberts the chance to reorganize British forces and prepare for a new offensive. New tactical guidelines were issued, numbers of mounted troops were vastly increased, and transport was reorganized to reduce dependency on rail lines. By February, Roberts had assembled a field force of approximately 45,000 men.[50] Leaving Buller to continue operations in Natal, Roberts deployed his force in the west with the intention of outflanking Boer positions at Kimberley and invading the Orange Free State. The Boers did not initially anticipate this movement, erroneously assuming that Roberts would be tied to the railway as Methuen had been and forced to make a new series of frontal attacks.[51] Instead, on 15 February a rapid, surprise advance by the British cavalry division under the leadership of John French burst through a thinly held Boer line at Klip Drift, rendering their overall position untenable and forcing them to abandon the siege.

Worse lay in store for the Boers. As their forces attempted to retreat, they found their path blocked by dismounted British cavalry. The Boers were stalled by this holding force, allowing the bulk of the pursuing British army to catch them by 17 February. Burdened with wagons, Boer leader Piet Cronjé judged that a breakout was impossible and instead chose to dig his troops in along the banks of the nearby Modder River. This fateful decision effectively doomed his force, which was surrounded by the numerically superior British and subjected to a nine-day siege that became known as the Battle of Paardeberg. Although British attempts to storm the entrenched Boer position were beaten back with heavy losses, a combination of artillery bombardment, disease, and starvation ultimately forced Cronjé to surrender his entire force of 4,000 men on 27 February. The loss of so many men was a severe blow for the Boer war effort, and it opened the road to Bloemfontein, capital of the Orange Free State.

At the same time that Roberts was operating around Kimberley, Buller's army was engaged in a series of hard-fought battles in Natal. Although a breakthrough attempt at the Battle of Vaal Krantz (5–7 February 1900) had been poorly handled and beaten back, the attritional nature of the fighting and improving British tactics were a growing cause of concern for the Boers. Buller's offensive continued with a series of attacks, collectively known as the Battle of the Tugela Heights, between 12 and 27 February. Despite some early successes, the Boer defenders were ultimately overwhelmed by the British, who demonstrated considerable tactical skill in combining artillery fire and infantry assaults. On 28 February, the siege of Ladysmith was lifted as lead elements of Buller's force arrived in the town.

The tide of the war had turned against the Boers.[52] Roberts continued his advance into Boer territory, pushing through demoralized resistance at the Battle of Poplar Grove on 7 March 1900 and occupying Bloemfontein on 13 March. Throughout South Africa, the Boer war effort appeared to be collapsing. Mafeking was relieved on 17 May, whereas Johannesburg and Pretoria were both occupied without a fight on 31 May and 5 June, respectively. Surviving Boer forces were driven away from Pretoria at the Battle of Diamond Hill on 11–12 June 1900. The remains of the Boer government relocated to the eastern town of Machadodorp, but the British advanced against the area in August, breaking through the Boer defensive line at the Battle of Bergendal on 27 August 1900 and capturing the town without a fight the following day. After this string of successes, Lord Roberts proclaimed the entirety of South Africa to be British territory. Roberts returned to England as a hero in November, passing command to Lord Horatio Kitchener.

By conventional standards, the war was over. The British had an overwhelming numerical advantage, the Boer capitals had fallen, and the Boer armies seemed incapable of making an organized stand. However, there were weaknesses in the British position that the Boers were able to exploit. The geographical vastness of South Africa combined with the largely rural make-up of much of the Afrikaner population made physical occupation virtually impossible, which meant large swathes of territory were essentially beyond British control. Given that the Boers still retained considerable mobility by virtue of being mounted, they could easily maneuver through these ungoverned areas and emerge unexpectedly in British territory. Indeed, Boer mobility was improving throughout 1900 as commandos chose to abandon their slow-moving field artillery and shed themselves of encumbering wagons. Using their speed, Boer commandos could strike isolated British posts and then retreat into wilderness areas where any pursuit was easily eluded. In addition, although the British had a preponderance of troops, formations operating in the rear echelons were frequently made up of volunteer forces who had received limited training and were often poorly led.[53] These related conditions presented an ideal opportunity for the Boers to use guerrilla tactics against the British.

Guerrilla raids had been a growing feature of the war throughout 1900 and could achieve spectacular results. For example, in March, Christiaan De Wet had led a successful raid against the Bloemfontein waterworks, killing or capturing almost six hundred troops and cutting the water supply to the city for several days, exacerbating an outbreak of disease among occupying forces.[54] Increased guerrilla activity throughout May had prompted a major sweep of the countryside in search of De Wet's commando, in what became known as the "First De Wet Hunt." However, the mobile Boers were able to evade the pursuit columns, and De Wet would remain a thorn in the side of the British throughout the war. Inspired by De Wet's example and recognizing the futility of conventional methods, by September 1900 the surviving Boer commandos had embraced guerrilla warfare as a means to carry on the fight.

The British were perplexed by this continued Boer resistance. Lord Roberts had initially hoped to deal with it by forcing surrendering Boers to hand over weapons and sign a proclamation announcing that they would not take up arms again.[55] When this policy failed to stem guerrilla operations, Roberts authorized a scorched-earth policy against Afrikaner farms thought to be supporting guerrillas. This controversial policy began in June 1900 and was considerably extended by Kitchener as the guerrilla war intensified in the latter part of the year. In an attempt to further deprive Boer guerrillas of support and to deal with the refugees created by the farm burnings, the British forced Afrikaner civilians into concentration camps.[56] Overcrowded and under-resourced, these controversial camps soon became notorious for high mortality rates, creating a global scandal and arguably hardening Boer resistance. The British also undertook regular sweeps, deploying all-arms columns to scour an area of Boer guerrillas, attempting to kill or capture as many as possible in the process. However, these operations were manpower intensive and often produced limited results in terms of inflicting casualties on the Boers. Furthermore, although the sweep might clear the Boers from an area for a time, the inability to provide effective garrisons in the vast country meant that there was little to prevent the Boers from returning in the future. Sweep operations also carried risks for the British, as weak or isolated columns were vulnerable to sudden attacks from Boer commandos.

By October 1901, the British were exasperated by the seemingly endless Boer resistance and frustrated by the relatively poor results gained by sweep operations; in addition, stinging defeats suffered at the hands of enterprising commandos remained a cause for concern. It was clear that the operations could no longer be considered a simple mopping-up exercise, and thus a policy shift was introduced. The British began to establish so-called protected areas that were based on larger cities, and then they would steadily work their way outward from these bases, driving the guerrillas away and restoring civilian normality to the cleared countryside. To support this activity and prevent the return of the guerrillas, the blockhouse system was introduced. A blockhouse was a simple fortified building constructed from earth and iron, originally designed by the Royal Engineers and generally built on a standard pattern. They were relatively cheap, easy to erect, and, crucially, able to withstand small-arms fire. Blockhouses had been in use as early as January 1901, when they were placed to guard key locations such as bridges and railways, but their usage had gradually been increasing throughout the year. Manned by small garrisons of around six men and a non-commissioned officer (NCO), the blockhouses were spread out in a long, thin line approximately a thousand yards apart, with barbed wire strung between them to prevent the enemy simply slipping past. By May 1902, there were more than eight thousand block-houses across South Africa.[57] This change in British strategy did not produce immediate results, but it gradually altered the shape of the guerrilla war. The blockhouse lines constrained mobility and thus began to deprive the Boers of their greatest strategic asset. The policy of working outward from the cities and securing those areas forced the commandos to operate in areas of wilderness, isolating them from sources of food, forage, and equipment. Shortages of weapons, ammunition, and clothing could to an extent be remedied by capturing them from the British, but food for the men and forage for the horses was harder to acquire. Sweep operations continued throughout the period, putting further pressure on the hard-pressed commandos and continuing to reduce their strength.

Although the Boer bittereinders continued to fight on, the tide of war had turned against them. Suffering a steady drip of casualties, hampered by lack of supplies, and constricted by the ever-growing blockhouse lines, the commandos were gradually losing the struggle. The Boers were still capable of startling victories, most notably at the Battle of Tweebosch on 7 March 1902, when a British column under the leadership of Lord Methuen was attacked and routed, with Methuen himself being captured.[58] However, even tactical successes such as these could do nothing to change the strategic balance, which was inexorably shifting in favor of the British. Recognizing the situation, the Boers sent a peace-seeking delegation to Pretoria in April 1902. Despite these initial feelers, fighting continued for several weeks until a more organized delegation including key guerrilla leaders was assembled to discuss peace in mid-May. After several days of negotiations, a peace treaty was signed on 31 May 1902. After almost three bloody years, the war was over at last. The

forces of the British Empire had suffered total casualties of nearly
a hundred thousand men; figures for the Boers are less precise, but
they put their dead at approximately nine thousand combatants
with an unknown number wounded. In addition, almost twenty-
eight thousand Afrikaner civilians had perished in concentration
camps.[59] Losses suffered among the black civilian population remain
unknown.

THE LEARNING PROCESS

Although the war had been immensely costly, in both human and
fiscal terms, the British Army had learned a great deal in the process. Throughout the struggle, the army had shown its capacity for
in-theater learning, gradually adapting its tactics to deal with the
unanticipated challenges of the war.

The low point of the British war effort undoubtedly came during the clashes of Black Week. All three battles in this period were
poorly handled.[60] Lacking operational mobility due to the shortage
of mounted troops, the British were forced to launch frontal attacks
against prepared defenses. The problems inherent in this unenvi-
able task were exacerbated due to the failure of reconnaissance to
identify the true strength or position of the Boer forces. Many of
the problems that followed stemmed from this inadequate reconnaissance. British attempts to gain a tactical advantage through the
use of heavy preliminary bombardments at Colenso and Magersfontein miscarried because the majority of the shelling was directed
at unoccupied areas of the Boer position. The ambitious use of
night advances at Stormberg and Magersfontein ultimately proved
disastrous: in both battles the British assault force was caught in
the open at daybreak, facing previously unidentified Boer defensive
lines. Similarly, at Colenso, the true location of the Boer position
was ascertained only as the British attackers came under fire from
previously hidden positions. The results of such blunders were predictable: in each of the Black Week battles, attacking British infantry was stopped dead by the fire of concealed Boers.

Nevertheless, the British gradually learned from their defeats
and changed their approach. Recognizing that direct attacks against
prepared Boer positions often struggled to make ground, Lord Roberts favored using widely extended infantry to launch diversionary

attacks that would draw attention, while British mounted forces turned the flanks.[61] The Boers typically chose to withdraw, abandoning their prepared positions, once they became aware they had been outflanked, which won victories for the British at a low cost. However, it also allowed the Boers to escape relatively intact; consequently, they were able to adopt guerrilla tactics beginning in the latter part of 1900.

In Natal, the rugged terrain made such flanking attacks largely impossible, and Buller's army was forced to fight through Boer positions step by step. Although the army suffered defeats at Colenso, Spion Kop, and Vaal Krantz, it learned from its experiences. The lessons learned led to the development of a new tactical approach based on close cooperation between infantry and artillery, with howitzers playing a particularly important role. This new tactical approach was evident in the series of battles for control of Tugela Heights in February 1900 that ultimately broke the Boer siege of Ladysmith.[62] During these battles, British artillery fire plans were carefully organized, and in contrast to the ineffective preparatory bombardments of 1899, the guns continued to fire in support of the advancing infantry to the very last minute, suppressing the Boer riflemen and allowing the infantry advance to close to decisive range and storm the position.

Although the British were able to adapt tactically and ultimately defeat the Boers, the length and difficulty of the struggle laid bare numerous strategic and tactical weaknesses as well as serious organizational flaws. The immense difficulty the professional British Army experienced in trying to defeat an enemy composed almost entirely of untrained militia raised grave doubts over its ability to perform against a formally organized and trained European foe. The exposure of tactical and operational shortcomings within all three service branches of the British Army led to a great deal of introspection in the immediate aftermath of the conflict. Many preconceived ideas—which were often based on the study of the earlier Franco-Prussian War—did not survive the test of combat on the veldt. Equipment was revised and improved, and the nature of combat in an age of smokeless powder and magazine rifles received debate and consideration from within the service. The war did not pass unnoticed by armies on the continent, and foreign writers, particularly in Germany, also weighed in with their opinions on the perceived lessons of the war.[63] However, the varied nature of the fighting—encompassing siege operations, set piece battles, and a protracted guerrilla campaign, all taking place across a vast geographical area—made analysis difficult. A consensus on clear-cut lessons did not immediately emerge, and interservice rivalry, social snobbery, and the continuing struggle between cliques within the officer corps confused the issues still further. A further limitation was the fact that the British Army lagged far behind the prestigious Royal Navy in allocation of funds and resources. Reforms were set in motion, but discussion and debate on the lessons to be learned continued and some of the changes either were not carried through to their full potential or were neglected entirely. Indeed, the 1902–1914 period was consistently characterized by a struggle between the reformists and the traditionalists, not only within the British Army but also within Edwardian society as a whole.[64] A disturbing sense of overall British decline resulted in an impulse toward the idea of national efficiency within the country to maintain Britain's place among rival continental and world powers, with the poor performance in the Boer War serving to drive this feeling home within the British Army.

Attempting to derive and implement reforms from the South Africa experience would occupy the British Army for the next twelve years. Although the process of reform was often difficult, it ultimately proved of great value when the army went to war in 1914. Writing in 1921, one veteran of the First World War summed up the importance of the South African war, commenting, "Paul Kruger [president of the Transvaal who had declared war in 1899] was the best friend the British Army ever had."[65]

2

DOCTRINE AND ETHOS

Throughout the Victorian era, the British Army was distinctly averse to committing itself to any formal, written doctrine. Proposals to create a General Staff similar to those possessed by France and Germany had been rejected by the Hartington Commission in the 1890s, preventing the development of a higher organization within the army that could have imposed a common doctrine from the top down.[1] Instead, a profusion of tactical ideas existed, meaning that tactics and training often varied considerably from battalion to battalion and new ideas and methods were localized. Tactics were influenced by a multitude of factors, including local combat experience in colonial actions, the attitudes of commanding officers, and the availability of suitable ground upon which to train. Drill manuals contained some useful ideas, but the lack of an overall doctrine in training meant that adherence to faulty, outdated concepts often continued unchecked. Training was principally focused on simple drill, with financial stringency and restrictions on maneuvers meaning that training at brigade level and above was a rare occurrence. Indeed, of the brigades dispatched to South Africa, only the battalions of Major-General Sir Henry Hildyard's 2 Brigade had been formed together and had the chance to train as a unit in peacetime.[2]

The early defeats in the opening months of the Boer War revealed the flaws in some of the pre-war ideas, especially when British troops were confronted with the challenge of crossing a fire-swept zone in the face of a virtually invisible enemy. In this new form of warfare, the close control and tight formations that had been victorious in conflicts against primitively armed colonial foes proved to be sources of weakness. Furthermore, cherished concepts such as strict discipline and unthinking obedience to orders were of limited value in a conflict where officers and men were often widely separated and forced to rely on their own initiative to an unprecedented degree. In addition, the stress of modern combat, particularly the disturbing experience of being under rapid fire from invisible foes, placed great demands on the troops' morale. The number of British regulars who surrendered in combat revealed that even hard-drilled and well-disciplined long-service soldiers were not immune to cracking under the pressures imposed by modern firepower.

Ultimately, the flexibility of the British Army and its ability to learn in-theater made it successful in adapting to the peculiar conditions of the Boer War. Nonetheless, in the aftermath of the conflict, the British grappled with a wide variety of new ideas, which often led to acrimonious debates within the individual combat arms. Arching above this debate was the acknowledgement that modern firepower required an overhaul of training attitudes, particularly regarding improving the quality of the individual soldier and the overall initiative of the army. Although rigid control and close formations could be of value in so-called savage warfare, against foes with modern weapons it was necessary for the army to develop a new training ethos that was based on skill and initiative as much as drill and obedience. These ideas contributed to the ongoing debate, common to all European armies of the era, regarding potential solutions to the problem of crossing the fire-swept zone and delivering an assault. The doctrinal responses to this issue in the pre–First World War period have been a popular subject for historians. Whereas the German Army has drawn considerable praise for its doctrine, the British Army has often been castigated for advancing little from its Victorian ethos, which ultimately led to defeats and heavy casualties in the battles of the First World War.[3] The Boer War has sometimes been seen as a negative influence in this regard, trapping the army in a small-war mentality that proved inappropriate when faced by the vast scale of 1914.[4]

However, more recently it has been suggested that although the British struggled to create a workable operational doctrine, at brigade level and below the BEF was tactically advanced in understanding the problems posed by modern fire.[5] The relative success of the BEF in the defensive battles of 1914, particularly Ypres, lends support to the idea that the British Army emerged as a tactically skillful force in the aftermath of the Boer War, although weaknesses undoubtedly existed at an operational level. In addition, the unique imperial role of the British Army meant that copying German or French operational methods would have been inappropriate for the type of campaigns that the army was likely to fight, limiting the flexibility and adaptability that was required in colonial campaigns.

It is my purpose in this chapter to add to the ongoing debate on the nature of British Army doctrine in the pre–First World War period by demonstrating how the experience of the Boer War contributed to a new ethos based on skill, intelligence, and initiative, which contributed to overall tactical effectiveness. However, the slow and hesitant process of instituting a General Staff and the unique demands of policing the empire meant that creating a formal, written doctrine proved largely impossible. This lack of formal doctrine created peculiar training difficulties for the British Army in the Edwardian period and limited the development of operational thinking. My analysis of the British Army in this period centers on three aspects: first, the change in training ethos to encourage high levels of initiative; second, the difficulties that prevented the development of a formal doctrine; and finally, the willpower versus firepower debate that encouraged a belief in the offensive, arguably to excessive levels. Although flaws remained, the emphasis on skill and initiative that developed from the South African conflict was an appropriate tactical response to the challenges posed by modern weapons. The focus on individual skill emerged principally as a response to the difficulties of maintaining command and control in widely dispersed infantry formations, but it developed further in the 1902–1914 period, ultimately forming a cornerstone of training for the entire British Army. Indeed, the combination of individual skill and thorough training allowed the BEF to perform well in battle against the Germans in 1914. However, the failure to develop a formal doctrine created certain long-term problems that became apparent during the First World War.

INITIATIVE

The idea of improving the initiative and skill of the individual British soldier was not a new concept on the eve of the Boer War. Indeed, as early as 1803, Sir John Moore had introduced innovative skirmish training that led to the creation of the regular army's first permanently constituted light infantry regiments. However, although certain elite formations benefitted from such enlightened ideas, throughout the Victorian era the majority of the army continued to train on lines of strict discipline, unquestioning obedience, and close control. These concepts served the British Army well in wars against poorly armed foes, such as the Zulus and the Mahdists, but by the 1890s there was a growing concern that these rigid tactics were potentially vulnerable against rifle-equipped opposition, such as the tribes of the North-West Frontier.[6] The 1896 edition of *Infantry Drill* picked up on this point, stating, "The conditions of modern warfare render it imperative that all ranks should be taught to think, and, subject to general instructions and accepted principles, to act for themselves."[7] However, this single sentence apparently had limited influence on training in the British Army prior to the Boer War. For example, William Gatacre was highly critical of the lack of intelligence shown by the ordinary soldier during the Tirah campaign of 1898, whereas other officers were scathing about the stultifying and outdated drill that made up the majority of training in the late 1890s.[8] Furthermore, the apparent benefits of improved initiative were considered doubtful by some officers. Even the forward-thinking Colonel G. F. R. Henderson had concerns about the concept, attributing Prussian setbacks in 1870 to "the impetuosity of all ranks and the excessive independence of the subordinate leaders" and feeling that too much initiative would cause basic drill book principles to be "cast to the winds."[9]

However, the war in South Africa provided stark evidence of the need to improve the intelligence and initiative of the individual soldier. As will be discussed in greater detail in subsequent chapters, the range and effectiveness of Boer firepower caused the abandonment of close-order formations in favor of widely extended lines, making it harder for officers to keep their men in hand and under control. Furthermore, the accuracy of modern rifles and the lack of smoke on the battlefield meant officers who shunned cover and tried to set an example for their troops became prime targets for Boer marksmen. Lord Methuen noted that after the Battle of Modder River, "the truth is that when no-one can get on a horse with any safety within 2,000 yards of the enemy, orders cannot be conveyed," and officer attrition soon became so severe that badges of rank and swords were abandoned to avoid drawing undue fire.[10] In these circumstances, handling larger formations became extremely difficult. Passing orders to front-line officers who were virtually indistinguishable from their men was a challenge for messengers, especially as they were forced to advance "from boulder to boulder" on their way to the front to avoid Boer snipers.[11] Even in the firing line itself, wide extensions made the conveyance of vocal commands difficult, with men at the fringes of the formation often unable either to identify their commanding officer because of his plain uniform or to hear his shouts over the sounds of combat. Whistle calls and identification badges worn on the collar or back of the uniform were suggested to remedy these issues, but these were improvised solutions that were far from ideal.[12] These command problems were so acute that one veteran officer considered that handling a single battalion under Boer War conditions was harder than handling an entire brigade in earlier years.[13]

This loss of control created a series of related problems that cascaded down the command structure of the British Army in South Africa, revealing the weakness of pre-war instruction. Deprived of orders from higher ranks, junior officers such as captains and subalterns suddenly found themselves facing far more responsibility than had been anticipated in peacetime training.[14] Inexperienced officers often struggled to cope with these unexpected demands, and Major-General A. H. Paget felt that in the case of many junior commanders, "it was perfectly obvious that they dreaded responsibility."[15] Inevitably, these officers looked to their NCOs for support in such circumstances, in some cases to excessive levels. Colonel Forbes MacBean noted that inexperienced officers "would almost rather take an old colour sergeant's opinion than develop one of their own."[16] Unfortunately, NCOs lacked any real schooling in command duties, and

although the rate of attrition often forced them to take the place of
officer casualties in combat, this was not a job for which they had
been prepared in peacetime training.[17] The difficulties of command
and control experienced by junior officers and NCOs filtered down
to the men themselves, who had often been trained to look toward
their officers for all instructions and therefore were not expected to
act on their own initiative.[18] Although the dependence of men on
officers could vary from battalion to battalion, at its worst it risked
leaving the soldiers utterly paralyzed in the absence of direct orders.[19] One anonymous officer described NCOs and men as being
"like a flock of sheep" when deprived of their officers, feeling that
defeats and lost opportunities throughout the conflict could often
be traced to this key problem.[20] This problem was especially noticeable in combat firing, as pre-war musketry training had largely been
based on the assumption that in action it would always be possible
for an officer to point out the target and announce the range.[21] When
battlefield confusion or officer casualties meant that such orders
were not forthcoming, the soldiers' shooting could prove exceptionally poor.[22]

Such issues were not necessarily universal throughout the army
during the Boer War, with certain formations benefitting from strong
leadership and training that reduced confusion. When the 1st Sher-
wood Foresters arrived in South Africa in December 1899, it was
put through rapid and rigorous training to prepare it for "the class
of warfare" it was expected to face, reducing battlefield confusion
when it went into action.[23] Nevertheless, the problems of command
and control in the Boer War were widespread and attracted a great
deal of attention within the army.

A critical issue for many junior officers in the war was a system of peacetime training that had left them with little work to do
and granted limited opportunities to exercise command. The eight-
company battalion system, the need to provide drafts for India, and
related manpower shortages meant that officers rarely possessed
a command worth the name. Hence, the officers interfered in the
work of subordinates, enforcing conformity at the expense of responsibility. Lieutenant Colonel A. W. A. Pollock summed up this
attitude as follows: "Zeal amongst us is displayed chiefly in worry-
ing those below us in rank, and scheming to avoid being ourselves
worried by those above us."[24] This culture of interference bore bitter

fruit in the Boer War. Schooled in a system where a superior officer was always close at hand to criticize mistakes, junior officers were often left crippled by the fear that any fault might earn them a reprimand or even lead to them being "Stellenbosched."[25] Sir Howard Vincent bemoaned that peacetime training attitudes were carried over into the war itself, with errors made in action being "mercilessly" seized on by "officer desk critics," causing some leaders in the field to prefer passive inaction rather than risking punishment for failure in combat.[26] Horace Smith-Dorrien gave voice to similar sentiments in a diary entry for 5 March 1901, writing, "I wish this war would end, as so far I have not been found out in any glorious mistakes, and should like to 'stand' as one says at cards when one has a fair hand and doesn't care to risk taking more for fear of losing everything."[27]

In the aftermath of the conflict, evidence presented before the Elgin Commission was virtually unanimous in calling for officers and men to be trained to accept greater responsibility and demonstrate more individual initiative.[28] Most felt that in addition to offsetting command paralysis in the absence of orders, cultivating intelligence and initiative would prove crucial in allowing troops to attack across fire-swept areas. In the face of modern rifle fire, density of formation and sheer weight of assault could no longer be relied on to succeed without the risk of prohibitive casualties. Avoiding such severe losses was particularly important for Britain, which relied on a small volunteer army that could not absorb casualties as easily as the mass forces of the continent. However, avoidance of heavy losses in turn raised the issue of how to maintain morale during an assault. Dense formations and close officer control had traditionally been the solution to keep morale high and prevent routs, with the troops drawing confidence from the presence of comrades and fearing the shame of being seen to panic. Conversely, extended formations, invisible foes, and potential isolation from officers placed far greater strain on the men than ever before.[29] Faced with these related issues, officers such as Lieutenant-General Sir Ian Hamilton felt that the solution lay in the development of a small but elite army, based around highly trained soldiers who could be relied on to press forward individually or in groups, laying covering fire for comrades and seizing advantages presented by local cover.[30] Instead of dense formations bolstering morale, superior training would give the men confidence in their own weapons and abilities. Similar views were advanced by William Gatacre, who believed such a spirit had been developing by the latter stages of the Boer War. Gatacre argued that successful attacks now depended less on the actions of nearby officers and more "on the initiative of the best non-commissioned officers and men who become local leaders."[31] G. F. R. Henderson seized upon the idea of NCOs being at the heart of attack tactics, with sergeants handling small squads of men in the absence of local officers.[32] Colonel J. H. A. MacDonald also endorsed the concept, noticing that intermingling of units during combat further limited the influence of officers; instead, he suggested training infantry companies to emphasize the formation of small groups under leaders specially drawn from the best NCOs and men.[33] Indeed, the role of NCOs had been paramount in both infantry and cavalry in the latter stages of the Boer War, with officer shortages meaning that it was estimated around 70 percent of cavalry squadrons were led by NCOs.[34]

In the aftermath of the Boer War, the British Army was seized by a spirit of reform that promised improvements to the key command difficulties experienced in combat. Extended battlefronts meant that the company was now considered the largest formation that could be controlled by a single officer, and although manpower problems still remained, there was a conscious effort to give captains and subalterns more responsibilities and encourage them to exercise their leadership skills in peacetime.[35] Whereas the 1896 *Drill Book* had first suggested the need for greater intelligence amongst all ranks, *Combined Training 1902* placed new emphasis on the issue, including how it was to be achieved:

Success in war cannot be expected unless all ranks have been trained in peace to use their wits. Generals and commanding officers are, therefore, not only to encourage their subordinates in so doing by affording them constant opportunities of acting on their own responsibility but, they will also check all practices which interfere with the free exercise of their judgment, and will break down, by every means in their power, the paralyzing habit of an unreasoning and mechanical adherence to the letter of orders and to routine, when acting under service conditions.[36]

Officers of both infantry companies and cavalry squadrons were given more tactical responsibilities and were expected to take a personal interest in improving the training of their own formations.[37] For example, for most of the nineteenth century the training of subalterns had been a role traditionally managed by the battalion colonel, but to foster closer company-level cooperation it was now incorporated into a captain's duties.[38] The increased role of junior officers and emphasis on initiative also encouraged a practical attitude toward training. Whereas prior to the Boer War it had been noted that the British regimental officer was "expected to make himself acquainted with the most absurdly unimportant details . . . there was but little necessity for him to be a soldier," in 1905 John French summed up the new attitude when he stated that junior officer training should make a clear distinction between "the 'cram' which aims at success in examination, and the inculcation of instinctive knowledge which aims at success in the field."[39] After an inspection of field artillery on Salisbury Plain, the camp commandant echoed similar sentiments, ruminating that "Nothing in my experience is more conducive to failure than a contentment with being word perfect in the Drill Book."[40] Although this change in ethos took time to produce results, there was much praise for junior officers' eagerness to learn. Keenness and a growing sense of professionalism were noted as becoming apparent among officers in the years following the Boer War, leading to improved instruction for the men and greater initiative at all levels.[41] Lord Methuen had rich praise for the work of permanently constituted divisions and brigades at the 1904 maneuvers, commenting, "One noticed complete decentralisation; the orders were given and it was taken for granted that they would be carried out intelligently. There was a complete absence of fuss, and officers and men took interest and used their individual intelligence."[42]

Although the process was not without its flaws, particularly the continuing need to provide drafts for India that drained away manpower and reduced training efficiency, there was a steady process of development throughout the period. By the middle years of the Edwardian era, there were discernable improvements in overall leadership quality, described as a "great step" by the inspector general of forces in 1907.[43]

Matching the reform of the role of junior officers, in the years following the Boer War there was a concerted effort to improve the quality of NCOs and men. Leo Amery summed up the intention of the reforms in 1903, noting that "The passive, automatic discipline of the ear must give place to the active, conscious discipline of the mind and of the will."[44] Brigadier General Michael Rimington echoed similar sentiments at the 1906 General Staff Conference: "The keynote of our training is always the same: *Develop the individual initiative of every officer, non-commissioned officer and man.*"[45] To this end, company officers were expected to become instructors rather than simple drill masters, encouraging the troops to show initiative and skill rather than mechanical obedience.[46] For example, musketry training placed new emphasis on individual accuracy and ability to estimate ranges, moving away from volleys and iron fire discipline that had been common prior to the Boer War. Innovative training exercises were introduced that meant that men were given the chance to demonstrate their initiative in situations approximating service conditions; even though some flaws remained in these maneuvers, particularly their small scale, they represented a considerable advance in overall training ethos. The quality of the regular British soldier steadily improved over the period, and by 1912, the inspector general of forces was pleased to report that he considered that for "individual efficiency" the British infantryman was the best in the world, attracting admiration from foreign observers.[47] In the same year, Lieutenant Colonel Campbell urged his fellow officers not to underestimate the importance of the average private, who he felt was now capable of winning a firefight even in the absence of direct orders—a clear improvement from the situation prevailing during the Boer War.[48] NCOs were also singled out for development. As previously discussed, several prominent officers saw NCOs as being a key element in future tactics, and the idea of a "staff college for noncommissioned officers" had been suggested to the Elgin Commission.[49] Acting on this proposal, an NCO school based in Salisbury Command was founded in 1904, with a mixed syllabus that encouraged greater command and combat responsibilities for sergeants.[50]

The reform of individual training was an essential component in creating the famously elite infantry of the BEF, but the process was not without difficulties or tensions. Whereas encouraging greater standards of skill amidst junior officers was largely a question of training reform, improving the NCOs and men was a more complex matter that touched on the raw nerve of social prejudice. There was a widespread fear of social degeneration created by urbanization during the Edwardian period, a concern that was worsened by the fact that the British Army did much of its recruiting from the lowest strata of society, often drawing on poorly fed and ill-educated men. During the Boer War, physical standards had been lowered to help recruitment, with the result that the British Army in South Africa was the smallest in physical terms that the country deployed during the nineteenth and twentieth centuries.[51] Boers were amazed by the difference in height between officers and men and were distinctly unimpressed by the physical standard of the some of the British soldiers, one burgher considering that "They had neither the accent nor the gait of Christians."[52] Later drafts of recruits and volunteers sent to South Africa often proved to be physically weak and tactically poor—notably the second contingent of Imperial Yeomanry—raising further prejudices about the capability of urbanized British citizens to make useful soldiers.[53]

The contradictory factors of lingering mistrust of the social class from which much of the army was drawn and a desire to encourage skill and initiative among the men caused the British Army to undergo what M. A. Ramsay termed "a paradigmatic crisis" as it searched for tactical solutions to the problems of modern warfare.[54] Even during the Boer War, there had been concerns that the degree of individuality allowed to men had become excessive. For example, James Grierson worried that officers and men had become too casual in tolerating nonregulation clothing in the field, and one anonymous officer felt that traditional ideas of drill, steadiness, and discipline had ultimately been the key in overcoming the skillful but ill-disciplined Boers.[55] In the aftermath of the conflict, some officers, such as Ian Hamilton, actually saw the army as an instrument of social regeneration, taking the lowest members of society and turning them into healthy, intelligent, and patriotic soldiers.[56] However, others had little faith in the working class and considered the new spirit of initiative to be positively dangerous. An anonymous officer complained in 1903, "The soldier has no more right to perpetual individuality than the operative, the mechanic or the domestic servant. What factory manager, engineer or housekeeper would allow independence of action to either of these classes?"[57]

This mistrust of the lower classes placed limitations on some of the reforms, particularly with regard to the role of NCOs. For example, the training given at the NCO School at Salisbury Plain was heralded as a great success, but by 1906 the school had been abolished, even though the Army Council admitted it had carried out "good and useful work" and the inspector general considered it "excellent."[58] Lack of funding was cited as the principal reason for its closure, but the Army Council made further justifications, including that the syllabus could be taught within regiments and that the attendance of NCOs at the school placed a burden on the companies from which they were drawn.[59] However, it has been suggested that the desire to maintain command in the hands of the officer class and avoid any dilution of power to NCOs of a lower social status was the fundamental reason that the tactical development of NCOs became marginalized in the pre–First World War period.[60] Promotion from the ranks actually declined during the Edwardian era, and the role of NCOs was not developed to the same extent that was apparent among junior officers and men.[61] Social status remained an important aspect to command, with one prize-winning essay published in 1914 arguing, "The 'habit to command' is largely hereditary," while another officer felt that it would be impossible to expect NCOs to be capable of the same intellectual standards expected from officers unless they were drawn from the same social class.[62]

Edwardian society was greatly defined by the class structure, and it was highly unlikely that a conservative, hierarchical institution such as the army would adopt egalitarian methods in peacetime. However, although modern historians have sometimes attributed military failures in 1914 to the existence of an anachronistic and elitist officer class, this interpretation is overly narrow and ignores the considerable improvement in British Army tactics that took place prior to the First World War.[63] Although social prejudice created certain tensions and limited the development of the tactical role played by NCOs, it did not stop overall improvements taking place in training for all ranks during the 1902–1914 period.

The shock of the Boer War caused a fundamental shift in attitudes toward training. Junior officers of all arms took a keener interest in the profession and were expected to show greater initiative and skill, and the men benefited from more advanced training. A private from the York and Lancaster Regiment recalled the confidence inspired by the presence of veteran NCOs in 1914, particularly the "old sweats" who had fought in colonial actions, concluding, "They were fine chaps, and good soldiers."[64] Writing some years after the First World War, Cyril Falls contrasted the hastily trained British soldiers of 1917 with more experienced troops of an earlier era, noting, "When he really was a trained soldier, the British non-commissioned officer was unsurpassed in skill and initiative."[65]

German sources sometimes attributed the tactical skills of the BEF to the presence of large numbers of colonial veterans.[66] This was not the case; indeed, the BEF of August 1914 was made up of around 60 percent reservists, few of whom had seen action.[67] In fact, the skills of the BEF had been developed as a result of changes in attitude and training in the aftermath of the Boer War. The tactical improvements that are discussed in later chapters were ultimately dependent on this new training ethos.

THE ABSENCE OF FORMAL DOCTRINE

Although there was a significant development in individual officer and soldier quality from 1899 to 1914, some major issues remained unresolved. Perhaps the most serious of these was the thorny issue of devising and implementing a formal doctrine. The Boer War had broken down a number of barriers that had prevented the creation of a doctrine in the Victorian era. For much of the nineteenth century the army had fought so-called small wars around the globe, with lessons learned in action having little impact beyond the immediate participants. The potential problems created by this absence of doctrine were highlighted by Redvers Buller, who observed that inexperienced officers were often left bewildered in action: "There is scarcely one officer in a hundred who has been taught any rule which would guide him in deciding how to act when confronted by the problem so frequent in war: 'I have my orders, but what ought I to do?'"[68]

The Boer War offered an opportunity to correct this flaw. In contrast to the small wars of previous years, the conflict in South Africa ultimately involved the majority of the British Army, giving the advantage of a shared combat experience on which to base future development. Furthermore, the dismal planning, organization, and intelligence work that had been undertaken prior to the war revived the debate about the desirability of instituting a General Staff system.[69] This debate ultimately bore fruit in 1904, when the reforms recommended by the Esher Committee swept away the post of commander in chief and replaced it with Britain's first General Staff, headed by successful Boer War commander Lieutenant-General Sir Neville Gerald Lyttelton.

Shared combat experience and the creation of the General Staff laid valuable groundwork for developing key principles that would carry the British Army into the twentieth century, but there were several crucial difficulties that delayed and ultimately prevented the creation of a formal doctrine prior to the First World War. The greatest of these problems was the unique military responsibilities imposed by the need to police the world's largest empire. Potential enemies and theaters of operations varied enormously, with the army as likely to face crudely armed tribal foes as they were opposition equipped with modern rifles. Dealing with these imperial conflicts remained the principal duty of the British Army in the immediate aftermath of the Boer War. A struggle against European opposition was considered highly unlikely, with the possible exception of a clash with Russia if the latter chose to invade India.[70] Contemporaries recognized that even though the tactical lessons learned in South Africa were valuable, the sheer variety of foes presented unique problems for the formation of a formal doctrine based on the example of a single conflict. One Boer War veteran officer complained of the dangers of being "tied down to hard and fast rules," while Major-General J. F. Maurice summed up the problems as follows: "I venture to think that there is a danger in our assuming that we can, from this one war [the Boer War], deduce all the lessons which will be applicable to the work of the British Army. . . . I maintain that the British Army is under a condition of difficulty . . . that exists for no other Army in the world, and we must face and recognize the fact that we cannot attempt to stereotype our tactics."[71]

Training manuals of the Edwardian period reflect the reluctance to create a formal doctrine, highlighting general principles but leaving considerable leeway for interpretation among officers. This practice ensured the tactical flexibility necessary for facing a wide variety of enemies, but it created a certain degree of confusion and inconsistency in training. As will be discussed in later chapters, these problems manifested themselves in the differing methods used by various commands regarding fundamental tactics, such as the width of infantry extensions and the deployment of artillery in covered or open positions. Although such difficulties were of limited importance in small colonial actions in which relatively low numbers of troops would be deployed, the growing threat from Germany and the risk of a large-scale European war suggested the need for a formal doctrine within the British Army.

However, the creation of any central doctrine was constrained not only by the need to remain flexible for a huge variety of potential foes, but also by concerns that it could potentially stifle officer initiative and cause a recurrence of the problems that had bedeviled the British Army in South Africa.[72] Indeed, the desire to improve the independence of junior officers and men in the years following the Boer War was so strong that it sometimes became counterproductive. In 1905, John French praised the spirit evident in company training but cautioned that giving captains the opportunity to exercise their initiative meant that bad habits and "manifestly wrong" methods could develop. However, mindful of the need to encourage individual command skills among junior officers, battalion colonels were reluctant to point out errors, causing French to highlight the fact that "some 'guidance' (rather than 'interference') is imperatively called for."[73]

This problem was common in the British Army throughout the period: local methods were tolerated, which led to the development of subtly different tactics in separate commands and divisions. In 1907, the Duke of Connaught expressed concerns that there was a "go as you please" attitude toward tactics, and that the lack of central doctrine created a "tendency to [form] cliques around particular Generals, from which the Army has suffered in the past."[74] This problem remained largely unresolved, arguably growing worse as the Boer War faded from memory. John French noted in 1911 that "The South African War and the lessons learnt from it had the effect of starting a new school of thought, which for some years gave a great impetus to training, and revived interest and initiative among officers. This seems to have died away into theory. We have a superfluity of literature on training, and a mass of theory is thrown at the heads of officers which they do their best to assimilate, but which has little visible effect."[75]

Other officers agreed with this assessment, noting that despite the amount of literature produced, it provided little central direction and thus tended to confuse rather than clarify. Brigadier General F. C. Carter bemoaned the disease of "*cacoethes scribendi,*"[76] complaining that "Every spring and autumn lengthy and verbose paraphrases of our Field Service Regulations are issued from several of the Command, Divisional, and Brigade Headquarters. These only tend to confuse and exasperate commanding and other officers. . . . I have seen no less than 14 of these paraphrases, called 'Hints on Training,' mostly of two printed foolscap pages, all issued in one year from a Divisional General Staff Officer."[77] This mass of often contradictory literature did not serve to create a uniform doctrine, and diversity of method remained. Official training manuals offered sound guiding principles but rejected formal doctrine. *Infantry Training 1905* was particularly strident on the issue, stating,

> It is impossible to lay down a fixed and unvarying system of attack or defence. Although such system might appear capable of modification to meet different conditions, yet constant practice in a stereotypical formation inevitably leads to want of elasticity, accustoms all ranks to work by rule rather than by the exercise of their wits, and cramps both initiative and intelligence. . . . It is therefore strictly forbidden either to formulate or to practise a normal form of either attack or defence.[78]

Despite the caution about fixed methods of attack, one clear principle that was emphasized in official manuals throughout the era was the need for close cooperation of all arms. This teamwork had been the key to victory in the Boer War, particularly in Natal, where cooperation between infantry and artillery had eventually allowed the British to break through the Boer lines. Equally, in the more open terrain of the Orange Free State, Lord Roberts's combination of frontal infantry attacks and turning movements with mounted forces had driven the Boers back at relatively low cost. *Combined Training 1905* embodied these concepts in a particularly clear paragraph that had echoes of the experience of South Africa:

Mounted troops and infantry compel the enemy to disclose his position and thereby afford a target to the artillery, whilst the latter by their fire enable infantry to approach the hostile position. Infantry, unaccompanied by mounted troops, is hampered by ignorance of the enemy's movements, cannot move in security, and is unable to reap the fruits of victory; unaccompanied by artillery, it is unable to reply to fire beyond rifle range, and is generally powerless against entrenchments. On the other hand, without artillery or machine guns, even the most mobile cavalry, unless they possess a marked numerical superiority, cannot be relied upon to drive back the hostile horsemen; while artillery, left to itself, is helpless.[79]

Combined Training went on to urge that all officers should gain some knowledge of the principles of employment of other arms.[80] The theme was continued in *Field Service Regulations 1909*, with the paragraph on combined arms being repeated almost verbatim.[81] However, although these training manuals urged closer cooperation, little was done to suggest a systematic manner in which it could be achieved. For example, *Infantry Training 1905* devoted three paragraphs to cooperation with artillery, emphasizing its importance but offering no real advice on how it could be developed.[82] The failure to create a true doctrine for all arms cooperation was a serious weakness for the British Army. Without systematic guidance, the individual arms tended to learn within their own framework, and developing closer links took time and effort to bear fruit. This state of affairs was particularly true of infantry and artillery, which is discussed in greater depth in subsequent chapters.

Many historians have praised the issue of *Field Service Regulations 1909*, with Jay Luvaas contending that it effectively created a uniform doctrine and Corelli Barnett arguing that without it, the enormous expansion of the British Army in the First World War would have resulted in utter chaos.[83] John Dunlop considered the work to be "of the greatest value for the inculcation of one central doctrine."[84] In fact, although *Field Service Regulations* was an important advance in British military thinking, it did not represent the creation of a formal written doctrine, and it continued the trend of rejecting the concept. The opening chapter of the manual stated,

"The fundamental principles of war are neither very numerous nor in themselves very abstruse, but the application of them is difficult and cannot be made subject to rules."[85] *Field Service Regulations* continued to place great emphasis on cooperation between the arms, noting, "*The full power of an army can be exerted only when all its parts act in close combination,*" but although the manual encouraged close links, it did little to ensure unity of method among arms or divisions.[86] For example, in 1912 the inspector general of forces praised the quality of *Field Service Regulations* and its accompanying service manuals but identified four critical tactical problems that were still open to substantial interpretation, noting that this ambiguity meant there was still "opportunity [for] individuals to put their own views into practice."[87] Furthermore, during a 1912 inspection, it was found that 2nd, 3rd, and 4th Divisions each had their own preferred method of attack that differed considerably from one another, causing the inspector general to complain that even though junior officers and men were at a peak of efficiency, the army as a whole had not achieved "anything approaching uniformity of practice, which is so divergent in different divisions that it would be difficult for them to combine into an army that acts with full effect."[88] However, the Army Council expressed little concern at the criticism, noting that *Field Service Regulations* clearly stated that methods should vary according to circumstances, and that therefore such variation in training was, in fact, to be considered "essential."[89] It was somewhat blithely assumed that in the event of a combined operation between the formations, the divisions would be acting under the orders of a higher authority and thus be able to regulate their methods to achieve their directed objectives.[90]

While official manuals continued to emphasize the attributes of flexibility and a rejection of formal rules, the British General Staff offered an opportunity to create a school of thought among the intellectual elite of the officer class that could ultimately emerge into a doctrine. On the continent, the presence of a General Staff system encouraged the development of operational doctrine, providing leadership from above that filtered down throughout the army. However, in Britain the newly formed General Staff experienced a number of teething troubles that slowed its development and limited its ability to create doctrine. As the first ever chief of General Staff, Neville Gerald Lyttelton proved to be a great disappointment.

Although he had done well as a commander in Natal during the Boer War, he was promoted beyond his abilities and offered no real leadership for the General Staff. Charles Repington, the influential military correspondent of the *Times*, was scathing about Lyttelton, writing in 1906, "old N.G.'s idea of happiness is to have no questions asked . . . he rated men according to their capacity for leaving him alone . . . he and many of his officers are the laughing stock of the Army and a fraud upon the public."[91] In addition to the weak leadership of Lyttelton, the General Staff was initially plagued by organizational problems and petty squabbles, delaying its true development.[92] Indeed, it has been argued that the General Staff did not constitute a true corps of elite, intellectual soldiers until at least 1908, when Lyttelton was replaced by William Nicholson.[93]

Though the General Staff played an important role in developing training manuals and held regular conferences to discuss tactical and operational problems, these measures did little to solve the problems of a lack of doctrine and diversity of method noticeable in the British Army. Part of the problem lay in the fact that the General Staff was somewhat disconnected from the lower-ranking officers of the British Army. In 1907, the Duke of Connaught complained that the General Staff did not provide leadership that filtered down, arguing that the body was "out of touch" with the army as a whole and in danger of being viewed as "just another War Office organisation."[94] It has been argued the entire army in this period was in the grip of a so-called cult of rank that limited debate between senior commanders and junior officers, a factor that seriously impaired the ability of the General Staff to devise a doctrine that would be accepted and implemented at lower levels.[95] For example, in 1905, a proposal to publish the reports on staff tours for the benefit of junior officers was rejected on the grounds that they would "probably be too difficult for the Regimental officer."[96] The result of this dislocation was that General Staff ideas sometimes ran counter to the prevailing ethos at lower levels. For example, whereas initiative and flexibility were emphasized at battalion level throughout the Edwardian period, in 1910 Douglas Haig expressed concern at ideas put forward at the staff conference of that year, writing, "I already see from your discussion at the Staff Coll. Confer. a tendency to split hairs, and a desire for *precise* rules to guide officers in every conceivable situation in war. This wants watching."[97]

Faced with the need to remain flexible to face a variety of enemies around the globe and lacking strong direction from the fledgling General Staff, the British Army was neither willing nor able to develop a formal operational doctrine prior to the First World War. Instead any ideas of doctrine were couched in loose and general terms, with wide room for interpretation. For example, Michael Rimington described a doctrine that permeated all ranks as "essential to success in war," going on to echo *Field Service Regulations* in stating "The doctrine is 'THE UNION OF ARMS AND THE RESOLUTE OFFENSIVE.'"[98] Although the British Army was undoubtedly moving toward closer cooperation between arms, particularly infantry and artillery, the considerable variance of tactical methods in each of the six BEF divisions placed limits on how much could be achieved prior to the First World War. Martin Samuels and Tim Travers have criticized the failure to develop a formal doctrine, arguing that it allowed backward ideas to flourish and contrasting it with the success of the German General Staff.[99] However, Travers also acknowledged that in 1914 the BEF as a whole emphasized a "sensible and flexible" approach to war that avoided stereotypical tactics, with the main problems lying in implementation rather than theory.[100] More recently it has been suggested that although the British Army undoubtedly suffered command problems at higher levels in 1914, at a tactical level it was considerably more advanced.[101]

This dichotomy between tactical skill and operational weakness was influenced by the experience of the Boer War. The struggle in South Africa had highlighted numerous weaknesses in the training of officers and men and had clearly demonstrated the tactical command problems that existed on a modern battlefield. However, the uniqueness of the Boers' fighting style as well as the relative brevity of the conventional stage of the war meant that there was little opportunity to learn operational-level lessons that could prove useful in the scale of conflict that a European war would entail. Furthermore, the Boer War did not fundamentally alter the duties of the British Army, which remained a small force designed to police the empire rather than engage in mass-scale warfare. The doctrinal lessons learned in South Africa were principally aimed at ensuring success in the next major colonial war, rather than in a vast European struggle.[102] This fact has caused some historians to be critical of the tactical approach that emerged as a result of the Boer War, with G. R. Searle arguing that it meant reformers "often became convinced of the merits of measures that later proved to be irrelevant, if not positively harmful. . . . British soldiers had engaged in a mobile, open war, in which small groups of men were obliged to assume a large amount of responsibility for their own actions . . . in short, South Africa did not provide the best possible preparation for the battlefields of northern France and Flanders."[103] However, the Boer War lessons regarding the need to develop skill, intelligence, and initiative among all ranks were of universal value. The tactical difficulties on the Western Front were not a result of erroneous Boer War lessons but, rather, were often attributable to the incomplete implementation of such concepts.[104]

Furthermore, in 1914, the high tactical quality of the regular BEF was of critical importance in surviving and ultimately blunting the onslaught of the Germans through Belgium and France. Whereas the operational handling of the British Army during this period has drawn criticism, the skill and professionalism of the army has attracted widespread praise.[105] Although the ethos of the British Army in this period had been geared toward colonial policing duties, at a tactical level it demonstrated considerable flexibility and performed well in the opening months of the First World War. The elite nature of the BEF was a direct result of the new training ethos that emerged as a result of the Boer War, replacing unthinking obedience, dread of responsibility, and strict discipline with individual initiative and skill at arms.

In the opening months of the First World War, such attributes were vital in allowing the outnumbered British Army to perform well against their German opposites. John Bourne has described the battles of 1914 as "soldiers' battles," with critical decision making taking place "at the 'sharp end' among formations of company level or even below," and it was here that the tactical skill of the BEF was at its most prominent.[106] However, the small size of the army and the absence of any formal doctrine meant that once the regular army had effectively been destroyed at the end of 1914, much knowledge was lost, meaning the new volunteer divisions were forced to learn painful and bloody lessons afresh. Many talented young officers of the BEF were killed in the fighting of 1914, and the surviving regular cadre was too small to provide a useful base for the massive expansion that followed.[107] Early training of the "New Armies" was particularly poor, with many of the problems that had been identified by the Elgin Commission reemerging, particularly lack of initiative in the absence of direct orders.[108] It would take the bitter experience of combat in 1916 and 1917 before an effective doctrine was crafted that was suitable for the mass warfare of the Western Front. Many of the skills necessary for victory in the First World War, particularly improved squad-level tactics and closer cooperation of infantry and artillery, had been identified in the Boer War. However, though many improvements had been made in the 1902–1914 period, the failure to codify the concepts into a formal doctrine seriously hampered the training of the massively expanded British Army and forced them to endure a bloody learning curve until final victory in 1918.

THE PRIMACY OF THE OFFENSIVE

In addition to prompting a wide-ranging reform of the training ethos of the British Army, the Boer War also played a key role in the debate over the viability of frontal assault tactics in the face of modern firepower. The discussion regarding how to press an attack successfully in the face of smokeless magazine rifles, machine guns, entrenchments, and artillery was common to all major armies of the period. Although advocates of both offensive and defensive methods enjoyed periods of ascendency, by 1914 a surprising consensus on the issue had emerged across Europe, which ultimately marked a retrograde step for the British Army from the lessons learned in the Boer War.

Concern over the effectiveness of the latest weapons had been growing within military circles throughout the latter part of the nineteenth century. Battles in the American Civil War (1861–65), the Franco-Prussian War (1870–71), and the Russo-Turkish War (1877–78) had all shown the difficulties of pressing the attack against well-armed and entrenched defenders, with even successful assaults suffering heavy causalities. However, the colonial duties of the British Army meant that encountering foes armed with modern weapons was relatively rare; thus, devising solutions to the problems of attack was a lower priority than it was for continental armies.[109]

However, although the British had little experience in facing modern firepower, the effectiveness of their own weapons against tribal foes had been proved throughout the Victorian era. Frederick Maurice cited Omdurman as a counterpoint to continental thinkers who argued that numbers and determination could overcome fire, noting, "If any accumulation of numbers or any supreme readiness to sacrifice life could enable a body of attacking troops to advance in front against modern infantry and artillery fire, beyond doubt the Dervishes would have broken our line at Omdurman. Therefore that battle gives, under this aspect, food for much reflection."[110] Nonetheless, even though there were concerns over the effectiveness of modern weapons, there was little consensus on how serious a problem this effectiveness might pose. Even the forward-thinking G. F. R. Henderson considered that "Shrapnel, Maxims and the small bore do not seem to increase the butcher's bill to the extent some would have us believe," although he acknowledged that the effect of fire on troops in the open would be "very great."[111]

The experience of the Boer War starkly revealed that the more cautious analysts of the Victorian army had been correct. At Magersfontein, the Highland Brigade was left pinned down on an open plain for hours, with small groups at various ranges between two hundred and six hundred yards from the Boer line unable to advance or retreat. Leo Amery wrote after the war that "efforts to rush the trenches were still made from time to time, but gallantry was powerless in the face of the overwhelming advantage of position . . . Rarely have troops gone through so severe an ordeal."[112] At the Battle of Paardeberg, Horace Smith-Dorrien witnessed a succession of attacks across open ground against the entrenched Boer laager come to grief, recalling one attempt in the following terms: "It was a gallant charge, gallantly led, but the fact that not one of them got within 300 yards of the enemy is sufficient proof of its futility."[113] These early setbacks showed clearly that frontal attacks against well-positioned Boers could succeed only with strong artillery support, wide infantry extensions, and skillful tactics.

Upon assuming command in South Africa, Lord Roberts adopted a different strategy for dealing with the Boers. Whereas Buller, Gatacre, and Methuen had been forced by geography, limited supply lines, and lack of mobile troops into making frontal assaults, Roberts possessed far larger numbers of cavalry and aimed to maneuver the Boers out of strong positions rather than batter his way through them. Frontal attacks were made by widely extended lines and aimed to hold the Boers in place, while flanking forces turned them out of their positions.[114] The strategy repeatedly forced the Boers back, allowing Roberts to relieve Kimberley and seize his objectives in the form of the cities of Bloemfontein and Pretoria without suffering the kind of defeats suffered by Buller in Natal. However, with the exception of the capture of Cronjé's laager at Paardeberg, it also allowed the Boer forces to escape from battle relatively intact. Continental writers, particularly in Germany, were contemptuous of this approach. The German official history of the war complained that "Lord Roberts's system throughout the whole campaign was to manoeuvre rather than to fight" and lambasted the British for being unwilling to risk heavy casualties in pursuit of a decisive victory.[115] Lord Roberts responded, arguing, "I manoeuvred in order to be able to fight the Boers on my own and not their terms," noting that the Boers would have been delighted to face frontal British attacks in prepared positions as at Magersfontein.[116]

Although many continental critics remained unimpressed, it was respect for firepower that came to encapsulate British offensive thinking in the years immediately following the Boer War. The experience of fighting in South Africa caused G. F. R. Henderson to revise his earlier opinions on modern weapons, writing in 1900, "A direct (or frontal) attack against good troops well posted, always a desperate undertaking, has now become suicidal."[117] Ian Hamilton echoed similar sentiments, feeling that old-fashioned, European-style attacks relying on mass were likely to fail and instead advocating the use of flanking movements and enfilade fire in the assault.[118] Some officers such as C. E. Callwell and B. F. S. Baden-Powell[119] went further, declaring that weapon quality now placed a decisive advantage in the hands of the defender, although such opinions were at the fringes of the debate.[120] Although there was an acknowledgement within the army that offensives would be more difficult under modern conditions, it was felt that though offering a passive defense might win local victories, it would ultimately lead to defeat through failure to capitalize on them. The Boers were cited as an example of this tendency. Despite winning a string of tactical victories against the British in the early part of the war, their failure to follow up their success was seen by some as being fatal.[121] As one British officer summed up, to remain purely on the defensive was "to suffer war, not make it."[122]

Therefore the ethos that emerged from the Boer War continued to place emphasis on the offensive as the path to ultimate victory, but the methods to be used were influenced by the bitter experiences of fighting in the Tugela and Modder River campaigns. Rejecting simple brute force, official manuals suggested the use of maneuvers in the style of Lord Roberts combined with the close artillery cooperation pioneered in Natal. *Infantry Training 1902* was skeptical about the use of frontal attacks across open ground, suggesting turning movements would yield better results for far fewer casualties.[123] Well-trained, skillful troops and extended formations were to reduce casualties during the advance, with great attention paid to the use of cover. As one officer commented in 1903, "If the old attack formations resembled the advancing tide, the new one will recall a number of parallel or converging streams rushing forward, as the surface of the ground permits."[124] If the enemy was particularly well entrenched and had secure flanks, direct assault was rejected and instead an approach by sap—covered trench—was advocated, such as that used at Paardeberg.[125] Indeed, the use of saps to close with an entrenched enemy formed the main focus for the 1906 maneuvers in India.[126]

However, a number of factors meant that the newfound respect for firepower gradually became eroded as the Edwardian era continued. The popularity of aggressive tactics remained high throughout European armies during this period, creating a virtual cult of the offensive in the French army and becoming a major influence for both the British and the Germans. This development has been widely analyzed by historians, including John Ellis, Michael Howard, M. A. Ramsay, and Tim Travers.[127] Though points of difference remain, a general consensus exists on the idea that military leaders saw the offensive as granting moral superiority, allowing courageous men to overcome well-armed but passive opponents through strength of will. Britain never became as devoted to the spirit of the offensive as the French, but a variety of influences in the years prior to the First World War meant that the British Army gradually began to lose sight of the lessons learned in South Africa.

One of the key influences throughout this period related to the new spirit of tactical initiative. From the eighteenth century onward, there had been concerns that once troops were given the chance to seek their own cover, getting them to move again would be extremely difficult, if not impossible. These issues were of particular concern to the British Army as it moved away from close control toward extended formations and local initiative. Doubts remained about the ability of the British lower classes to live up to the new tactical standards expected of the post–Boer War army, particularly how to maintain morale and ensure an advance when officers were not close at hand. Although thorough training, strong low-level leadership, and esprit de corps were seen as important factors, it was also considered essential that the men should be highly motivated.[128] High levels of individual motivation were seen as a form of discipline in themselves. Douglas Haig extolled the virtues of "courage, energy, determination, endurance, perseverance, and unselfishness," noting that "Without these qualities, which mean *discipline*, no combination will be possible."[129] To this end, the belief in the offensive and the exultation of moral strength became complementary ideas. To physically press a frontal attack in the face of modern weapons required great courage, and the determination to assume the offensive was held to give the attacker a distinct moral advantage over the enemy.[130]

Nevertheless, the bitter experience of the Boer War had shown that even courageous and highly disciplined regular soldiers could be stopped by the fire of magazine rifles. Acknowledgment of this fact may have continued to predominate in the British Army had it not been for the events of the Russo-Japanese War. During the conflict in Manchuria, Russian forces had assumed a generally defensive posture, fighting from behind earthworks and attempting to weather a string of Japanese attacks. The fire-swept zone in this conflict was even deadlier than it had been in the Boer War, with machine guns and large quantities of artillery adding substantial strength to the defender. The Japanese were often forced to approach via sap, moving under cover of darkness to within assault range of the Russian trenches.[131] Even with such preparations, attacks against Russian positions tended to be bloody affairs; however, despite suffering heavy casualties, the Japanese attacks were often successful. This success led many European observers to create a two-level analysis. On one hand, the tactical lessons emphasized the increase of firepower, the requirement for invisibility, and the high cost of assaults, but at a strategic level it was seen to demonstrate the power of the offensive to overcome the passive defensive, even if the defenders held a numerical advantage and the benefit of field works.[132] Indeed, the tactical observations seemed to confirm many of the lessons of the Boer War regarding firepower, entrenchment, and concealment.

British observers were generally cautious about the success of Japanese assault tactics. One officer concluded that the tactics of both armies "consisted chiefly of hard pounding, and the Japanese pounded hardest."[133] Ian Hamilton admired the speed of Japanese infantry rushes, but he attributed much of their success to the abysmal marksmanship of the Russians, contending that against well-trained British troops, "I do not see how the Japanese could hope to sprint across the last 300 yards."[134] Officers from the Royal Engineers noted that even successful attacks had taken several days of hard fighting, with particularly heavy losses in the initial assault waves.[135] One Royal Engineer commented that future attack tactics "will involve an appalling amount of spade work" but felt that this was the only way it would be possible to close with an entrenched enemy without prohibitive casualties.[136]

Yet, although the majority of tactical observations stressed the difficulty of assault and the heavy casualties it would entail, the fact the Japanese had won the Russo-Japanese War with an offensive strategy was seen as the ultimate vindication of the power of the attack.[137] Tactical observers placed importance on the use of entrenchment and close artillery support on the offensive, but these key factors were sometimes neglected by analysts, who often saw them as being of secondary importance to willpower and morale.[138] For example, the Japanese suffered 48,000 casualties in assaults against the defenses of Port Arthur compared with 28,200 casualties suffered by the Russians, but the eventual success of the Japanese attacks was held up as proof that morale could overcome the material advantages enjoyed by the defenders of fortifications.[139] Even the commander of the Russian forces in Manchuria, General Kuropatkin, supported this idea, writing after the war, "our moral strength was less than that of the Japanese. . . . This lack of martial spirit, of moral exaltation, and of heroic impulse, affected particularly our stubbornness in battle. In many cases we did not have sufficient resolution to conquer such antagonists as the Japanese."[140] The Japanese warrior spirit of *Bushido* was admired by European observers, and their willingness to take severe casualties in frontal attacks was contrasted favorably against the British preference for flanking

moves in the Boer War. German critic Major William Balck felt that
the Japanese had succeeded precisely because they had rejected British tactics and had instead "pushed doggedly forward like angry bull
dogs, never halting, until, bleeding and exhausted, they had fastened
themselves on the enemy and won the victory."[141] In the aftermath
of the Russo-Japanese War, such views became popular throughout
Europe, particularly in France. Although the Boer War had seemed
to demonstrate the power of modern weapons, the lessons of that
conflict had never been completely accepted in France or Germany,
and historians have suggested that this resurgence in the belief that
willpower and morale could overcome fixed defenses represented
the existence of preconceived ideas that had not been modified by
the South African war.[142]

The situation was somewhat different for the British Army,
which had the benefit of having practical experience in the Boer
War. Although British assessments drawn from the Russo-Japanese
War regarding the offensive were more cautious than those that
developed on the continent, they had the unfortunate effect of sti-
fling the trend of thinking that had emerged from the South African
conflict.[143] As in the French army, willpower was emphasized over
firepower by some officers. Even Ian Hamilton argued that "Blind-
ness to moral forces and worship of material forces inevitably lead
in war to destruction."[144] *Field Service Regulations* echoed similar
sentiments, stating, "Success in war depends more on moral than
physical qualities. Skill cannot compensate for want of courage, energy and determination," although it also sounded a note of caution for those who might take such ideas to extremes, adding that
"even high moral qualities may not avail without careful preparation and skilful direction."[145] The belief that sheer determination
could force men across fire-swept ground encouraged some officers
to express greater confidence about the success of the attack in the
face of modern weapons, rejecting the pessimistic appraisal that
had emerged in 1902. These related factors contributed to a subtle
change of wording from *Combined Training 1905* to *Field Service
Regulations 1909*, placing new emphasis on the final "assault"
rather than the development of superior firepower.[146] In a similar
manner, the emphasis on flank attacks that had been featured in earlier manuals was changed to an emphasis on finding the weak spot
in the enemy line and delivering a decisive assault at that point.[147]

The rejection of the South African experience seemed to reach a peak at the 1910 General Staff conference, when Brigadier General Lancelot Kiggell offered an opinion that apparently dismissed the Boer War at a stroke:

> After the Boer War the general opinion was that the result of the battle would for the future depend on fire-arms alone, and that the sword and the bayonet were played out. But this idea is erroneous and was proved so in the late war in Manchuria. Everyone admits that. Victory is won actually by the bayonet, or by fear of it, which amounts to the same thing so far as the conduct of the attack is concerned. This fact was proved beyond doubt in the late war. I think the whole question rather hangs on that; and if we accept the view that victory is actually won by the bayonet, it settles the point.[148]

When taken out of context, this quote appears to provide a clear illustration of backward thinking within the British Army.[149] Yet, the statement was actually made during a discussion on the importance of using fire to facilitate movement, with Kiggell offering his thoughts on the reasons why soldiers may "dissociate movement from fire" and how such issues could be overcome.[150]

Indeed, at brigade level and below, a belief in "fire and movement" and a respect for modern firepower remained central principles.[151] As a result, the cult of the offensive that gripped the French never truly emerged in the British Army, though individual officers sometimes favored such ideas.[152] Discussions at General Staff Conferences in 1911 and again in 1914 raised the possibility of copying various methods used by the French infantry in the attack but concluded that such tactics were impractical and incompatible with the bulk of British regulations; thus, such tactics were dismissed.[153] Furthermore, there were contrary voices within the army who criticized the dedication to aggressive tactics. Major-General May bemoaned that determination to attack "threatens to become a stereotypical phrase . . . This is so everywhere, although there are not wanting signs that the vogue is less unquestioned than it was."[154] The belief that courage alone could carry men forward also received criticism. Major Rooke discussed the issue in early 1914, echoing sentiments expressed by Maurice's earlier appraisal of Omdurman: "It is clear that however much the attacking troops may be 'trained above the fear of death,' this itself will not prevent their being struck by the enemy's bullets, and may not improbably even increase their losses since such troops are likely to expose themselves unduly."[155]

Attitudes toward the offensive were malleable throughout the period. In the aftermath of the Boer War, there was pessimism and caution regarding attacks against modern weapons, but the attitude was reversed following the apparent success of the Japanese in Manchuria. However, from 1912 onward, the trend once again began to turn against dedication to moral forces and the offensive at all costs.[156] It remains questionable to what extent the ideas of the absolute offensive became popular at the tactical level of the British Army, and its influence appears to have been limited in brigade and battalion work.[157]

Nevertheless, views from the continent, doubts about the courage of lower-class troops, and the misinterpretation of examples from the Manchurian war had the negative effect of causing the British Army to forget some of its own South African experiences. The cautious assessment that had emerged in 1902 was gradually eroded, downgrading the importance of firepower and movement and replacing it with a belief in moral supremacy and willpower. Though the British were more cautious about the implications of firepower than some of the continental nations, the belief that willpower could triumph over modern weapons was a dangerous line of thought. In expressing belief in the value of moral forces, advocates of the offensive were in danger of forgetting the experiences of the Boer War, where courageous and hard-drilled regulars had often been unable to make any progress against untrained farmers armed with modern rifles. Fortunately for the British Army, such views did not go unchallenged and did not develop into a firm doctrine as they did for the French. However, their growing popularity following the Russo-Japanese War represented a clear regression in thought from the cautious but intelligent assessment of the offensive that had developed in the aftermath of the Boer War. Although the regular BEF fought on the defensive for virtually all its major battles, in the later years of the First World War the failure to ally commensurate tactical and operational skill to courage in the offensive often led to tragic consequences. The root of such thinking lay in the pre-1914 era; thus, the rejection of the lessons regarding firepower and willpower that emerged from the Boer War must count as an error for the British Army.

CONCLUSIONS

The British Army of 1914 was unique in many ways. Despite the growing threat from Germany in the latter part of the Edwardian era, the army remained a colonial police force that faced potential deployment to locations all across the empire. Confronted with this challenging role, the British Army developed along quite different lines than the mass armies of the continent, emphasizing skill in low-level tactics and encouraging diversity of method among its divisions but lacking an operational doctrine. Training manuals for individual service arms and the army as a whole followed this trend, emphasizing adaptability and flexibility rather than providing a written doctrine. In organizational and operational terms, the army remained wedded to small-war principles, but its professionalism, training, and tactical flexibility meant that it performed well in 1914, despite being heavily outnumbered.

The Boer War had played a key role in shaping the army's development along these lines. In terms of operational lessons, the Boer War provided limited guidance. The conventional stage of the war had lasted less than a year, turning into a mobile guerrilla conflict following the fall of the Boer capitals. However, the hard lessons learned by the British in the early battles showed the need for skill and initiative at all levels and demonstrated the difficulties associated with frontal attacks against modern firepower. These ideas came to form the linchpin of the British Army's tactical development in the years immediately following the war, encouraging a new dedication to training that allowed the army to develop many of the new tactical ideas that are discussed in the following chapters. By 1914, this change in training ethos had produced elite infantrymen who were capable of an unprecedented rate of aimed fire, skillful in the use of the ground, and capable of operating in extended formations.

The British Army of the First World War has sometimes been criticized in comparison with the German army, most notably by Martin Samuels, who contrasted German operational success against British incompetence.[158] However, in 1914, the British and German armies had strikingly different roles. As previously discussed, the colonial duties of the British Army emphasized small-scale tactical principles and lacked formal operational doctrine. Conversely, the German army had virtually no colonial duties and had long anticipated a vast European conflict against France and Russia. The focus on this coming continental struggle encouraged the German army to develop detailed operational plans for the defeat of her future enemies. However, this focus on operational-level planning had become something of a fetish in the latter part of the Edwardian period, virtually to the exclusion of other considerations.[159] Bruce Gudmundsson has argued that by 1914, this narrow focus on operations meant that tactics had been relegated to a mere "subsidiary art" in the German army, and Steven D. Jackman has highlighted the fact that old-fashioned thinking and conservative attitudes could predominate to a surprising degree at tactical levels, with reactionary officers encouraging close control, dense formations, and rigid drill.[160] Although much of the German army was well trained in 1914, its tactics could sometimes prove surprisingly anachronistic. British soldiers expressed their amazement at the appearance of close-order columns during the Battle of Mons and inflicted dreadful casualties on dense formations at the First Battle of Ypres.[161] The contrast in infantry tactics adopted by the two armies is illustrative of the fact that the British had learned crucial lessons in South Africa, translating them into useful tactical principles that served them well in 1914.

The British Army was also distinct from that of the French. Although the French army possessed a colonial branch, some sections of the army had blamed defeat in in the Franco-Prussian War on the influence of colonial officers, who had developed great reputations in imperial wars but had failed in combat against the Germans. The simmering tensions between colonial soldiers and the metropolitan army remained unresolved in the pre–First World War period, preventing any real interchange of tactical ideas. The army was also hampered by political pressure from ever-changing governments, who disliked the authoritarian aspect of the military and preferred the concept of patriotism replacing discipline.[162] This preference contributed to a rejection of doctrine by the French army who, expressing similar sentiments to the British, feared it would stifle initiative.[163] Unfortunately, while the British Army was able to develop effective low-level tactics from the Boer War experience, the French had no comparable examples to provide a base for tactical development. Lacking guidance from above or experience from below, the French army reacted by seizing on the cult of the offensive, a fashionable view that emerged at lower levels and spread throughout the rest of the army.[164] Inspired by this idea, French training and tactics revolved almost entirely around the *offensive a outrance* (offensive to excess), rejecting doctrine and tactics that took into account modern firepower. British observers in 1912 noted with disquiet, "the French infantry displayed marked inferiority to our own in minor tactics. There was not . . . anything like the same efficiency in fire direction and control. The infantry, like the cavalry, did not seem to realize what modern rifle fire was like."[165] The belief in the offensive a outrance bore bitter fruit in the opening months of the First World War, when the French army suffered more than 300,000 casualties, mainly caused by reckless attacks against German positions.

Although certain sections of the British Army had placed similar faith in courage and the bayonet in the aftermath of the Russo-Japanese War, such ideas did not become universal. Although these ideas did lead to a modification of the cautious but realistic attack tactics of South Africa, this reform was never taken to the extremes that prevailed in the French army, and at a tactical level there remained a belief in fire and movement and a respect for modern weapons.

However, although the British Army had a number of strengths in 1914, it also had weaknesses. In remaining a colonial army that emphasized flexibility, it ensured it could perform a wide number of roles, including successfully engaging the German army in 1914. Nevertheless, the focus on flexibility combined with a lack of operational doctrine created considerable diversity of method among the various divisions. The British Army had no experience in fighting such a large-scale conflict, and lack of operational experience caused serious errors. For example, during the Battle of the Aisne in September, a lack of urgency and direction from higher command led to a piecemeal and inadequate attack. The *Official History* was scathing on this issue, noting, "There was no plan, no objective, no arrangements for cooperation, and the divisions blundered into battle."[166]

The most serious example of operational failings came during the initial stages of the Great Retreat. The withdrawal from Mons was poorly managed by John French and his staff, with inadequate direction causing I and II Corps to drift apart, thus presenting the Germans with a great opportunity to destroy them in detail. Although the stand at the Battle of Le Cateau proved to be critical in holding off German pursuit, the fact that Smith-Dorrien erroneously assumed his right flank was supported by Haig's I Corps presented the Germans with a great opportunity to encircle and destroy an entire half of the BEF.[167] Fortunately for the British, a combination of tactical skill on the part of the BEF, the fog of war, flawed German reconnaissance, and command errors on the part of the Germans prevented this encirclement taking place.[168]

Early battles of the First World War emphasized the ethos of the British Army: tactically adept with strong leadership from junior officers, but less astute operationally, with limited influence from higher command and disappointing levels of cooperation between the two corps. In the event, professionalism and tactical skill ensured survival, but only after a costly delaying action at Le Cateau that could well have ended disastrously.

3

INFANTRY

On the eve of the Boer War, British infantry had a well-deserved reputation for courage, discipline, and success. At the heart of imperial campaigns, the infantry had swept most colonial opposition from battlefields across the globe. In the Boer War, however, fighting an opponent that was armed with smokeless magazine rifles and was occupying concealed positions, British troops often found themselves pinned down by accurate rifle fire and unable to make significant progress. Over the course of the war, infantry units were forced to abandon a number of preconceived tactical ideas and adapt new, unanticipated solutions to ensure victory. By the close of hostilities, although the British had devised a system that was successful in defeating the Boers, it was clear that the infantry had many lessons to digest.

Of the three main combat arms of the British Army, it was the infantry who learned the most from the experience of war on the veldt. Whereas the cavalry were initially small in numbers and later hampered by tremendous problems with horse supply, and the artillery saw its opportunities for action decline after the fall of Bloemfontein and Pretoria, infantry played a part in the opening battles of 1899 and remained in the front line until the end of the war in 1902.

By the close of this period of hard fighting, a number of serious weaknesses in pre-war tactics and training had been starkly revealed, and a need for reform to meet the challenges posed by modern firepower was readily apparent.

The issue was not whether reform was needed, but what kind and how it was to be implemented. Conditions in South Africa had been unusual, with the flat, barren terrain and clear atmosphere combining to make rifle fire highly effective, particularly at long range. These conditions made extrapolation of lessons difficult, and as revealed by the findings of the Elgin Commission, the army lacked a unanimous opinion on what tactical direction to take in the years following the war in South Africa.

In addition, persistent structural problems such as the lack of men available for training in the average company and the drain of drafts for India placed certain limits on the extent to which tactics could be improved. Since the Cardwell reforms in 1871, British regiments had consisted of two linked battalions, one of which would be stationed in Britain and provide a source of recruitment, while the other would be sent to India to serve as part of the garrison. In the nineteenth century, ensuring the security of India was seen as the primary role for the British Army, and the home battalions were expected to regularly provide trained drafts for their Indian partners. Hence, forces based in Britain were constantly short of men, being forced to send their best soldiers abroad each year. The lack of men and the negative impact it had on training was cited as a serious issue by several witnesses who addressed the Elgin Commission.[1]

However, in spite of these limitations, by 1914 the infantry of the British Army had reached a peak of excellence. Edward Spiers has noted that the infantry had reached a standard "never before achieved in the British Army and unequalled among the contemporary armies in Europe."[2] Clearly, in achieving this level of skill, the army had undergone a considerable improvement from the Victorian force that had been embarrassed by the Boers. In this chapter my goal is to demonstrate that the seeds of the tactical reforms that allowed the BEF of 1914 to become such an elite army were laid during and immediately after the Boer War. Although I acknowledge that the experience of combat in South Africa was somewhat ambiguous and open to debate, I argue that key lessons of modern warfare painfully learned on the veldt were absorbed into the tactical framework of the infantry.

Martin Van Creveld has suggested that the years 1830–1945 marked an epoch of war he terms "The Age of Systems." He has argued that the growth of battlefield firepower in this era produced three key tactical reactions in armies worldwide, particular in the infantry branch. In an attempt to increase the survivability of infantry in the face of modern weapons, there was a much greater appreciation of cover, including the use of field entrenchments and earthworks to protect troops from incoming fire. Allied to this was a recourse to camouflage and concealment as opposed to colorful uniforms and bright equipment, making the individual infantryman a less distinct target than in previous eras. Units also began to adopt dispersed formations, moving away from shoulder-to-shoulder formations and vastly reducing the number of soldiers per square yard of front line.[3] While armies around the world were gradually moving toward these tactical concepts in the years prior to the First World War, the British Army's experience of conflict in South Africa gave it an important head start. All the tactical precepts suggested by Van Creveld were identified as important to victory during the Boer War and would provide the British Army with a vital framework upon which to build some of the most elite infantry in Europe in the period prior to 1914.

Therefore, in this chapter I analyze the tactical development of the infantry of the British Army during the period 1902 to 1914. Taking the experience of the Boer War as a base, I argue that the infantry learned three crucial lessons in the 1899–1902 period: greater formation extension to cross the fire-swept zone, a need for improvement in marksmanship and fire tactics, and finally greater interest in the use of the earthworks and entrenchments. These subheadings provide a framework for analysis, demonstrating that although the tactical lessons of the South African war were neither entirely self-evident nor unchallenged, they gave the British infantry an important head start in the tactics that were to become necessary on twentieth-century battlefields.

EXTENSION AND CROSSING THE FIRE-SWEPT ZONE

The Boer War was a conflict that contained several unpleasant surprises for the British Army, but the increased deadliness of small-arms fire should not have been one of them. From the American Civil War onward, there had been a steady increase in the effectiveness of infantry firearms, with the Wars of German Unification and the Russo-Turkish War providing further evidence of the power of modern rifles. Infantry firepower had also revealed its considerable potential in earlier campaigns in South Africa against the Boers. Prior to the defeat at Majuba, the British had fought a number of small campaigns against the Boers, and although these had generally ended in victory, the British participants had been quick to note the unusual characteristics and skills of the average Boer. For example, in 1848 a small force led by Sir Harry Smith, a veteran of the Napoleonic Wars, had put down a Boer rebellion at Boomplaats. Although victorious, Smith described the skirmish as one of the most severe he had witnessed and declared of the Boer shooting: "a more rapid, fierce and well-directed fire I have never seen maintained."[4] Unfortunately, these early warnings on the military potential of the Boers were largely ignored, and such ignorance played a part in the ignominious defeat at the Battle of Majuba Hill in 1881. However, even after this debacle, little was learned from the experience outside of individual officers and units.

Given that the Boers had already demonstrated the effectiveness of their firepower in earlier wars against the British, there was no reason to underestimate them in 1899. Indeed, in some ways they were more formidable than ever before. A large-scale government-spending program had rearmed the Boers from 1895 onward with the latest magazine-loading Mauser rifles. These were excellent weapons, capable of long-range rapid fire on flat trajectories. Crucially, they also used smokeless powder that not only increased accuracy, but also meant that firing the weapon did not give away the marksman's position. The potential effect of smokeless powder in the hands of an opposing force had been recognized as posing new difficulties as early as 1892, but the failure to disseminate new tactical ideas within the Victorian army meant that these warnings had had little impact on the British Army as a whole by the time of the Boer War.[5]

Any lingering doubts about the military capacity of the Boers were dispelled by the opening engagements, especially the defeats of Black Week in December 1899. Although opinion on individual Boer marksmanship in this period varied considerably—from those who felt it was as good as before to others who felt it was "shockingly bad"—it was almost universally agreed that modern rifle firepower was now capable of causing casualties at extremely long ranges, while at closer distances the sheer volume of fire was as significant as its accuracy and made further advance exceptionally difficult.[6] In addition, smokeless ammunition created an apparently empty battlefield, denying troops a target to shoot at and placing a considerable psychological strain on soldiers.

For the infantry, the most pressing tactical problem was how best to cross this fire-swept zone to get into assaulting range of an entrenched and often invisible enemy. An anonymous officer offered a description of the changed nature of war:

> War is not what it was when armies manoeuvred in sight of each other, and when 600 yards was the limit of artillery fire. I smile when I think of the face of a man who is bungling an attempt to bite off the end of a cartridge, with one eye cocked all the time on the gentleman advancing at the double to avenge the death of "poor Bill." That was old-time fighting, and some sport about it too. Now Bill is killed at 2400 yards, and Bill's pal hasn't an idea where the shot was fired. That is modern warfare.[7]

To officers and men who had cut their teeth in colonial actions against poorly armed tribal foes, the new conditions of warfare were strikingly different. Colonel A. W. Thorneycroft noted that at first his men were dismissive of the potential effects of Boer fire, as past combat experience had shown them that tribal opposition "fires over your head as a rule."[8] In stark contrast, an officer who fought at the first engagement of the war, the Battle of Talana Hill (20 October 1899), left an account of the difficulty of facing modern rifle fire:

> I don't suppose I am ever likely to go through a more awful fire than broke out from the Boer line as we dashed forward. The ground in front of me was literally rising in dust from the bullets, and the din echoing between the hill and the wood below and among the rocks from the incessant fire of the Mausers seemed to blend with every other sound into a long drawn-out hideous roar . . . the whole ground we had already covered was strewn with bodies.[9]

In the face of such intense defensive fire, attacks were problematical. The problems were exacerbated by the lack of tactical options open to the British in the opening months of the conflict. As previously noted, lack of cavalry in the early part of the war meant that the infantry were forced into making relatively narrow frontal attacks. Even at best these attacks simply forced the Boers back to another defensive position with relatively few casualties compared with those suffered by the British. Lord Methuen's campaign to relieve the siege of Kimberly typified this kind of fighting, which was described by a journalist attached to his force as "nothing but an honest, straightforward British march up to a row of waiting rifles."[10]

Although study of the recent European wars had hinted at the difficulties inherent in attacking a determined, well-armed defender, this was the first practical experience the British had had facing modern firepower on a large scale, and it was soon found that the kind of close-order tactics that had been valuable in the Sudan and other colonial wars were a liability in South Africa. For example, at the Battle of Enslin[11] (25 November 1899) the Naval Brigade[12] made a brave but clumsy attack in relatively close order, Lord Methuen noting in his dispatches, "The fire here was very heavy, and the Naval Brigade suffered severely, keeping in too close formation . . . [and not] taking advantage of cover."[13] The brigade lost virtually all its officers and NCOs killed or wounded, with an overall casualty rate of more than 40 percent.[14] Even after this example, some officers still persisted with the use of close-order. At the Battle of Colenso (15 December 1899), Major-General Fitzroy Hart, a believer in keeping his men "well in hand," advanced his 5 Brigade toward the Boer positions in quarter columns, even going so far as to countermand an instruction from the commanding officer of one of his battalions to open into extended order.[15] The results were predictable, and not even the poetic words of Arthur Conan Doyle describing the brigade's attack could disguise the fact the formation was a serious tactical blunder: "the four regiments clubbed into one, with all military organisation rapidly disappearing, and nothing left but their gallant spirit."[16] Witnessing the attack, Redvers Buller offered a blunter description, describing it as "a devil of a mess."[17]

Although close-order formations had worked against colonial opposition that lacked modern weapons, existing British tactical thinking was not entirely ignorant of the threat of improved firepower, and close-order formations were not formally recommended for use against well-armed opposition. The 1896 edition of *Infantry Drill* suggested extending from close-order column formations at a range of approximately half a mile from the enemy, although naturally this round figure was open to interpretation and was not always followed.[18] In addition, the lack of doctrine in the British army and the profusion of tactical ideas based on individual regimental experience meant tactics and formations adopted for the attack varied considerably. A junior officer stationed with a British regiment in India noted that his battalion assault training in July 1899 consisted of the attacking line being separated into "tight little bunches of about twenty men each" advancing in a line to within two hundred yards of the enemy position. Though this was extension of a sort, it was hopelessly inadequate, and the officer recorded in his diary, "I could not believe it was serious practice for modern warfare. We should all have been wiped out."[19]

Nevertheless, the ideas of extension in *Infantry Drill 1896* were a move in the right tactical direction, and those officers who had prior experience of such formations, usually gained in fighting on the North-West Frontier, were able to make use of them against the Boers. For example, although William Penn Symons has been justifiably criticized for his strategic errors in the early stages of the war, it is often overlooked that his infantry initially advanced against the Boers at Talana Hill extended to as much as ten paces per man.[20] Perhaps the most prominent proponent of extension in the early stages of the Boer War was Ian Hamilton, a veteran of Majuba and the Tirah campaign, who was known for his unorthodox ideas on the nature of future warfare.[21] While stationed at Ladysmith prior to the outbreak of hostilities, he had begun training his brigade in some of the tactical ideas he had picked up on the North-West Frontier. When Hamilton was called on to commit his troops at the Battle of Elandslaagte (21 October 1899), the three lead companies of the 1st Devons attacked with a very large frontal extension of somewhere between 700 and 1,000 yards, with 450 yards between each successive line. The troops advanced forward by rushes, one section firing to cover the advance of the next.[22] These infantry tactics and formations at Elandslaagte helped contribute to a notable local victory for the British at relatively low cost and hinted at the future direction of tactical reform.

After the disasters of Black Week and the appointment of Lord Roberts to overall command of British forces in South Africa, formal tactical instructions regarding extension were introduced. One of Roberts's first actions was to issue a memorandum entitled "Notes for Guidance," which set out a number of tactical tips for the three major service arms based on the experience of the opening months of the war. These notes confirmed many of Hamilton's earlier tactical ideas, suggesting abandonment of close-order formations between 1,500 and 1,800 yards from the enemy, being prepared to have an extension of between six and eight paces per man, and making maximum use of cover.[23] In practice, extension and dispersion of formations went well beyond these guidelines on a number of occasions. At the Battle of Diamond Hill (11–12 June 1900), British infantry was noted as having an extension of thirty yards per man, and in many actions between ten and twenty yards was not uncommon.[24] These tactical precepts offered little that was of an entirely new nature, and their value against well-armed enemies had been identified during the Tirah campaign.[25] However, whereas the earlier campaign had been fought in a wild corner of India purely by forces stationed in the subcontinent, the Boer War was fought by virtually the entire regular army, plus numerous colonial and volunteer formations. In the past, the influence of colonial wars had been limited outside of the immediate participants, but the scale of the war in South Africa ensured that the impact of its tactical lessons was far wider than any previous imperial war.

The primary advantage of extension was that it provided a small, individual target that was less vulnerable to fire than a mass of men in a tight formation, but it also had other benefits. The first and arguably most important of these secondary benefits was that it allowed men to use their discretion and take advantage of cover during the advance. Taking cover during the attack was a controversial subject within the pre–Boer War British Army, and it was not widely practiced in peacetime. The army was proud of its reputation for "dash," and there was a spirit of resistance to any tactical method that threatened to reduce this much-prized attribute. Foreign observers were particularly surprised at this disdain of cover; Captain Slocum of the U.S. Army wrote, "The disregard of the British officer and soldier of all corps of ordinary precautions for his own safety is astonishing."[26] However, the experience of combat began to erode this attitude, and in the face of modern firepower, the need to make the most of cover to avoid heavy casualties soon became paramount. Lord Roberts's tactical memorandum had insisted that "Every advantage should be taken of cover," but lack of pre-war training meant that infantry instead had to learn by hard experience the potential value of taking shelter.[27] For inexperienced units, this situation could lead to almost comical errors. Major-General Sir Henry Colvile commented on his wartime experiences of such problems: "At first officers and men were very stupid about taking cover. I have seen men halted on a rise in full view of the enemy when a few paces forward or backward would have placed them in shelter, the reason being that to have taken this step would have broken the dressing of the line."[28]

Nevertheless, veteran troops soon became adept at taking cover when in action.[29] After experiencing a rough learning curve in early battles such as Colenso and Spion Kop, the infantry of Buller's army in Natal became particularly noted for their skill in taking up good positions.[30] At the Battle of Vaal Krantz, Neville Lyttelton remembered that his men had taken up positions "very cleverly" and suffered only relatively minor casualties, even though the Boer fire was so severe that one officer thought it was the wind rushing through nearby undergrowth instead of bullets.[31]

Dispersion facilitated the use of cover, but there would inevitably come a time when it was necessary to cross a stretch of open ground to reach the next point of shelter. In the Boer War, this step was most readily achieved by a system of rushes. Once again, peacetime training had not prepared the British Army well for this tactical requirement, and in the early stages of the war it was underused. Observing early operations in Natal, Captain Slocum commented, "The infantry never make rushes in their attacks, but march erect and calmly forward."[32] However, as the war continued, an appreciation of rush tactics soon developed. Typically led by an officer, a small group of men under cover would rise and sprint a short distance to the next piece of shelter. Although simple in theory, rushes were harder to perform in practice. Ian Hamilton's infantry had achieved success with rushes at the Battle of Elandslaagte, but a German volunteer who fought for the Boers remembered that as the war dragged on, veteran commandos began to learn how to predict when a rush was about to take place by the sudden cessation of fire that usually preceded it. This pause gave the Boers time to aim, and the veteran recalled, "Onsets such as these were almost always shattered . . . a few seconds were frequently enough to decide the matter."[33] How long to maintain a rush was also an issue open to debate. The Boer veteran considered that the British rushes had been too long and had given the burghers many opportunities to take aim and inflict casualties, but German observers felt that the British rushes were too short and did not gain sufficient ground for the risk entailed.[34] In the aftermath of the war, William Gatacre summed up the ideal infantry rush to be aimed for in training: "sudden, short, rapid and irregular in interval and strength, otherwise the defenders get many chances; each rush must be locally supported by comrades' fire till the runners have settled down ready to support the next group in turn."[35]

A corollary of the increased use of cover and concealment was a necessity for camouflage. The British Army had already adopted khaki as its standard overseas uniform color, but bright buttons and other prominently visible items of kit held the potential to give away a man's position, and as the war continued these were darkened or removed entirely.[36] Officers, often forced to scorn cover to set a courageous example for the men, were particularly prime targets, and attrition among them was extremely high. By late October 1899, British forces in Natal had lost seventy-three officers and three commanding officers, proportionally twice as many casualties as the men.[37] A contemporary source estimated the overall casualties for the men typically ranged between 3 and 6 percent, whereas casualties among officers were 12 to 30 percent.[38] Although a major cause of these casualties was the need for officers to demonstrate personal courage and lead their men by example, the carrying of swords and wearing of rank insignia were factors seen as attracting fire. One British observer said the wearing of the sword "was quickly recognised as a sort of legend 'Here I am an officer, shoot me' and [was] laid aside with colours and other relics of the past."[39] Officers in Lord Roberts's army carried rifles instead of swords, and by the time of Spion Kop the officers of Buller's force had removed all badges of rank to avoid drawing the attention of enemy sharpshooters.[40]

Although they faced a difficult learning curve, by the end of the war in South Africa, the British Army had learned more about facing modern firepower than any of their contemporaries. An army that had initially been wedded to a profusion of tactical ideas, many of them inappropriate for the conditions, had emerged as a highly skilled fighting force that had overcome a unique and determined enemy in difficult conditions. Whereas in the early battles of the war British infantry had sometimes attacked in narrow close formation and suffered as a consequence, by the latter stages they were capable of advancing in an extended order, taking advantage of available cover and maintaining forward momentum in a manner that had seemed impossible in the early months of the conflict. Although the fighting in South Africa was undoubtedly unusual—in terms of both atmospheric conditions and the unique military culture of the Boers—the lessons of concealment and dispersion learned by the British in this conflict placed them considerably in advance of European rivals.

British peacetime training soon changed to reflect the lessons of the Boer War, and the memory of the conflict remained paramount in the minds of many throughout the army. Concealment, cover, extension, and a respect of firepower were emphasized in infantry tactics. At Aldershot, officers were criticized for remaining mounted while too close to the firing line, whereas infantry were berated for bunching too closely during the attack and, in one unusual case, for being accompanied by a brass band.[41] Infantry were expected to take up an extension of six to twenty yards per man during the attack, and John French summed up the post-war attitude toward training and tactics when he stated, "Personally, I believe as strongly as ever in the wide extension of Infantry in the attack . . . The instinct of all infantry soldiers should be to take advantage of cover, and to avoid open ground."[42] The influence of the conflict could also linger in more subtle ways, as a training inspection report on 1st Division at Aldershot in 1904 revealed when it referred to hills as "kopjes" after the South African terminology.[43] In the immediate post-war years the training and tactics of the infantry were acknowledged to have improved considerably. Even staunch critics such as Leo Amery gave praise to the improvements, attributing much of the development to the presence of Boer War veterans among both officers and men.[44]

However, dissenting voices on the value of the war were raised even in its immediate aftermath. The unusual military characteristics of the Boers along with the uniquely clear atmosphere of South Africa, which allowed for shooting at extremely long ranges, were both cited as rendering the lessons of the war misleading. Henry Colvile summed up the views of many of the doubters: "It should be borne in mind that the conditions of warfare in South Africa were wholly exceptional, and it is unlikely that they will ever be reproduced. I do not think, therefore, that our tactics in South Africa, successful as they eventually were, have by any means solved the difficult question of how to reach the enemy's position in the face of modern smokeless magazine fire."[45]

Although a return to close-order shoulder-to-shoulder formations was never seriously advocated, a number of officers questioned the lessons of extension derived from South Africa. Those who challenged the value of the experience focused on the peculiar characteristics of the enemy. As previously noted, the Boers would not hold positions to the last extremity, did not launch counterattacks to retake lost ground, and would typically fall back if their opponents could not be stopped by rifle fire. As the Boers showed little inclination to resist close assault if the enemy were able to establish themselves at close range, it was relatively uncommon that the British needed to undertake the difficult process of reforming from wide extension into a thicker line that would carry weight in the firefight and the subsequent charge. This situation encouraged the use of a single, heavily extended but thin line that would be able to advance with minimal casualties, rather than a somewhat more densely packed line that would find it easier to assault. Lord Roberts noted that "Throughout the war the Boers were determined that there should be no hand to hand fighting," but observers both at home and abroad noted this would not be the case in Europe, where positions would be defended much more tenaciously and the cost to break through would be high.[46] F. N. Maude summed up these views in 1902, stating, "Against an enemy known to be adverse to counter-attacks, the extreme extension we adopted was justified by results, but it would be a very unsound generalisation to assume that similar extensions would answer against an active European drilled army."[47]

Some continental writers further criticized the British Army on the grounds that wide extension and flank attacks were an illogical reaction to fear of casualties. A German observer rejected these tactics, arguing that "The English . . . endeavoured to obtain decisive victories without serious loss. The first law of war is that lives of soldiers must be sacrificed without hesitation when the necessity arises."[48]

Such radical views achieved little support in the years immediately following the Boer War, when European conflicts were still far from the minds of most British Army officers. However, from 1905 onward the value of large extension began to be called into question. The core of this problem was a tactical paradox. Modern infantry fire, considered effective at distances of up to 1,400 yards, meant that dense formations were impractical for closing with the opposition; thus, wide extension was necessary.[49] However, although extension would allow the men to close with the hostile position, it did not provide enough strength at a point to actually overwhelm the enemy, either with firepower or via a close combat assault. Indeed, for fire superiority to be gained over the foe, it was widely believed a ratio of at least one man per yard was necessary.[50] How to cross the ground to get into a good fire position without suffering prohibitive casualties and then have enough strength to win the firefight and final assault was a paradox the British Army struggled with throughout the period. *Combined Training 1905* identified the problem without offering any real solutions. Noting that in the infantry attack "it is superiority of fire that renders the decision of the conflict possible," it went on to state that against a well-trained enemy, within eight hundred yards of their position "the ground over which the attack must pass is so closely swept by a sheet of lead as to be well-night impassable to troops in any other formation than lines of skirmishers."[51] Ultimately, the solution reached was a compromise. Under this system, infantry advanced in extended formations as far as possible. Once forced to ground and involved in the firefight, the firing line would be built up by supports and reserves advancing forward by rushes, covered by the fire of the original line. Therefore, the line only became dense at decisive range to ensure overwhelming infantry firepower.[52]

The Russo-Japanese War highlighted the difficulties associated with this tactical conundrum. The Japanese were often required to launch direct, frontal assaults against Russian earthworks, and although they were frequently repelled with heavy losses, in contrast to the Boer War, bayonet charges and hand-to-hand combat occurred on a surprisingly frequent basis.[53] Initially, the Japanese favored old-fashioned Prussian-style tactics, assaulting in relatively dense lines preceded by a swarm of skirmishers. A French observer commented on these formations, noting, "The losses were so ruinous that never again was this method of attack employed."[54] British observer Ian Hamilton also noted the terrible cost of using German assault tactics and was pleased to be told that "the Japanese are discarding German attack formations, and approximating more to those employed by us in South Africa."[55] By the time of the Battle of Mukden (20 February–10 March 1905), a Japanese officer reported that he was doubling the extension of his battalion from the distance set in pre-war guidelines.[56] Conversely, some German writers saw the ultimate success of Japanese frontal attacks, regardless of their cost in lives, as a vindication that the British had lacked the moral strength to absorb casualties making frontal assaults in South Africa.[57] The profusion of contradictory tactical lessons regarding infantry assault in the Russo-Japanese War did little to clarify the issue of extension.[58] Indeed, although the Japanese had moved toward using extensions of eight yards per man or more by 1905, in subsequent years their infantry training manuals turned against this practice and formations gradually increased in density.[59] There was abundant evidence that crossing the fire-swept zone was now even more difficult than in the Boer War, but equally the success of Japanese attacks against Russian earthworks suggested that close assault remained possible.

The successful Japanese frontal assaults and the local strength required to launch them contributed to the debate on the value of Boer War infantry tactics. Ideas that had been formed during the experience of combat in South Africa came under scrutiny during the following years, including the notion of arming officers with infantry rifles. This idea had been controversial for some time and had often been raised for Army Council consideration, but it was not until 1908 that it was officially decided to abandon the rifle and reinstate the sword as the personal weapon for officers.[60] More importantly, formations also came under critical examination in the aftermath of the Russo-Japanese War. Even reformers such as Ian Hamilton began to wonder if extended formations were being taken too far. Although Hamilton considered wide extensions "probably the best of the many good ideas derived from the South Africa War," he cautioned that even these tactics "will not bear being turned into a fetish."[61] While serving as inspector general of forces, John French echoed similar views on extension, arguing, "I think it is well worth serious consideration whether we are not overdoing the so-called lessons of the South African War as applied to possible European war against masses of trained soldiers."[62]

The tactical paradox of forming a strong firing line without suffering annihilating casualties beforehand still remained. Complaints were made that the infantry were able to advance splendidly in training, but that there was no attempt at any stage in the attack to close up a firing line at a depth greater than "three or four paces" per man.[63] The reaction against extension reached its peak in an article that appeared in 1912 in *Army Review*—a publication supported by the General Staff. Criticizing British assault training, the author, Brigadier-General F. C. Carter, felt in large part the flaws were due to "the fact that the fetish of 'over-extension' which, after the early disaster of the South African War, was set up as a God in the Temple of Mars, still claims some devotees among our senior officers."[64] Urging closer formations, Carter concluded the article as follows: "We must harden our hearts, as our forefathers did of old to the heavy losses that will occur . . . a steady advance of strong, disciplined and brave men, prepared to suffer losses, to use their bayonets with effect and to snatch victory from the jaws of death."[65]

Although Carter's viewpoint was somewhat extreme, he expressed tactical opinions that were not uncommon among continental armies or those who admired them. The Boer War had had relatively limited impact on formations of armies in Europe, and the Russo-Japanese War, with its bloody but successful attacks, seemed to be a vindication of traditional attack tactics to many in the German and French armies. Ironically, the author of the *Army Review* article cited as a supporting example work by F. N. Maude, the principal proponent of the pro-Prussian school in the Victorian era army. As in the Victorian era, the British Army grappled with influences from both the colonial experience of the Boer War and the ideas of continental thinkers. However, whereas in the nineteenth century the British had a great deal to learn about facing firepower as the Prussians had done in the Franco-Prussian War, by the Edwardian period it was the British Army who had the practical experience.

In 1903, a British observer of German maneuvers was surprised at their dense attacking lines, noting, "I pointed out the losses would be enormous. I was told they were prepared to lose, as they lost at Gravelotte."[66] Although there was a strand of thought within the British Army that a war against mass armies on the continent would require mass tactics, it was also well understood that the small numbers available to the BEF meant that any attempt to fight a continental conscript army on a like-for-like basis was unlikely to succeed.[67] A call to absorb casualties in mass attacks on the German or French model was not in keeping with the military or political goals of the small BEF. One anonymous officer summed up the problem, noting the British Army was "bound for political, financial and national reasons, to economise life, and to win our campaigns with the fewest possible casualties."[68] Therefore, in terms of reducing extension, the European influence was limited beyond a small number of adherents, much as the Prussian influence in the Victorian era army had been.[69]

Despite a number of calls for a counterreformation following the Russo-Japanese War, and the urging of officers such as Carter to follow the continental example, the British Army did not abandon extension; however, it was reduced from the standard adopted after the Boer War. In 1908 Ian Hamilton reported that extension in Southern Command had been reduced to a level slightly above that adopted by the Japanese in the war in the Far East, giving attacks "greater cohesion, flexibility, and driving power." However, he cautioned that "the reaction against the exaggerated extensions adopted during and immediately after the South African War has gone far enough" and felt "it is better for formations to be too open than too concentrated."[70] Lieutenant-General Charles Douglas echoed similar views in 1909: "I cannot help thinking that we are inclined to neglect some of the lessons of the South African War which are applicable to European warfare; lessons which we learnt by bitter experience."[71] By 1912 and 1913, reports from the inspector general of forces were also cautionary regarding overly dense advancing lines. The 1913 report complained, "I desire to emphasize very strongly a marked tendency in our present day infantry tactics to ignore the effect of fire during movement. Large bodies are frequently seen advancing under effective rifle and artillery fire bunched together in a manner that would entail very heavy casualties . . . attacks in this manner cannot hope to succeed."[72]

The Army Council stated that this problem would be addressed, further noting that it would be highlighted in a forthcoming revision of *Infantry Training*. However, the outbreak of war prevented the issuing of a new manual.[73]

The thorny problem of how to create a strong line from an extended formation to win fire superiority remained a contentious issue that was never entirely settled in the years prior to the First World War. In *Infantry Training 1911* the paradox remained, although there was now a greater emphasis on supporting fire from friendly infantry, machine guns, and artillery to facilitate the forward movement of supports and reformation for the final firefight.[74] In addition, the use of cover and short but rapid rushes to gain good positions were discussed at some length. Unlike extension, the use of these tactical movements had never been seriously challenged in the post–Boer War years, and they remained a fundamental part of British infantry tactics.

Despite the controversy over extension and its relative value, by the eve of the First World War, British infantry remained skillful at crossing the fire-swept zone. Problems persisted, especially with regard to the difficult task of thickening the line at the decisive moment; nevertheless, the necessity for dispersion, emphasized by the rough handling of close-order formations in the Boer War, remained a valuable and enduring lesson. Once war had broken out in Europe, the tactics for crossing ground that had worked in South Africa were often cited as good examples for the current conflict. *Notes from the Front*, a handbook of tactical advice printed and issued for the army after the opening months of hostilities in 1914, once again reiterated the value of extension, stating a formation with "8 or 10 paces intervals [is thought to be] the least vulnerable."[75] In addition, in a September 1914 memorandum, Brigadier-General Johnnie Gough called for increased usage of dispersed "loose and irregular elastic formations" as used in South Africa.[76]

Such tactics proved practical in combat. A sergeant in the King's Royal Rifle Corps remembered an attack on a German *jäger* (light infantry) battalion during the Battle of the Marne: "We went forward as we had been trained—one section would advance under covering fire of another section, leapfrogging each other as the others were firing to keep Jerry's heads down."[77] More than four hundred prisoners were taken. The sergeant recalled one prisoner telling him "your fire was so accurate we couldn't put our heads up to shoot at you."[78]

Compared with the French and German armies, who sometimes made use of close-order formations in the early part of the First World War, British extension tactics were considerably advanced. By combining extension tactics with the use of cover and rapid, irregular rushes from point to point, the British infantry was among the best prepared in Europe to face modern rifle fire on a tactical level. A French observer of the 1913 maneuvers felt that British attacks were "carried out in an excellent manner. . . . Infantry makes wonderful use of the ground, advances, as a rule, by short rushes and always at the double, and almost invariably fires from the lying down position."[79] The core principles of extension, cover, and rushes realized in the Boer War were a logical and appropriate tactical response to an extended fire-swept zone, and despite debate and controversy, the British Army still remembered the value of these important lessons at the outbreak of war in 1914.

MARKSMANSHIP AND FIRE TACTICS

One of the most remarked upon aspects of combat against the Boers throughout the nineteenth century was the effectiveness of the marksmanship possessed by the average burgher. The good shooting of Boers armed only with muskets had surprised participants in engagements in the 1840s, and by the time of Majuba in 1881 it was further improved by far better weaponry. Though there was a distinct lack of consensus on the overall quality of Boer marksmanship in 1899, the increased range and sheer volume of fire that could be produced by magazine rifles made even a poor marksman a potentially dangerous foe, especially at close range. In addition, the use of smokeless powder meant it was difficult for the British to return the fire, as there was no tell-tale puff of smoke to give away the firer's position. For British troops who were used to facing brave but reckless tribal opposition charging across the open, this was a rude awakening. Neville Lyttelton described the startling change in combat experience: "Few people have seen two battles in succession in such startling contrast as Omdurman and Colenso. In the first, 50,000 fanatics streamed across the open regardless of cover to certain death, while at Colenso I never saw a Boer all day till the battle was over, and it was our men who were the victims."[80]

British infantry in the Victorian period were poorly trained in marksmanship and were highly dependent on volley fire. For regular troops forty-two rounds were officially distributed per year for individual fire training, but these rounds were used against static targets at fixed distances up to eight hundred yards without the added pressure of a time limit.[81] Almost twice as many rounds, seventy-seven per year, were used on sectional volley practice against fixed targets at similar distances. A further eighty-one rounds in total were placed at the disposal of the company captain and battalion commander, but the use of this ammunition was entirely discretionary and was rarely used in more realistic practice, such as firing against surprise targets. For the keener officers, the allowance of extra rounds was often too small to effect significant improvement.[82] Volley firing was still seen by many within the British army as the essence of fire tactics, and although independent fire was seen to produce superior results on the firing range, it was felt that volleys came into their own once in the field.[83] The volley had proven its value against opponents who attacked *en masse,* such as the Mahdists; even against the Boers, at longer ranges volleys had a certain degree of suppressing effect and some tactical value. For example, at the Battle of Elandslaagte, the advance of the Devons was made in rushes, with supporting sections delivering volleys to keep down the Boers' fire.[84]

However, within six hundred yards and at closer ranges, the individual fire of the Boers, often termed "snap shooting," proved far more effective than the cumbersome volleys of the British. The volley was of limited use in inflicting casualties on a dispersed, well-concealed enemy in a good position or in earthworks. Furthermore, the extension and use of cover necessary for survival at close ranges meant it was difficult for officers to organize a volley, as their voices would often be lost in the din of fighting and to emerge from behind cover risked drawing the attention of Boer sharpshooters.[85] In such conditions, the Boers' more skillful individual shots held a clear advantage over the British. One officer remembered of this type of fighting: "where they [the Boers] beat us so completely was when we got onto kopjes at close quarters, say, a few hundred yards, a man could not put his finger up over a rock or ridge without being hit."[86]

A related problem was that the prevalence of volleys had created a very strict system of fire control, which emphasized holding fire for as long as possible during the advance. In 1899 it was expected that the infantry would not open fire until they were within approximately five hundred yards of the enemy's position.[87] Although this type of fire control had some justification against poorly armed opposition, the Boers with modern rifles were able to inflict casualties at ranges more than triple this distance. The result was that in the early stages of the war, British advances were sometimes forced to ground at nine hundred to a thousand yards from the enemy without the attackers having fired a shot.[88] Several early attacks took this course, with the British attempting to press onward against increasingly heavy fire, suffering casualties and ultimately being forced to ground before they even began the firefight in earnest.[89] Gaining infantry fire superiority from such a weak initial position was virtually impossible. Fire discipline and pre-war training also encouraged firing at obvious, visible targets on the basis that this would preserve ammunition and prevent fire from becoming wild. Unfortunately, this practice soon proved to be a weakness that the Boers were able to exploit. William Gatacre recalled, "On several occasions I saw our men wasting their ammunition at purposely prepared vacant trenches on kopjes, when the men who were doing the mischief were under cover in front or to a flank."[90]

The volley was generally unsuited for the nature of combat in the Boer War, but the standard of individual marksmanship possessed by the average British soldier varied immensely. Several officers suggested it was as good as, if not better than, that of the Boers when shooting at static objects at known ranges, but when engaging fleeting targets at unknown distances it suffered in comparison. The difficulties of firing at a well-concealed enemy were exacerbated by the unusual atmospheric conditions of South Africa, which made judging the range difficult. Even veteran officers were known to make considerable errors of judgment in this regard.[91] Such errors in judging distance were especially serious because the emphasis on collective fire meant individual soldiers were often dependent on an officer to call out the distance to the target for them and were poor at setting their own sights without instruction.[92] An anonymous Boer remembered capturing some British infantry, only to find, "Of 35 men whom we took prisoners, after they had fired at us up to

350 paces, not a single one had got his sight correct. Most of them had kept their sights fixed at 800 and 850 yards, because no order to change them had been given."[93]

Ruminating on the issue, the Boer veteran noted, "In this respect, the English, as far as we could ascertain, were not only quite unskilled, but what is worse, they had been trained on an utterly erroneous system."[94] The failure to correct rifle sights as the range changed was a persistent problem, especially prevalent among inexperienced or poorly trained men. For example, the ability of the Boers to make close-range mounted attacks during the later stages of the war was attributed by some officers to the inability of the British soldier to correct his sights to deal with a rapidly closing target.[95]

By the end of the conflict, the power of modern rifles in skillful hands was a lesson that was brought home in the strongest terms. An individual was now able to produce a tremendous rate of fire, and a small group of determined, skillful men in a good position could prove a formidable foe. For example, at the Battle of Bergendal on 27 August 1900, a group of Boers had taken up a strong position on a kopje, delivering effective fire against the attacking British. Neville Lyttelton, a participant at the battle, related, "It was so continuous that I thought there were quite 300 men in the kopje, but I doubt if there were 100."[96] On another occasion, prior to the Battle of Spion Kop, a British advance found itself under persistent and harassing sniper fire. Two battalions with artillery support were deployed to flush out the Boers, only to discover the fire had been coming from just three well-concealed burghers.[97]

For the infantry, the most important tactical development of the Boer War was realizing the power and effectiveness of these smokeless magazine rifles. The impressive firepower that could now be developed by even small numbers of skilled men hinted at the future. Ian Hamilton caught the mood of post-war reformers when he suggested that attacks would now be based on the determination and skill of a handful of men who would be able to work their way across the final five hundred yards into good positions. He argued, "If . . . the enemy's line is penetrated, even by a few men, the power of their modern armament will make their flanking fire so demoralising and effective that the position will either be abandoned forthwith, or so much attention will be concentrated on the intruders that an assault may become practicable all along the line."[98] Concluding this strand of thought, Hamilton laid down the necessary requirement for these tactics of the future, suggesting, "We want an army composed of men each of whom can be trusted to make the fullest possible use of the finest and most delicately adjusted rifle that can be made."[99]

Improving marksmanship clearly required a vast overhaul of the pre-war musketry regulations and training routine. The Victorian-era army had assigned a miserly quantity of ammunition for rifle practice and had focused almost entirely on shooting at static targets at known distances. In the aftermath of the Boer War, there was some call for marksmanship training to take place at long range with troops forced to estimate the distance themselves and set their sights accordingly.[100] This method was considered an effective way to simulate the South African experience, but such a system required very long target ranges and complex training. The ranges of infantry fire in South Africa had been enormous, with effective fire at two thousand yards being considered common by some, but this range was largely due to the exceptionally clear atmosphere of the country.[101] Other officers felt that these ranges were abnormal and that scoring hits at such a distance was more luck than judgment.[102] Ultimately, the issue was settled by Lord Roberts, who, taking the advice of the School of Musketry, saw the crucial area of fire as being at medium to close range, rather than at great distances.[103] "Effective" rifle range was thus defined as being between 1,400 to 600 yards, and less than 600 yards was considered "decisive."[104] It was at this latter range that Lord Roberts considered Boer shooting to have been most dominant over the British.[105]

Debate continued on the ranges at which the men should practice, and a 1904 committee from I Corps suggested that men should be trained to fire accurately at ranges up to a thousand yards. However, the School of Musketry rejected this view, arguing that "careful concentration of collective fire," rather than a handful of specially trained individuals, was best at achieving results at long range.[106] Trials showed that it took an expert marksman in favorable conditions an average of twelve rounds to hit a dummy that was lying in the prone position at six hundred yards; therefore, this distance was considered the maximum limit of useful individual fire.[107] Musketry training emphasized rapidity and accuracy of fire in this "decisive" six hundred-yard range throughout the period, up to the outbreak of the First World War.[108]

However, the process of improving marksmanship took time and was not without difficulties. Initially, lack of shooting ranges led to considerable overcrowding at those that were available, causing practice to become rushed and inefficient. Ammunition supply also became an issue. To improve the marksmanship of the men, the cartridge allowance for practice purposes was vastly increased, with a figure of three hundred rounds per year for each man being approved in 1903.[109] However, in 1906 the allowance of training ammunition was reduced because surplus supplies from the Boer War were running out and to maintain the existing level of supply would cost between £70,000 and £80,000 per annum. Although several members of the Army Council thought a reduction was feasible and even potentially beneficial, the move was almost unanimously opposed by the general officers commanding, who argued that it would be detrimental to training.[110] Nevertheless, financial considerations won out, and the ammunition allowance was reduced to two hundred and fifty rounds per man. However, even with these limitations, the amount of ammunition and effort expended on marksmanship training was still considerably more than on the continent.

The quality of individual musketry and the seriousness that was now attached to it was the most striking change in the British infantry in the aftermath of the Boer War. In 1903, one commentator praised improvements in training, noting that as a result the "British Army . . . is a better shooting force than the army of any Continental power."[111] In 1904, an anonymous officer noted with satisfaction, "The day has now quite gone by when the officer at the firing point brought down with him to the range, as a necessary part of his equipment, an easy-chair and a novel, and the officer in the butts if he hadn't a novel went to sleep . . . greater interest is now shown by everybody . . . the keenness displayed by all ranks is as great as could be desired."[112]

The old system of firing purely at static targets at fixed ranges was replaced with a far more challenging system. New exercises included concealed and surprise targets that could be raised and then collapsed at short notice, as well as moving targets, some of which were pulled by teams of horses travelling at the gallop.[113] Adapting to these new training methods took time, and early experiments with the method could produce embarrassing results. During an early attempt at using surprise targets in training during 1899, at least one company was so surprised by the sudden appearance of a twenty-second target that they failed to get a single shot off.[114] Nevertheless, these moving targets ultimately proved a great success and a huge improvement on the old methods. At Aldershot in 1909, a musketry course was laid out that included "every sort of appearing and disappearing target," and dummy attacks were made against a selection of them as part of competitive training.[115] These training techniques gave soldiers practice at meeting counterattacks and aiming at active-service-style targets and were considered by Aldershot commander Horace Smith-Dorrien to be "an unqualified success."[116]

Individual training encompassed a variety of exercises, including range shooting for accuracy, rapid-fire work, and firing the rifle with bayonet fixed. All exercises took place with the soldier either kneeling or lying prone, and they often featured a strict time limit.[117] A key goal of training was to develop the snap-shooting skills that had given the Boers such an advantage in firefights. An annual allowance of at least twenty-five rounds per man was assigned purely for such exercises. Soldiers would take cover and then engage surprise targets that would be raised for between four and six seconds.[118] Beyond individual target shooting, exercises included instruction in the ballistic qualities of rifles, practice in estimating ranges, and collective fire work alongside comrades.[119]

The culmination of musketry training was the "mad minute," an exercise in which a prone soldier was required to fire fifteen rounds at a target at least three hundred yards distant. To increase the difficulty, the soldier was only allowed to begin with four rounds in the magazine and one in the breach. Furthermore, although the Lee-Enfield rifle possessed a ten-round magazine capacity, reloading was permitted only in five-round increments during this exercise.[120] Achieving this feat was a source of considerable individual pride. Troops would spend evenings working the breach on their rifles to become accustomed to the rapid reloading necessary, and with practice a number of soldiers could deliver as many as twenty aimed rounds a minute.[121] The pre-1914 record stood at an astonishing thirty-eight rounds in sixty seconds, all of which hit the inner ring of the target.[122]

Men who were skillful shots could earn additional pay, and a coveted marksman badge was awarded to those who reached the appropriate musketry standard—both of which encouraged individual training. There were also widespread musketry competitions for both individuals and units.[123] In 1913, a memorandum cautioned that one particularly popular competition for individual rifleman was attracting so many entrants that it was becoming impossible to manage.[124] Collective exercises such as the Smith-Dorrien Competition for infantry and the Evelyn Wood Competition for infantry and cavalry also attracted considerable participation.[125]

In addition to the overhaul of training, the standard Lee-Enfield rifle was redesigned based on the experience of South Africa. This redesign resulted in the issue of the famous "short" Lee-Enfield[126] in the summer of 1903. This new rifle was designed to be easy to handle when firing from behind cover and thus more effective in snap-shooting engagements. Its comparatively short length allowed it to be used by both infantry and cavalry. The rifle and its later variations have been described subsequently as "the finest combat bolt-action rifle ever to see active service."[127] This improved equipment undoubtedly aided in the development of British marksmanship prior to 1914.

However, an enduring criticism of British musketry has been that the emphasis on marksmanship and rapidity was a response to the failure to provide sufficient machine guns to the infantry. In 1909 and 1910, the commandant of the School of Musketry, Major N. R. McMahon, argued in favor of increasing the number of machine guns per infantry battalion and introducing an automatic rifle to replace bolt-action weapons.[128] As will be discussed in greater depth later in this chapter, the request for additional machine guns was refused.

Frustrated by this development, McMahon argued that "We must train every soldier in our Army to become a 'human machine gun.' Every man must receive intensive training with his rifle, until he can fire—with reasonable accuracy—fifteen rounds a minute."[129] John Edmonds claimed in the British *Official History of the Great War* that the decision to focus on rapidity of rifle fire was taken in 1909 as a direct result of the denial of an appeal for additional machine guns for infantry.[130] Subsequently, this assertion has been repeated by several historians.[131]

However, this view is erroneous.[132] Although McMahon placed considerable emphasis on rapidity, it was not a new concept in musketry training. South African experience had clearly shown that sudden bursts of very intense fire were most effective at suppressing enemy fire during the attack or stopping an enemy advance when defending a position. School of Musketry training exercises showed that in favorable peacetime circumstances, soldiers could maintain this level of fire for only around four minutes without the fire becoming wild; under the stress of combat, the school estimated that this figure would be closer to a minute. From this estimate, the so-called mad minute was developed as a fire tactic to be used at critical moments during an action. The value of this tactic was discussed at the 1906 General Staff Conference, several years before the dispute arose over machine guns.[133] In other respects, McMahon maintained the direction of musketry reform that had begun in 1902, namely a focus on accuracy, shooting from cover, and snap shooting. His tenure as commandant at Hythe marked a further refinement of pre-existing musketry reforms rather a sudden revolution in thinking.

As well as making the individual soldier a good marksman, making effective tactical use of infantry fire was a keynote of British assault tactics in the years immediately following the Boer War. *Combined Training 1905* noted that fire action had increased greatly as a result of modern technology, going on to state, "All movements on the battlefield have but one end in view, the development of fire in greater volume and more effectively directed than that of the opposing force; and although the bayonet still plays an important part, it is superiority of fire that renders the decision of the conflict possible."[134]

As previously discussed, gaining this superiority of fire posed a problem regarding the best type of formation to adopt during the infantry attack. British musketry training was aimed at producing skillful individual marksman, capable of accurate and rapid fire at up to six hundred yards. However, a series of complex experiments at the School of Musketry discovered the unpalatable fact that between four hundred and five hundred yards' range, a dense firing line of average and indifferent shots possessed considerably greater firepower than an extended line of first-class marksmen. Although the extended line achieved a higher proportion of hits to rounds fired, the sheer volume of fire from the dense line typically inflicted overwhelming casualties on their extended opponents within a minute of fire being opened.[135]

This tactical problem highlighted the important fact that it was not enough to simply make men talented individual shots. Instead, it was crucial that high levels of individual skill were allied with an effective system of fire tactics that encouraged and allowed movement. Widespread use of earthworks meant that simply outshooting the enemy was not enough. This issue had been well illustrated at several actions in the Boer War, most noticeably during the Battle of Paardeberg (18–27 February 1900). After an initial day of uncoordinated and costly infantry attacks, the British had settled down to what was effectively a siege of Cronjé's laager. Although the British held fire superiority throughout most of the battle, the Boers suffered few casualties and were compelled to surrender only by the combination of starvation and the presence of infantry at just sixty-five yards' distance from their trenches threatening a fresh assault. The difficulty, if not impossibility, of using infantry firepower alone to move a determined enemy from a good position was further emphasized in the Russo-Japanese War.[136]

With these experiences in mind, British infantry fire tactics consisted of the two tightly connected elements of fire and movement. Both were mutually supporting within the infantry attack. Covering fire from one section of the line would allow other parts to advance. Once the advancing troops had taken up fire positions of their own, they would provide covering fire to allow the rest of the line to move. In this manner, the attackers would advance in bounds, with troops moving only when their comrades could provide covering fire. Ultimately, it was intended that the advancing infantry could take up progressively stronger fire positions and win superiority over the enemy. This concept was to be the keynote of fire tactics for the British throughout the 1902–1914 period. At the 1910 General Staff Conference, N.R. McMahon, spoke of "the importance of impressing on all soldiers that they must win their battles by movement, and must regard fire as a means enabling them to move. . . . [this represents] the decisive uses of fire."[137] Writing in 1912, an infantry officer summed up the attitude toward the issue throughout the era when he wrote, "Fire and movement . . . must never be dissociated in peace training and must be regarded as complementary in war."[138]

Regarding the importance of movement in fire combat, a notable change in British regulations was the subtle rewording in the discussion of the attack in *Field Service Regulations 1909* from the original in *Combined Training 1905*. Whereas *Combined Training* had stated, "Superiority of fire makes the decision possible," *Field Service Regulations* noted, "The climax of the infantry attack is the assault, which is made possible by superiority of fire."[139] This change has sometimes been portrayed as representing a backward step for the British Army.[140] However, the principle behind this alteration was relatively sound, as it aimed to emphasize the importance of using fire to allow movement, rather than merely as an end in itself. This emphasis was a conscious response to some of the problems faced in South Africa, where troops had often become stalled in firefights. N. R. McMahon spoke on such problems in 1910, stating, "We all remember that hundreds and thousands of rounds of ammunition were fired in South Africa when there was no attempt at movement on either side."[141]

Much like the efforts to improve individual marksmanship, efforts to replace the old system of fire tactics that had relied on close control and volleys took considerable time. However, progress was helped and supported by the work done at the School of Musketry at Hythe. By 1907 it was noted with satisfaction that not only was the program of instruction at Hythe excellent, but also that an interchange of ideas between the School of Musketry and the army practice camps was now becoming apparent.[142] Nevertheless, translating this teaching into practice could sometimes be difficult. For example, in 1910 there was considerable concern that volley fire appeared to be making a return within certain units. An alarmed inspector general noted that although in some cases officers who still favored old-fashioned methods were to blame, in most cases it resulted from a misinterpretation of teaching at Hythe, which suggested it was sometimes useful to use a simultaneous burst of rapid fire but had somehow had its teaching "twisted into the word 'fire' leading to an order to press the trigger several times in succession."[143] Steps were taken quickly to correct this retrograde development. In 1911, there was frustration that training in fire and movement was falling short of desired standards, despite the fact that much work and discussion on the concept had taken place. Officers were criticized for failing to "recognise that musketry and tactics are synonymous and cannot be separated. . . . Hythe teaching is so clear and definite on these points that it is incredible how little attention seems to be paid to them."[144] Yet from this low point, steady developments in fire tactics were observed in subsequent years. In 1912 and 1913 improvements were evident, and it was noted with satisfaction that the use of fire to facilitate movement was well understood in all battalions by 1913.[145]

The acid test of British musketry reform was to come in the battles of 1914. Although there are no official figures for German casualties at Mons, historians have estimated them as being between 2,000 and 10,000 men.[146] German commander Alexander von Kluck described his losses at Mons as "heavy."[147] Similar doubt exists over the casualties at Le Cateau.[148] However, in both cases it should be remembered that British artillery support in these early engagements was often lacking, particularly at Mons, and thus many of the German casualties at these engagement were likely to have been the result of rifle and machine gun fire.

British rifle tactics in these early battles showed that the effort devoted to musketry training had not been in vain. One British soldier at Mons recalled engaging a German column advancing in close order, noting, "The effect of the mad minute on such a target was electrical."[149] An anonymous sergeant from the Lincolnshire Regiment recalled that at Mons his company had held their fire: "We lay in our trenches with not a sound or a sight to tell them of what was before them." Opening fire at close range, the company surprised the Germans, who despite shaking into open formation and advancing by rushes, were ultimately pinned down. The sergeant related that while most of the company continued to fire in controlled bursts to keep the Germans pinned, "a few of the crack shots were told off to indulge in independent firing for the benefit of the Germans. That is another trick taught to us by Brother Boer, and our Germans did not like it at all."[150] The deployment of individual crack shots to pick out choice targets was also repeated at Le Cateau. An officer of the Hampshire Regiment related, "The best marksmen of D Company were able to pick off some of the machine gun crews and occasional officers who marked themselves out by carrying drawn swords."[151]

The ranges of rifle fire were shorter than they had been in the crystal-clear atmosphere of South Africa, but British fire could prove effective at considerable distance. At Le Cateau, the Gordon Highlanders opened fire at nine hundred yards, and although this inflicted few casualties, it delayed the German advance to such an extent that it took them more than an hour to advance to within four hundred yards.[152]

German accounts of the British fire give testimony to its effectiveness. Walter Bloem, a German officer at Mons, related an experience leading an infantry attack against the British. After a difficult advance by rushes to within a hundred and fifty yards of the British line, leaving behind them a meadow "dotted with little grey heaps," the Germans noted British infantry fire had virtually ceased. Bloem planned to launch a final thirty-yard long rush, but in a tactic similar to those used by the Boers, the British were waiting for Bloem's men to break cover. Bloem recounted, "The enemy must have been waiting for this moment to get us all together at close range, for immediately the line rose it was as if the hounds of hell had been loosed at us, barking, hammering as a mass of lead swept in amongst us . . . Voluntarily and in many cases involuntarily we all collapsed flat on the grass as if swept by a scythe."[153]

Recalling the fighting at Le Cateau, a jäger officer paid compliment to the British infantry: "They were wily soldiers, tough and tenacious fellows, with iron nerves, even when wounded. They shot well and understood how to use terrain with such skill that it was difficult even for jäger to detect them."[154]

At both Mons and Le Cateau, German artillery dominance forced the British infantry to fight with limited support from their long arm.[155] In these confused battles, although often lacking direction from higher command and in a difficult strategic position, British infantry acquitted themselves well against their German opponents. The emphasis on training accurate marksmanship against an the enemy within six hundred yards' range, which had been urged by Lord Roberts after the Boer War and supported by the School of Musketry, was vindicated during early First World War engagements. *Notes from the Front* reported that "A short field of fire (500 yards or less) has been found sufficient to check a German infantry attack" and successful defenses were mounted at even shorter distances.[156] British rifle fire would arguably prove most effective during the first Battle of Ypres, when it scythed down densely packed German reserve formations with such ferocity that it was attributed to machine gun fire.[157] A German official account of the battle stated, "The British, many of whom had fought in a colonial war against the most cunning of enemies in equally difficult country, allowed the attacker to come to close quarters and then opened a devastating fire at point-blank range from rifles and machine guns concealed in houses and trees."[158]

The improvement and success of British marksmanship in 1914 can be directly attributed to the lessons that had been learned so painfully against the Boers in South Africa. The Boers had taught the British hard lessons regarding the power of accurate rifle fire and the necessity for extended formations in 1899, but to the credit of the British Army these lessons had not been ignored and instead formed a linchpin of infantry tactics. Their value was emphasized in the battles of 1914, when it was the Germans who were forced to experience some of the problems of attacking skillful marksmen in good positions.

MACHINE GUNS

Whereas the Boer War taught valuable lessons regarding the necessity of improving individual marksmanship and fire tactics, its influence on the development of the machine gun was largely negative. As previously discussed, in 1909 the School of Musketry began lobbying for a vast increase in machine guns per infantry battalion. The failure to meet these demands meant that the British infantry of 1914 went to war with just two machine guns per battalion, a fact that has been cited by numerous historians as a serious material weakness.[159]

Perhaps the money may have been more readily available for machine guns had their performance in South Africa been more impressive. Machine guns had proved extremely valuable in struggles against tribal foes, allowing a handful of Europeans to inflict crippling casualties on the brave but crudely armed tribesmen. However, when committed to action against a well-armed and carefully concealed opponent in South Africa, results were disappointing. The Boers fought from behind cover and refused to provide the kind of massed target that the Mahdists had done in the Sudan. Furthermore, many of the British machine guns in South Africa were mounted on so-called galloping carriages rather than tripods. These wheeled carriages made them easier to move but presented a far larger target.

How best to use machine guns in the Boer War was a tactical problem to which no definite answer was ever found. Some officers favored pushing the guns right into the infantry firing line, where targets would be more visible and friendly troops would be encouraged by the sound of the weapon in action.[160] Yet this tactic was deprecated by others, who felt bringing the gun so far forward made it too easy for the Boers to silence it with either rifle or artillery fire. For example, at the Battle of Modder River, the machine gun of the 1st Scots Guards was brought in to close-range action, but it was knocked out in less than five minutes by Boer pom-pom gun[161] fire.[162] Reliability was also an issue, with jams and breakdowns frequent throughout the campaign. One officer who fought at Modder River reported his battalion's gun had jammed an incredible twenty-nine times during the course of the engagement.[163] Lack of technical training within the gun crews meant that repairing mechanical problems in the field was difficult and sometimes even impossible.[164]

Views on the value and practicality of the machine gun remained varied throughout the war. Problems of where to deploy the weapon in an advance, its relative vulnerability, and the lack of good targets presented by the Boers meant that many officers saw it as more useful in defense than in attack.[165] A handful of adherents emerged from South Africa, one officer stating somewhat prophetically, "The effects cannot be exaggerated, and if understood tactically the machine gun dominates the whole question of attack in the future . . . neglect of proper tactical use of machine guns, was the most important lesson of the war," but opinions such as these were in a distinct minority.[166] A more common view was that although the gun was valuable in both attack and defense against enemies who operated in dense masses, it was useful only in defense against opposition who made use of cover and entrenchment.[167]

The Russo-Japanese War tended to confirm rather than dispel these ideas. The Russians had made the most of machine guns in the early stages of the war, and their effectiveness when deployed in a defensive role was undoubtedly great.[168] The Japanese subsequently placed greater emphasis on the weapon and used it in an offensive role, where it proved useful in suppressing Russian trenches during attacks. However, its employment in this manner did little to shake the tactical orthodoxy surrounding the weapon. Commenting on his wartime experiences, a Japanese officer noted, "For the commander to use the gun as a substitute for infantry fire shows ignorance of its nature" and considered the ammunition consumption was so great that to use it purely to suppress an enemy trench was wasteful, with artillery being capable of doing the same job more efficiently and at much longer range.[169] Nevertheless, armies on the continent, especially that of Germany, took an increased interest in the weapon and began moving toward increasing their establishments of machine guns.[170]

In Britain, assessments of the weapon remained mixed. Machine gun allocation was doubled to two guns per battalion for both infantry and cavalry in the aftermath of the Boer War.[171] However, tactical interest in the weapon waned despite the efforts of a number of officers who emphasized the value of the machine gun and encouraged its use. For example, a 1901 committee assembled to assess the value and organization of machine guns and pom-pom guns in the future ignored its remit and omitted discussion of the machine gun altogether.[172] After a brief spell of interest and allocation to the cavalry and mounted infantry, pom-pom guns soon fell from favor, being unwieldy and relatively ineffective at inflicting casualties. By 1905, discussion of the pom-pom as anything other than a range-finding device had ceased, and the weapons themselves were apparently withdrawn. Conversely, machine guns remained in service with infantry and cavalry, but training in the weapon lagged behind European armies for several years. In Britain, a period of only nine months was allocated to train a machine gunner versus three years on the continent.[173] At a 1909 lecture, one officer summed up the problem of the gun's poor reputation:

No doubt this is due very largely to the discredit into which the Maxim gun fell in South Africa . . . they were perfectly useless and had to be abandoned; had we known as much about it as we do now different tactics would have prevailed. . . . The way the guns are handled on manoeuvres, the way they are attacked, leads one to believe that people take very little account of them. At present half the mistakes in the training at manoeuvres are due to no-one knowing where the machine gun is, and certainly not caring.[174]

Training did begin to show improvement from 1910 onward, with experiments taking place involving overhead fire and organization of machine guns into brigades.[175] However, despite proposals from the School of Musketry to increase the quota of weapons, including the addition of light machine guns to infantry battalions, growing interest in the weapon came too late to ensure senior officers accepted these ideas. John Ellis has been highly critical of this decision, arguing the rejection of machine guns was based on anachronistic attitudes in the officer class and was not a rational response to either technical or financial considerations.[176] However, Shelford Bidwell and Dominick Graham have convincingly challenged this interpretation, arguing that financial considerations played a far larger role than Ellis allows. The British Army had only recently rearmed its artillery at considerable expense and had also adopted a new short Lee-Enfield rifle. In addition, discussions were underway to change the caliber of the infantry rifle, which would entail further costs. The Liberal government was committed to reducing the cost of the army where possible, and in such circumstances a large-scale rearmament of the machine gun branch was financially impractical even though there was evidence that Britain was lagging behind European rivals in this regard.[177]

Perhaps if the machine gun had had a better reputation this might have encouraged its development and expenditure upon it; however, as has been shown, it performed poorly in South Africa and its role in the Russo-Japanese War seemed to confirm the idea that it was best used as a weapon of defense. Unfortunately for the British infantry, the Boer War experience was largely negative in this regard and did little to encourage the adoption of a weapon that would become crucial in the First World War.

ENTRENCHMENT

Prior to the Boer War, the onerous task of storming enemy trenches was a relatively rarity in colonial warfare, although the British did have some experience of assaulting earthworks. Organized opposition in Egypt had made use of trenches, and Britain's tribal foes sometimes sought recourse to the employment of hill forts and other methods of basic fortification. However, the Boers were to provide a rude awakening with the complexity and the depth of their trenches, which provided excellent protection against both British artillery and rifle fire. Furthermore, by making use of large amounts

of native labor, the Boers were able to construct complex entrenchments in a relatively short time frame. One British veteran recalled
that "Bitter experience has shown us that to give the Boer time was
to ensure an elaborate system of trenches and obstacles being added
to his defensive assets."[178]

The shelter these earthworks provided was highly impressive.
The trenches dug by the Boers at the Battle of Paardeberg provided
such cover that casualties among the burghers were relatively low
despite being under the regular bombardment of field and heavy
artillery for more than a week. Inspecting the trenches after the
surrender of Cronjé's laager, Lord Roberts commented, "They had
constructed their trenches in an extraordinarily skilful manner.
Deep narrow trenches, with each side well hollowed out, in which
they got complete shelter from shellfire, and if their food could
have lasted, they might have defied this large force for some time
to come."[179]

As well as providing excellent protection from incoming fire,
Boer trenches were often extremely well concealed. Combined with
smokeless powder, this concealment made locating the enemy before and even during an attack a considerable challenge. On several occasions, including the major engagements at Modder River
and Colenso, British forces were largely ignorant of the location of
Boer entrenchments until the battle was underway. Most famously
of all, at the Battle of Magersfontein the Boers had decided against
placing their trenches on the summit of the kopje and instead sited
them at the base. This unexpected move allowed the flat-trajectory
Boer rifles an excellent field of fire across the open plain in front
of them.[180] Equally, the tactic completely deceived Lord Methuen
and his force. Prior to the attack, the real Boer trenches were not
discovered; instead, British artillery carried out a heavy, two-hour
bombardment of the largely deserted kopje. Total Boer casualties
from this shelling were just three men wounded.[181] The subsequent
night attack against the kopje miscarried disastrously, with delays
and confusion causing the British to be caught in close-order formation several hundred yards short of the hidden Boer line at dawn.[182]
It was only when the British assault force came under withering
fire that the true location of the Boer position was revealed. Leo
Amery considered the placement of the Boer trenches at this battle

"one of the boldest and most original conceptions in the history of war," and although subsequent historians have been less impressed with the originality of the idea, there is no denying it came as an extremely unpleasant shock for the British.[183]

In stark contrast to the Boers, British infantry expertise in constructing trenches was noticeably lacking. Pre-war infantry regulations recognized only two kinds of shelter trenches: the "half-hour" and the "hour," named for the amount of time it was expected to take for them to be constructed.[184] These trenches were tiny compared with those of the Boers, being only one and a half feet deep, and although it was considered possible to increase their size if time permitted, in reality this was rarely practiced in peacetime for fear of leaving dangerous obstacles behind for cavalry, or because of concerns that the land on which the training was taking place was privately owned.[185] In 1900, Sir Howard Vincent was scathing over this lack of training, writing, "I think at some manoeuvres they have a piece of tape to represent a trench, or something of that sort. That is the ridiculous farce which is played, and all because we cannot compensate some farmer or must not disturb some squire's game, or something of that kind."[186]

More detailed and serious entrenchment work was considered to be the domain of the Royal Engineers, and the infantry was greatly dependent on them in this regard.[187] Although a proportion of infantry carried a small entrenching spade, heavier tools were carried on pack animals and in local transport, being distributed only when digging in was considered necessary.[188] However, both types of tools were considered poor for work on anything other than soft ground. Henry Hildyard, who had commanded one of the best-trained brigades at the outset of the Boer War, remembered that the tools were "universally condemned" by both junior officers and men.[189] Indeed, his troops had much preferred Boer picks and shovels and had taken them for their own use whenever the opportunity presented itself.[190]

Poor equipment, limited training, and overreliance on the Royal Engineers had created a distinctly negative attitude toward the effort required to entrench properly. Much as there had been a disinclination to take cover in the early part of the war, initially many men were resentful of the labor required to entrench and saw little value in it.[191] An anonymous general in the field was reported as complaining of British troops, "I believe if our people were here for a month they would never entrench."[192] Major-General H. M. L. Rundle issued a memo in mid-1900 that summed up many of the problems associated with the attitude toward entrenchment: "Up to date I have failed to see intelligent use made of entrenchments by Brigadiers or by the troops under their command; they appear to think that a few stones hastily gathered together or 6in. of earth hastily scraped up at haphazard is adequate protection against modern gun and rifle fire."[193]

The poor understanding and attitude toward entrenchment in the Boer War was neatly expressed in a famous tactical treatise entitled *The Defence of Duffer's Drift*, where the unfortunate protagonist is called upon to organize a defensive position, only to be repeatedly defeated through simple yet unforeseen errors. Among others, these errors include making a shallow bullet-proof trench that is vulnerable to artillery, making a completely straight trench that is too easily enfiladed, and failing to conceal a trench line, allowing the Boers to observe a planned ambush from miles away. The author summed up this final point as follows: "To surprise the enemy is a great advantage . . . If you wish to obtain this advantage, *conceal* your position. Though for promotion it may be sound to advertise your position, for defence it is not."[194]

As with the reluctance to take cover, experience under fire gradually began to erode the poor attitude toward entrenchment. Boer methods were admired and imitated.[195] Rundle felt that the examination of the Boer trenches at Paardeberg created a sensation throughout much of Lord Roberts's army, and its design was subsequently adopted throughout his divisions.[196] The unpleasant experience of being shelled and under heavy rifle fire soon encouraged greater efforts with the spade, as the consequences of inadequate preparation were often fatal.[197] By the latter stages of the war, entrenchment was greatly improved, as Major-General Hubert Plumer recalled,

> They [Plumer's men] were very good at it, they were very intelligent, and in fact it did not require at the end of the war to tell them to entrench themselves; they always did it as a matter of course. We took up a position, and expected after an hour or so to find our men entrenched, and with very rare

exceptions it was so; but at the beginning of the war we had to explain to them how very important it was and what a difference it would make.[198]

Conflicting ideas on methods of entrenchment emerged in the aftermath of the Boer War. Although skill at digging in had steadily improved, the standard British entrenching tool remained universally reviled. James Grierson felt the tool could be abandoned entirely, arguing it was impossible to dig in under fire and that it would always be possible to bring up mules carrying shovels and picks when necessary.[199] Equally, Ian Hamilton expressed concerns that although entrenchment was valuable, the carrying of heavy tools by infantry would reduce their mobility too much.[200] The old system of tools being brought to the front when necessary persisted until the Russo-Japanese War. Examples from this conflict highlighted the fact that entrenchment had gained considerably in importance, in both attack and defense. Ruminating on the experience, the Duke of Connaught cautioned, "It would appear that it is unsafe in modern war to trust entirely in carts or pack animals for the transport of entrenching tools."[201] Moves toward creating a more efficient entrenching tool proceeded slowly, but by 1907 a superior pattern had been devised and was carried by men and NCOs. Heavier equipment such as picks continued to be carried on pack animals and in carts.[202]

In terms of training and practical work, the army initially placed a great deal of thought and effort into improving entrenching methods and tactics. Entrenchment was particularly emphasized during training at Aldershot, where there were facilities for digging and constructing thorough trench lines. Divisions were praised for their detailed work that took into account the experiences of the Boer War, particularly in terms of cleverly siting trenches and providing concealment and covered approaches.[203] The standards by which the work was judged were extremely high. For example, a trench constructed by a battalion from 2nd Division was picked out for criticism, the inspector noting, "It is perhaps hypercritical . . . but some trenches on the heather were concealed with bracken when a mixture of fern and heather would have been better."[204] While in command at Aldershot, John French repeatedly emphasized the need for skill in the use of trenches, writing in 1905, "I would strongly impress upon infantry officers that the skilful use of entrenchments is one of the most powerful weapons in their armoury, and I urge them here, also, to recall their own experiences and impress upon their minds the lesson which these have taught."[205]

Aldershot was well suited for training in entrenchment, possessing government-owned land that could be dug up and worked on as required. Soil at Aldershot was sandy and thus easily worked, although the loose nature of the earth could prove problematic when constructing deeper entrenchments. However, for other elements of the British Army this was not the case. In particular, Southern Command was almost completely lacking in appropriate ground for entrenchment training.[206]

A further problem was that as the years passed by, the quality of training in entrenchment declined, with elementary aspects being poorly understood and an overemphasis being placed on elaborate schemes. In a 1910 report, John French complained, "I do not believe that instruction in the practical, thorough entrenching of positions receives adequate attention, although a few years ago it was a prominent feature of all our larger exercises and manoeuvres."[207] Despite being an issue singled out for improvement by the Army Council, problems with entrenching continued to be identified right up until the outbreak of the First World War. Individual spade work was considered good, but there remained limited tactical thought in the placement of trenches and only minor consideration given to the steps necessary for them to be occupied for long-term periods.[208] Little improvement was evident by 1913, and it was considered that infantry had regressed in this regard.[209]

A number of factors were responsible for the disregard of the lessons that had been learned in South Africa. Ian Hamilton identified as an influence the natural turnover in the numbers of men and junior officers who had seen action, noting in 1908 that "[in the last three years] there has been an inevitable steady process of replacing war-trained subalterns, sergeants and corporals by young officers and non-commissioned officers of similar rank who have not as yet been able to profit by the experiences of field service."[210]

This process continued throughout the pre–First World War period, and by 1914, 46,291 men of the BEF had less than two years' experience with the colors.[211] Just as soldiers who served in the Boer War had been inclined to regard entrenchment as tedious and time consuming until they actually experienced combat, so these new soldiers and junior officers were inclined to form the same opinion in peacetime. The tedium of the work was further increased by the fact that any trenches constructed during maneuvers needed to be filled back in afterward. One officer noted that it was "disheartening to troops to know that the more they dig the more they will have to put back."[212]

The need to compensate landowners for damage caused by entrenching during maneuvers remained unresolved throughout the period and was a serious barrier to realistic training. At large-scale maneuvers on privately owned land, trenches were often signified by markers such as tape and ground sheets. At the 1909 maneuvers, a particular incident was singled out for criticism, with the report noting it was a "somewhat common procedure": "One battalion on the Red side, when attacking a Blue position, gained a fire position, put down its tape, advanced a short distance, put down its tape again, delivered an assault which was ruled to have failed, and were sent back when it again put down its tape."[213]

At maneuvers in 1910, it was noted that on several occasions infantry launched frontal assaults on defenders apparently lying in open fields, only to be informed by the umpires that the defenders were to be considered entrenched.[214] The situation was never satisfactorily resolved. A General Staff discussion of the problem in 1912 was forced to conclude that "At best, any entrenchment done must be limited to what causes no permanent damage—in other words to digging where digging does no harm, provided the trenches etc. are filled in again immediately."[215]

A further problem for the British Army was the increasing emphasis on the offensive, to the point where passive defense was considered fatal for any hope of success. Infantry training manuals emphasized the importance of the offensive, downgrading the value of strong entrenchments and seeing them as being of use primarily in terms of reducing the number of men needed to hold a position, which would allow more troops to be used in a counterattack. *Field Service Regulations 1909* stated, "The choice of a position and its preparation must be made with a *view to economizing the power expended on defence in order that the power of offence may be increased."*[216] It is likely that this great focus on the offensive contributed to the general apathy toward entrenchment work that pervaded British training in the latter stages of the period.

Of all the key lessons learned by the infantry in South Africa, entrenchment had the least lasting influence. Although in the years immediately following the Boer War entrenchment was well practiced and understood, the tactical use of earthworks underwent something of a regression in the latter part of the Edwardian period, despite the example of the Russo-Japanese War proving it was more important than ever. Overemphasis on the offensive, a decline in the numbers of war-hardened soldiers, and a lack of facilities on which to train all played a part in the fading of these important lessons. Nevertheless, the standard of entrenching in the infantry had come a considerable way from the virtually nonexistent level it had been at in 1899 prior to the Boer War.

The First World War would ultimately require a revision of entrenchment methods and tactics as trenches became the dominant aspect of the battlefield, but in the early months of the war the experience of the Boer War helped to give the British infantry a basic grounding in entrenchment tactics. Some units benefited from the presence of Boer War veterans who insisted on deeper and more complex entrenchments, with one sergeant recalling that his company had constructed deep, concealed trenches at Mons, noting that this was "a trick we learned from the Boers, I believe."[217]

However, other regiments were not so fortunate and suffered accordingly from German artillery fire. The intense heat of August 1914, the exhaustion caused by marching, and the confusion inherent in the retreat from Mons meant that entrenchment was often inadequate, with troops reluctant to dig in or in some cases becoming separated from their tools.[218] Sometimes elementary mistakes identified in South Africa were repeated; for example, at Le Cateau the trenches of the 2nd Scottish Borders were clearly visible because of the presence of recently turned earth. This visibility attracted such heavy artillery fire that they chose to abandon their earthworks and shelter in the open.[219] The ferocity of German artillery fire in 1914 came as an unpleasant shock for the British and necessitated the reiteration of the lessons of concealment and depth for trenches that had originally been identified in South Africa but that had unfortunately declined during the years of peace that followed.[220]

CONCLUSION

From 1902 to 1914, the infantry of the British Army experienced a vast overhaul of training and tactics. The BEF of 1914 was tactically almost unrecognizable from the army that had been defeated by the Boers at Colenso, Magersfontein, and Stormberg in 1899. Whereas the Victorian infantry system had placed faith in volley firing and cumbersome, linear formations, the army of 1914 utilized flexible tactics that emphasized dispersion, intelligent use of the ground, and skillful marksmanship.

Despite the persistence of some tactical and material weaknesses, the British infantry of 1914 were far better trained to wage modern war than they had been in 1899. The lessons of the Boer War were sometimes ambiguous and often challenged, but the key themes of dispersion, use of ground, maximization of infantry fire power, and the value of spade work emerged from the conflict and became the core tactical principles for the infantry.

With hindsight, it is possible to identify aspects of the reforms that did not develop as fully as perhaps they should have. In particular, the failure to equip the infantry with machine guns in greater numbers was undoubtedly an unfortunate decision; however, as has been demonstrated, a combination of financial restrictions and the poor performance of the weapon in South Africa militated against its wider adoption. In placing emphasis on such errors, there is a danger of ignoring or marginalizing the fact that as a whole, British infantry tactics and training improved markedly in the 1902–1914 period. Not only were useful tactical lessons derived from South Africa, but the need for improved training to ensure they were absorbed by the army was also identified and successfully implemented.

The process of infantry reform begun by the Boer War had born fruit by the outbreak of the First World War, and the experience gained in South Africa led directly to the creation of the highly trained BEF infantryman of 1914. The ability to fight in dispersed formation and produce very rapid and accurate rifle fire came from reforms introduced as a direct result of the Boer War. In the confused opening battles of 1914, these skills were to be decisive in allowing the British Army to fight successfully against the numerically superior Germans.

Throughout the battles of 1914, the British infantry were forced to bear the brunt of much of the fighting. At Mons the artillery lacked adequate positions to deploy, while at Le Cateau the gunners struggled to cope against overwhelming numbers of German guns, throwing the emphasis of the battle onto the foot soldier. In a similar manner, during the Battle of Ypres, artillery support was often rationed because of a chronic shortage of shells for the guns. The impressive performance of the infantry during these vital defensive battles is testament to their much-improved tactics of both fire and formation. British performance in these early battles gave the Old Contemptibles an enduring reputation for skill and determination that proved that many of the hard lessons of the Boer War had been well learned.

4

ARTILLERY

T he Boer War was a rude awakening for the entire British Army, but the arm that received the greatest surprise was the Royal Artillery. The gunners had to look back several decades to the Crimean War (1854–56) to find a conflict in which they faced an enemy who was comparably armed, and years of small-scale colonial warfare had left little room for the artillery, which generally had a very limited combat role against crudely armed foes. Lacking practical experience of fighting against technologically equal enemies, the gunners based much of their doctrine on German writing, which drew examples from the Franco-Prussian War. Unfortunately, many of these ideas were to prove irrelevant to artillery combat on the veldt.

Although the Royal Artillery possessed a substantial numerical advantage over the handful of guns available to the Boers, in the early battles of the war the British were often disappointed by the performance of their long arm. The Boer gunners refused to conform to expectations of battle derived from the Franco-Prussian War, which suggested guns of both sides should engage in a preliminary artillery duel against one another in the open. Instead, the Boers made the most of concealment, long range, and dispersion to continuously harass the British, despite the best efforts of the Royal Artillery to locate and destroy them. Although the physical damage inflicted by the Boer guns was small, its impact on morale was considerable. The apparent effectiveness of Boer artillery tactics was greatly magnified by the British press, further heaping humiliation on the Royal Artillery.

These embarrassments and the press reaction to them caused the government to approve a complete overhaul of the Royal Artillery's equipment, with new guns and howitzers for both field and heavy artillery being introduced. In technical terms, particularly range and rate of fire, the guns of 1914 represented an enormous advancement from those with which the British had gone to war in 1899. However, the difficulty for the Royal Artillery in the years following the Boer War was designing workable tactics and doctrine to take advantage of these new weapons. The Boer War had shaken many long-held ideas in the artillery, and a variety of replacement theories struggled for prominence in the years preceding the First World War. Although ideas from the war in South Africa were initially dominant, as the period progressed there were concerns that the conditions on the veldt and the nature of Boer artillery were radically different from those likely to be encountered in a potential European conflict. Therefore, influences from the continent and the Russo-Japanese War became popular, further complicating the process of developing new tactics. Technological changes were fundamentally altering the use of field artillery, and the permanent introduction of heavy guns into the field marked a new tactical element that had been seen only on rare occasions in previous wars. At the same time the gunners were grappling with these changes, there was a gradual but growing recognition that on a fire-swept battlefield, artillery would become the dominant weapon.

Whereas the infantry of the BEF have won much praise from historians for their development in the aftermath of the Boer War, the Royal Artillery of 1914 has not received such universal admiration. Although there were valuable tactical ideas within the artillery, an apparent lack of consensus on their value meant that a level of uncertainty over correct artillery doctrine persisted throughout the period.[1] Robert Scales has been critical of the artillery, arguing that too much faith was placed in the lessons of the Boer War, blinding the gunners to developments on the continent.[2] Edward Spiers has taken a more balanced view, feeling that the artillery possessed a well-considered doctrine by the eve of the First World War. However, Spiers suggests this doctrine was not due to the Boer War experience but was instead formed by the "fortuitous coincidence" of the examples of the Russo-Japanese War and closer links with the French military following the entente of 1904.[3]

The variety of historical opinion concerning the effectiveness of the Royal Artillery in 1914 mirrors the lack of consensus that existed within the arm during the pre–First World War period. A formal artillery doctrine was not established in the aftermath of the Boer War. Instead, flexibility of method was encouraged, which allowed certain outdated ideas to survive right up until the First World War. Nevertheless, in spite of this problem, the Royal Artillery advanced enormously in terms of tactics from 1899 to 1914 and fought tenaciously against vastly superior numbers of German guns in the opening battles of 1914.

In this chapter, discussion is structured around several important developments within the artillery branch during the 1902–1914 period, all of which had their roots in the experiences of the Boer War. I cover the ongoing debate within the Royal Artillery over the potential usefulness of long-range fire and how best to incorporate the new branch of heavy artillery into the existing tactical framework. In addition, I analyze the vociferous debate over whether engaging from concealed positions or using close-range deployment in the open was the correct method to employ, and I also discuss the development of the relatively new indirect support weapon in the form of the field howitzer. The final part of the chapter concentrates on arguably the greatest tactical problem that faced artillerymen, namely how best to support infantry, especially during the attack. Taking these themes as a base, in this chapter I demonstrate how the Boer War provided a crucial impetus for artillery reform. Although the lessons from South Africa sometimes proved to be misleading, its tactical influence provided a crucial starting point for future development. Further shaped by examples from Manchuria and the continent, the Royal Artillery was able to develop tactics by 1914 that were a considerable advance on the faulty ideas with which it had gone to war against the Boers.

LONG-RANGE FIRE AND HEAVY GUNS

On the eve of the Boer War, the Royal Artillery remained wedded to tactical ideas developed by the Germans during the Franco-Prussian War. Part of the Prussian experience was that long-range fire was generally ineffective; therefore, they felt shooting at ranges above 1,800 yards should be avoided if possible.[4] Although modern artillery pieces of the 1890s were technically capable of delivering fire at far longer ranges, it was generally believed that any shots beyond observable distance would be wasted; thus, the Royal Artillery worked toward securing maximum accuracy and effect at shorter ranges. To this end, the practice range at Okehampton was just 1,500 yards long in 1897, although it had been increased to 2,148 yards by 1899.[5] Other arms endorsed such ideas. The infantry anticipated 3,000 yards to be the extreme "useful range" of hostile artillery and did not expect to come under fire at greater distances.[6] The limited experience the artillery had gained in fighting against colonial foes had done nothing to shake this faith in close-range action, and indeed the guns had often fought at point-blank distances against the Zulus and the Mahdists. Although time would prove this faith in close-range artillery to be a weakness against the Boers, on the eve of the conflict there was felt to be little cause for concern. Even staunch critic Leo Amery felt the British artillery was "perhaps the best trained in Europe" prior to the war.[7]

Unfortunately for the Royal Artillery, lessons drawn from a war fought thirty years earlier and limited experience against poorly armed foes had done little to prepare the arm for combat against an enemy equipped with modern weapons. Small-arms fire against gun crews had been a growing feature of warfare from the American Civil War onward, and the latest long-range, smokeless rifles made close-range tactics extremely dangerous for the artillerymen. However, among many colonial veterans this fact went unrecognized. Captain N. F. Gordon related a conversation with a handful of officers in Natal prior to them seeing action, where one veteran of so-called small wars offered the opinion that "long and medium ranges would hardly ever be necessary, that the motto for the mounted artilleryman should be 'Push forward, push forward' and that endeavours should be made to first come into action 500 yards to 800 yards from the objective, which should ensure success to your own side and be very bad indeed for the enemy."[8]

However, in the face of modern small-arms fire, these tactics were dangerously out of date. This fact was brought into stark focus in the early months of the Boer War, when an attempt to make use of the kind of daring tactics that had worked in so-called savage warfare failed disastrously. At the Battle of Colenso, Colonel Charles Long took two batteries of field artillery into close-range action in the open against an entrenched Boer position, without any friendly infantry support. Redvers Buller subsequently put the range as "1,200 yards, and I believe within 300 yards of the enemy's rifle pits."[9] Long had fought at Omdurman, where he had caught the eye with the daring handling of his guns, and he was reported by a journalist as expressing the opinion on the voyage to South Africa that "the only way to smash these beggars is to rush in on them."[10] Although this approach may have been appropriate in the Sudan, where the Mahdists had typically been armed with hand-to-hand weapons and fought in the open, at Colenso the Boers were equipped with modern rifles and fought from concealed trenches. At such close range, the contest was an unequal one despite the courage of the gunners. Long was seriously wounded, and crews and horses suffered heavy losses. The batteries managed to sustain the action for almost an hour before mounting casualties forced the gunners to fall back, abandoning their weapons in the open.[11] Valiant attempts to recover the lost pieces followed, resulting in further casualties, including the death of Freddy Roberts, Lord Roberts's only son. However, despite the best efforts of a number of volunteers, only two of the twelve abandoned guns were brought back to British lines. The Boers dragged the remainder away in the night, completing a humiliating reverse for the British, especially for the artillerymen, who prided themselves on preventing the loss of guns in action.[12] Explaining his tactics, Long later claimed that he had been confused by the atmospheric conditions and had approached closer to the Boers than he had originally intended.[13] Some years after the war he also somewhat uncharitably blamed Buller for not giving him more precise guidance, relating to another officer that when Buller pointed out the position he wanted Long to occupy, "his damned, fat thumb covered three square miles of the map!"[14] It remains unclear how and why Long blundered into such a dangerous position, but it is likely that the reckless charge was the product of the misleading experiences from numerous wars against ill-armed opposition.

Long's disaster at Colenso was not repeated by other batteries, but the dangers posed by infantry fire remained serious. At the Battle of Elandslaagte, Boer marksmen wounded several gunners, including the commander of one battery, and at the Battle of Stormberg, while covering the British retreat, 77th Battery came under such intense rifle fire that its commanding officer gave the order for the gunners to kneel while working the guns.[15] It was clear that old methods inspired by the Franco-Prussian War and colonial actions were no longer adequate in the face of well-armed infantry. Significantly, when Lord Roberts took charge in South Africa, the very first point relating to artillery in his "Notes for Guidance" was the following: "At the commencement of an action Artillery should not be ordered to take up a position until it has been ascertained by scouts to be clear of the enemy and out of range of Infantry fire."[16] With Boer rifle fire considered capable of inflicting casualties at 1,500 yards or more, this forced the guns to rely on longer-ranged fire than it had been possible to practice at Okehampton for much of the pre-war period, and it represented quite a shock to artillerymen who had not considered small-arms fire to be dangerous at more than a thousand yards.[17]

However, a further problem regarding appropriate ranges confronted the artillery. Despite the varied experience of imperial conflict, a significant gap in British military knowledge was methods of combat against enemy guns. Foes encountered in colonial actions had lacked any meaningful artillery, and the example of fighting the Russians in the Crimea was rendered largely irrelevant by the tremendous technological advancements that had occurred during the following decades. The Boer War would represent the first time in almost fifty years that the Royal Artillery faced a foe with comparable, and in some respects superior, weapons. As the Boers could not financially sustain a gun-for-gun arms race with Britain prior to the war, emphasis had been placed on gaining qualitative advantages by importing the most modern European artillery. Weapons used by the Boers included 75 mm field guns from French and German manufacturers, plus the notorious Creusot 155 mm, nicknamed "Long Tom" by the British.[18] These weapons were manned by the Transvaal's *Staadtsartillerie* and the Orange Free State's *Artillerie Korps*.

Amounting in total to a little more than a thousand men, these two small formations represented the only professional element of the militia-based Boer military. Although some historians have considered that the level of tactics among the Boer gunners did not match the quality of their equipment, more recent scholarship has argued that following the botched Jameson Raid in 1895, the artillerists took their duties very seriously and worked hard to improve their gunnery and tactical handling.[19]

Of these weapons, the one that was to create the most profound shock and have the longest lasting influence on the British was the Long Tom. The 155 mm was essentially a fortress gun designed to be placed in a fixed mounting. British intelligence had identified their presence in the Boer arsenal but assumed they were to be used in recently constructed fortifications around Pretoria, noting that they were "not really mobile guns at all."[20] However, against all expectations, the Boers were able to bring these weapons into the field and maintained such mobility with them that the British were never able to capture one intact. Combined with the weapon's inherent range, the uniquely clear atmospheric conditions of South Africa meant that these Long Toms could deliver surprisingly accurate fire at ranges of ten thousand yards and beyond. Even the smaller field pieces of the Boers were typically used to fire at long ranges, refusing to engage the British in a straightforward gun duel and instead relying on distant, harassing fire.[21]

The actual effectiveness of this long-range shooting was a matter of some debate within the British Army. The Boers suffered persistent problems with their fuses, which meant their shells often burst in the ground or not at all, seriously reducing their effectiveness. However, when the fuses were correct and the ammunition worked properly, they were capable of inflicting damage at unprecedented ranges. Lord Roberts related an example of a Boer shell fired from around seven miles away hitting a Volunteer company of the Gordon Highlanders, killing and wounding eighteen men, and an artillery officer remembered a single Boer shell causing twenty-one casualties at approximately ten thousand yards.[22] Nevertheless, such shots were rare, and casualties from very long range fire were limited. Ruminating on this fire, one officer noted that Boer shells regularly "burst with marvellous accuracy, but, for the most part, entirely harmlessly."[23] General Sir Henry Brackenbury expressed a more critical view of the value of the Long Toms: "I do not think the physical effect of the Boer heavy guns was ever anything at all. They never did any serious harm of any sort, and nothing was so astonishing to me, and I think to many others among us, as the extraordinary moral effect which the presence of these big guns had upon our troops, especially the cavalry."[24]

Despite Brackenbury's surprise, it must be remembered that being under hostile artillery fire was a new and uniquely frightening experience for much of the British Army. Having not faced artillery in more than fifty years, it was perhaps inevitable that being shelled by long-range guns would exert a disproportionate effect. Rear-Admiral Hedworth Lambton, commanding the Naval detachment trapped at Ladysmith, highlighted the problem: "What really caused the depression was the extraordinary ignorance of the power of Long Tom. So far as I can make out there was hardly a single soldier who had ever seen a big gun, and the exaggerated apprehension of this gun was really very marked."[25]

How to deal with this long-range fire was a problem for the British. Standard field artillery armament was the fifteen-pound gun, with the horse artillery possessing a smaller, more mobile twelve-pound gun, both of which were out-ranged by the 155 mm despite the best efforts of Royal Artillery officers to deliver effective counter battery fire. The absence of a mobile, long-range gun was a clear gap in the equipment of the British Army, a legacy of years of colonial war against opponents who possessed no real artillery of their own and could thus be engaged at close range.

Lacking suitable equipment, the British brought 4.7 inch naval guns into the field as an emergency stop gap to deal with Boer 155 mm, mounting them on improvised carriages taken from heavy howitzers.[26] These pieces certainly possessed comparable range to the Long Toms and were able to engage at up to 11,000 yards, although 8,000 yards was generally considered the limit of truly effective range.[27] However, they had never been intended for field use, and as with all improvised weapons they suffered from certain drawbacks, particularly regarding their heavy carriage and consequent lack of mobility. Despite matching the Long Toms for range, the 4.7 inch guns did not win universal praise. Artillerymen themselves recognized that bringing the weapon into the field was essentially a compromise solution, and few were satisfied that it had achieved an acceptable balance of power, range, and mobility.[28] Other officers had even stronger criticisms. For example, Lieutenant-General Archibald Hunter was especially scathing, recounting that the shooting of the 4.7 inch guns manned by naval crews in Ladysmith was so bad "that I offered to take the girls out of the school to come and serve the guns, and make as good practice."[29] Some older artillerymen felt the press had blown the danger of long-range fire out of all proportion, and that using the 4.7 inch guns at all was a waste of resources and ammunition. One retired gunner complained in 1900, "The public are very much exercised because we do not fire at from 8,000 to 10,000 yards. What is the good of firing at from 8,000 to 10,000 yards? How much is that? From 4.5 to 6.5 miles. . . . I say it is perfectly impossible to make accurate practice at such distances. . . . I think these great ranges have been utterly useless, and I hope, for Heaven's sake, we shall not copy them."[30]

Nevertheless, the 4.7 inch gun also drew praise, particularly from the infantry, who appreciated its ability to engage the Boer long-range guns on equal terms. Henry Hildyard considered that "The heavier guns in use have proved of great value. The 4.7 inch Naval Gun is the only one that can compete with the Boer guns in range, and any fire [force?] operating without them feels itself, in a certain sense, in an inferiority."[31] Commanding officers such as Redvers Buller and Lieutenant-General Sir Charles Warren also singled out the 4.7 inch for praise, particularly in support of infantry attacks.[32] Although the actual equipment was regarded with a somewhat circumspect eye by many soldiers, other officers saw the value of long-range fire as being one of the most important lessons to be drawn from the Boer War.[33] Even the critical Archibald Hunter noted, "I think one of the chief lessons of the war that the Boers taught us is how to move guns of positions about and use them as field artillery."[34] It was also a point of concern that the Boers had sprung such a surprise on the British with their long-range guns, and there were fears that it could happen again with disastrous results if the Royal Artillery was not properly equipped. Artilleryman Major-General Sir G.H. Marshall recognized that "as long as the Boers or anybody else have a long range gun against us we are bound, even if only for the moral effect, to have a gun of equal range."[35]

The need for artillery to engage at greater ranges, both to avoid the effects of small-arms fire and also to deal with long-range enemy artillery, soon received official endorsement, with the new attitude toward combat distances being reflected in post-war drill books. Whereas prior to the war, it had been considered that 2,500–3,500 yards was "medium to distant" range, in 1902 artillery range tables put "distant" range as 4,500–6,000 yards.[36] "Effective" range was considered to be 2,000–3,500 yards, with ranges below this termed "decisive." Heavy batteries were given a separate ranging table that put their maximum range at 10,000 yards. These ranging standards were first introduced in 1902 and remained in force throughout the period up to the outbreak of the First World War.[37] To facilitate training at these new ranges, Okehampton had its target area extended, with the distance more than doubled from the 1897 length to 3,209 yards in 1902.[38] By 1904, the artillery training range at Salisbury Plain stood at an impressive 4,000 yards.[39]

Although the older fifteen-pound field gun had been able to achieve ranges beyond pre-war expectations in South Africa, for the gunners to deliver effective fire consistently at such distances required new equipment. Artillerymen had been agitating for a rearmament program in the years prior to the Boer War, and the shock of the opening six months caused the government to approve a complete overhaul of artillery weapons. However, the experience of combat in South Africa generated a considerable debate on the nature of any future field artillery. The capacity of the Boers to bring very large weapons into the field and keep them mobile had been well matched by the British ability to keep 4.7 inch guns and heavy howitzers moving, even during antiguerrilla operations where mobility was considered a crucial asset. Despite their weight, these heavy pieces acquired a good reputation among column commanders, and their popularity was such that attempts to remove the guns from columns were met with fierce resistance.[40] In the years following the end of the war, an emerging school of thought argued that the Boer War had shown that very heavy weapons could prove mobile enough for the purposes of infantry support, and therefore heavy artillery should become the new form of field artillery. Ian Hamilton was an early champion of this viewpoint, relating to the Elgin Commission that "I hold very strong views that there is no longer any room for Field Artillery in a modern army . . . It is uselessly mobile for the infantry."[41] Other officers echoed this idea, with Leslie Rundle considering that "we go for too light a gun. I do not think horses galloping about is [sic] necessary in modern warfare.... I want to see heavy field artillery brought in and dragged up by mules, traction engines, or anything that would do it; that would be my tendency."[42] Although the advocacy of using of heavy pieces for field artillery was not a unanimous view, it did reflect a more general desire for improved range and especially firepower in the artillery that was common throughout the army.

This urge for greater firepower ultimately bore fruit in the adoption of the eighteen-pound gun for field artillery and the thirteen-pound gun for horse artillery. When its introduction was mooted, the eighteen-pounder was considerably more powerful in terms of shell weight than any gun in its class then in service in Europe, but it was also heavier. There were concerns over the fact that the gun was too heavy and not in line with typical European artillery equipment, with the secretary of state bemoaning that such a heavy weapon did not "conform to the rest of the world" and suggesting that setting out on a separate path would only end with Britain having to revert to European standard at great cost.[43] However, the example of the Boer War was cited in response, with the adjutant general pointing out that "The great majority of officers who saw service were of the opinion that both Horse and Field Artillery guns should have greater range, and that the Field Artillery should have greater shell power."[44] By this point Ian Hamilton had moderated his views on heavy guns for field artillery after witnessing the difficulties experienced by the Japanese moving heavy pieces into action in Manchuria, and he contributed to the discussion via letter endorsing the eighteen-pounder as a good compromise.[45] After a considerable debate between the government and the Army Council, the new guns were somewhat reluctantly accepted by the secretary of state.[46]

A technical response to the problems encountered in South Africa, the new weapons were nevertheless modern and powerful when the designs were accepted in 1904. In terms of range and weight of shell, the guns were excellent and compared favorably with field guns then deployed by France, Germany, and Russia. Shields were fitted as standard to the weapons for the first time in the Royal Artillery, providing some protection for the crew, particularly from shrapnel and small-arms fire, and encouraging the gunners to operate the gun while crouched. However, despite their apparent quality, the new guns suffered from certain drawbacks that are discussed in greater detail later in this chapter.

In addition to rearming the field and horse artillery, a better weapon for the newly formed heavy branch was required. The 4.7 inch was an unsatisfactory compromise, and although it remained in service for several years after the end of hostilities, as early as 1900 Lord Roberts had called for a new heavy gun and laid down the simple requirements as follows: "Range 10,000 yards, weight behind the team not more than 4 tons, shell of as large a capacity as possible."[47] A committee to consider this replacement was appointed in October 1902.[48] Ultimately, this process resulted in the design, approval, and subsequent introduction of the sixty-pound gun in 1905–1906. Compared with the difficulties of introducing the guns for field and horse artillery, the process of design for this heavy weapon was remarkably painless, the gun matching the specifications assigned by Lord Roberts in all respects except for an unavoidable extra half ton of weight.[49]

Equipped with all these new, longer-ranged weapons, the immediate issue facing the British was how to devise a doctrine for their usage. This task was especially difficult in the case of the heavy artillery, which had been born as a result of the Boer War and as such had to draw virtually all its arguments for employment from this conflict.[50] The sixty-pounder was a design that owed almost everything to the experience of the veldt.[51] It was a flat-trajectory gun, using heavy shrapnel as its principal ammunition, and although it also carried a proportion of lyddite ammunition for dealing with hard targets, the primary role of the weapon was as a man killer rather than a material destroyer. This role was very much inspired by the usage of heavy guns in South Africa, where, with the exception of entrenchments, the opportunities for material destruction had been relatively limited. The veldt lacked built-up urban areas or even large stretches of woodland where high explosive could be used with great effect. Furthermore, the poor performance of lyddite explosive from heavy guns prejudiced many officers against its use and encouraged the use of shrapnel instead.[52] Although heavy guns had been used to pound Boer trenches, their main duty had been to try and silence enemy artillery and sweep rear areas at great distances. Regarding this topic, one officer wrote shortly after the war, "Our

South Africa experience has shewn us that the principle which we have long recognised as true in the case of the field gun, is equally so in the case of all guns used in the field, viz., that the gun is a man killing weapon, and shrapnel should therefore be its principal projectile."[53]

The sensation created by the Boers' use of long-range fire lingered in the memories of many soldiers. Officers had been shocked at the tremendous fear created by the shooting of the Long Toms in the early stages of the war and hoped to create similar panic among potential enemies.[54] To further facilitate this idea, some advocated copying Boer methods of extreme dispersion of heavy guns, to the point of using them as individual sniper-style weapons. Winston Churchill was an early advocate of such tactics, but some officers also saw potential value, especially for terrifying colonial foes.[55] However, most artillerymen were disparaging of the concept, noting that it was wasteful of ammunition and produced a very limited physical effect when compared with concentrated fire.[56]

Nevertheless, the Boer War did give birth to some useful ideas for the employment of heavy guns. Although Boer counter battery fire had been considered ineffective, this ineffectiveness was generally caused by faulty ammunition rather than poor shooting. Equipped with better fuses, heavy guns held the potential to inflict severe damage on exposed field batteries, which would be unable to return fire because of the long range.[57] Although this advantage would be most pronounced when fighting on the defensive, methods of using heavy guns to silence enemy artillery in the attack were also considered, as this would allow the lighter guns to concentrate on enemy infantry. There had been some examples of this method in the Boer War, with the Battle of Alleman's Nek on 11 June 1900 cited by one officer as a good example: "Our infantry had to cross an open plain to attack what looked like an impregnable position . . . [but] the Boer guns were silenced by heavy guns; the 7th and 64th Field Batteries changed position under the cover of fire of our heavy guns, so as to enfilade the Boer position. . . . This was practically the turning point of the action."[58]

However, in contrast to these ideas, there was a distinct school of thought that was prejudiced against the use of long-range fire and saw little real future for heavy weapons. There were concerns that the extreme ranges encountered in South Africa were unlikely to be repeated elsewhere, especially in Europe. The atmosphere on the veldt had been remarkably clear, allowing observation at great distances, but in Europe this would not be the case. As well as hazy conditions, the presence of villages, towns, and woodland on the continent would further reduce the visible range. Some officers countered this argument by pointing out conditions in parts of the empire were similar to those that had been found in South Africa, but the assertion that ranges in Europe would be so short as to devalue long-range fire and limit the use of guns capable of it remained a constant theme throughout the era.[59]

With many officers seeing a limited role for long-range fire in the future, allocating a precise doctrinal role for heavy guns proved difficult. This difficulty was further exacerbated by the unusual organizational position of the heavy artillery. Although the sixty-pounder was a mobile gun capable of field operations, its size and weight meant that men of the Royal Garrison Artillery provided the crew. Hence, the weapon fell between two stools, being expected to perform in the field but not being manned by the Royal Field Artillery itself and therefore occupying an anomalous position not entirely within the purview of either branch. The initial training of Royal Garrison Artillery troops was in manning fortifications and heavy weapons on the seacoast. Inevitably, this meant it took time to train the gunners in the skills needed for duties in the field, and early results were embarrassing. After watching the heavy guns at work at Okehampton in 1905, the camp commandant Colonel W. E. Blewitt was scathing, noting their standard of fire discipline was little more than "elementary"; he went on to state, "Seeing the batteries left the impression on my mind that they had been only taught to fire very slowly at a 6 foot target."[60]

Furthermore, the size and slow speed of the heavy guns made them a burden on commanders during maneuvers, where time was often of the essence. One gunner remembered how during the maneuvers of 1903, "it came to be a by-word not to get blocked by the 'cow' guns."[61] The danger of becoming stuck behind the slow-moving weapons caused commanders to place them at the rear of marching columns, but this wasted much of their tactical value. By engaging enemy guns, the heavy artillery could be expected to open up the battle, but if they were too far to the rear of a column then either time would be lost bringing them forward or they would be

forced to deploy rapidly in a potentially inadequate position.[62] At
the 1904 maneuvers, an officer reported the deleterious effects this
had had: "The eight 4.7 inch guns . . . marched astern of the whole
army corps when this was advancing by a single road, and, thanks
to the drivers being on foot, they could not hurry to the front for action when fighting began and when the situation offered them a rare
opportunity."[63]

An additional, unresolved problem was the lack of space on maneuvers to really demonstrate the potential of heavy weapons. Artillerymen had soon identified that a distinct asset of these guns was
the ability to deliver enfilade or oblique fire by virtue of their great
range. Rather than being forced to engage directly against enemy
lines, they could be pushed out to a flank, enabling their fire to rake
the foe at an angle. *Combined Training* picked up on the value of
this idea and identified it as a key role of heavy artillery.[64] However,
although using the gun at such an angle was a fine tactical idea,
implementing it in the cramped confines of the maneuver areas
proved to be difficult.[65] Some success was achieved in the 1906 maneuvers at Aldershot, where heavy guns enfiladed a defensive position considered to be impregnable from the front, but problems in
achieving this kind of effect and having it recognized on maneuvers
remained throughout the period.[66] Furthermore, by deploying at
great distances and out of sight of much of the army, heavy artillery
struggled to have its work recognized by the umpires. Judging the
effect of long-range fire from heavy guns during maneuvers could
prove problematic, especially as the fast pace of the exercises meant
that targets were often fleeting.

Although the quality of battery training among the gunners
improved markedly over the period, there was little matching development of their role at maneuvers. The infantry rarely had the
opportunity to train alongside the heavy pieces. General Belfield,
commanding 4th Division, complained in 1908: "One is not blessed
in the Fourth Division with having a heavy battery, except for a very
short period in the year, and then one must do one's best to try and
ascertain how best to employ it."[67]

The situation showed little sign of improvement throughout the
pre-war years. Although the batteries were able to develop greater
accuracy and skill on the field, in terms of work alongside the infantry, little advancement was made. The commanding officer of the

35th Heavy Battery noted with disappointment in 1909 that "the use of Heavy Artillery has gradually become neglected, until at the last manoeuvres it was scarcely (advisedly) used at all."[68]

The devaluing of long-range fire in the aftermath of the Boer War left the role of heavy artillery poorly defined, and the experience of the Russo-Japanese War did little to clarify the issue. The great use of earthworks and difficulty in taking them showed a need for heavier guns to smash trenches, but as one Russian participant noted "flat-trajectory weapons would be useless. . . . These conditions imperatively demand the employment of high angle fire."[69] Designed as a long-range man killer and counter battery weapon, the sixty-pounder was not the type of gun that could break down complex earthworks. Robert Scales has been critical of this aspect of the gun's design and compared it unfavorably with heavy German weapons that were designed to destroy material.[70] However, this criticism is somewhat unfair. The British rearmed in the aftermath of the Boer War in the anticipation of using the weapons in a future colonial struggle against a wide variety of potential opponents, whereas the Germans could equip their batteries with the express intention of using them to destroy French and Belgian fortifications in Europe.[71] The colonial duties of the British required them to possess weapons that would be appropriate for deployment around the globe, and thus the sixty-pounder was designed to be suitable in a variety of conflicts. The British were well aware of the need to engage trenches and fortifications and never intended the sixty-pounder to be a substitute for the howitzer, which was expected to deal with enemy earthworks. Indeed, the British kept the sixty-pounder gun in service with minor modifications throughout the First World War, where it was principally used as a counter battery weapon, and it remained in use up until 1944. In 1914 they served the British well, with John Terraine considering the sixty-pounder to be of "inestimable value" in the opening battles.[72] For example, at the Battle of Le Cateau, the Heavy Batteries of 3rd and 5th Divisions were positioned some distance behind the front lines and tasked with counter battery work. Difficulties of observation meant that it was hard to gauge effectiveness, but German attempts to silence them were ineffective and the sixty-pounders were able to provide valuable covering fire during the British withdrawal.[73] Unfortunately, the heavy guns of 4th Division had not arrived on the battlefield and their absence was "felt acutely" during counter battery work.[74]

Beyond technical considerations, a further criticism is that the British did not develop a clear enough doctrine for use of their heavy artillery once they had been equipped with it. The guns were in short supply, with just a four-gun battery being assigned per regular division at the outbreak of war, reflecting the fact the BEF was not a mass army on the continental model.[75] Although the old idea of using sniper guns had long since fallen from favor, a section of two sixty-pounders was still seen as the main tactical unit, derived from the Boer tactics of dispersion in the face of greater numbers of enemy guns.[76] Ideas on the tactical employment of heavy artillery were rooted in the experiences of South Africa. *Field Service Regulations 1909* described its role in action in the following terms: "Its principal duty is to engage shielded artillery with oblique fire, to enfilade targets which the lighter guns can only reach with frontal fire, to search distant localities in which supports or reserves are concealed, to destroy buildings or other protections occupied by the enemy, and in the final stage to support the assault by fire converging on the most important points."[77]

The tactics suggested by the manuals were fundamentally sound, and some of these valuable ideas had been further developed in the pre–First World War period, particularly the potential use of heavy guns to render enemy entrenchments untenable via enfilade fire and the use of long-range weapons to eliminate lighter field guns.[78] The lessons of the Boer War on the use of heavy guns may have been deceptive regarding the extreme range at which they could engage in the clear atmosphere of South Africa, but in many respects the British grasped the potential value of using them to deal with enemy artillery and sweep rear areas. The examples themselves were not misleading, but translating them into effective practice proved difficult in the cramped confines of British maneuvering areas. Indeed, the greatest weakness in the BEF regarding heavy artillery was a lack of numbers and a failure to integrate the guns into wider tactical thinking. Instead, these valuable weapons were often neglected in maneuvers because of their slow speed and were typically left to their own devices. For these reasons, the links between infantry and heavy artillery saw little improvement during the 1899–1914 period. The British Army of 1914 relied on the Field Artillery for infantry support, with the heavy guns remaining as specialist pieces that were poorly understood by the infantry.[79]

Nevertheless, although British use of heavy artillery suffered from some technical and tactical weaknesses, it remained considerably superior to that of France. The French placed almost complete faith in their powerful 75 mm field gun and neglected heavy weapons until the very eve of the war.[80] In 1912, British observers were distinctly unimpressed with French attempts to put heavy guns into the field, noting that of four types of guns deployed at maneuvers, two were at an experimental phase, and the other two were antiquated weapons dating from 1878 and 1884, respectively.[81] By the time serious efforts were made to equip with heavy guns, it was too late for the French Army. The heavy guns that were available were possessed in very limited numbers, and confusion reigned over their usage.[82] A French officer noted in 1913, "We have heavy artillery. Do we have a doctrine for the employment of this heavy artillery? It does not appear so. Ask one hundred officers picked at random of all ranks and arms: 'What is heavy artillery? What is it used for? How is it used? Whom does it support? Where is it positioned?' The odds are 100–1 that you get no answer or that the same question will be asked of you."[83]

The failure to equip with heavy artillery was a critical flaw in the French Army of 1914. Their shorter-ranged field guns were unable to deliver counter battery fire against the long-range German weapons and consequently were often smashed to pieces by shelling from heavy German batteries.[84] Pre-war belief in France that it was not worth the effort in firing beyond visible range proved to be a serious tactical weakness in 1914 and cost their artillery dearly.[85]

Although the Royal Artillery had experienced a reaction against the extreme ranges encountered in South Africa, this school of thought did not gain ascendency and produced limited overall effect. The artillery range tables of 1914 were identical to those of 1902, suggesting that there was still official belief in the value of long-range fire throughout the period. Despite flaws that remained in the usage of heavy guns with the wider army, the lesson of the Boer War that artillery could engage effectively at long range remained. Whereas the French placed almost complete faith in close-range action, the British did not forget the example of South Africa and thus were somewhat better prepared for the tactical problems of artillery combat in 1914, although they were not so well-equipped as the Germans in this regard. Long Tom had been an unpleasant surprise for the British, but the artillery had adapted well to the expectation of long-range action and proved a tenacious foe for the Germans in the opening weeks of the First World War. Despite its limited numbers, the sixty-pound gun proved a valuable asset, being the only weapon in the British arsenal that had the range to engage the devastating 15 cm howitzers deployed by the Germans.[86] However, the sixty-pounder may have been even more useful had greater efforts been made to forge closer links between the heavy artillery and the infantry in the years prior to the outbreak of war, and the failure to capitalize on this must be counted as an opportunity missed by the British Army.

CONCEALMENT

On the eve of the Boer War, an expectation held throughout the British Army was that any major battle would begin with a preliminary artillery duel. The opposing artillery would deploy in the open and attempt to pound one another into submission, the winner then having a virtually free rein to distribute his fire across the battlefield, with the loser forced to shelter his surviving guns and use them as and when possible. As with much thinking within the Royal Artillery, this idea was drawn from the Franco-Prussian War, where German artillery had typically overwhelmed the French guns before the battle was joined in earnest. [87]

However, the Boers were not wedded to any European doctrine and had no intention of conforming to this unrealistic expectation. Although the Boers possessed certain qualitative advantages over the British artillery, in numerical terms they were hopelessly outmatched and faced certain destruction if they attempted to engage the British in an open duel. Instead, the Boer gunners chose to take advantage of the smokeless powder that gave their rifle-armed comrades such an unexpected advantage. Fighting from concealed positions, with no smoke puffs to indicate the direction of fire, the Boer artillery proved incredibly difficult for the British gunners to locate. This failure to track down Boer artillery was perhaps even more humiliating for the British than being outranged. Whereas the gunners could cite material weaknesses for being unable to reply to long-range fire, in terms of silencing a concealed enemy they had no such excuse.

As well as firing from cover, the Boers used additional methods to frustrate attempts to knock out their weapons. Multiple positions were usually prepared for the guns, so that if the British located one, the gun could be moved to another and resume fire. Entrenchments and emplacements for the gun and crews were considered essential. If the gun position was located, the crew would shelter in these dugouts, waiting for the British fire to lift before manning their weapons once more.[88] One Boer gunner ruminated that without them, "it is probable not a man of us would have been left" owing to volume of fire the numerically superior British guns could deliver.[89] Simple tricks were also used to confuse the British, including firing a concealed smokeless gun from one position and simultaneously detonating a flask of black powder at a separate, false point. The eye was inevitably drawn to the smoke discharge, causing the British to waste their fire at a decoy position while the real gun continued to operate unmolested. This ruse proved to be so prevalent that attention was called to it in an official memorandum issued by Lord Roberts.[90]

During the early part of the war, the British used observation balloons in an attempt to locate the position of Boer trenches and guns. Balloons proved most useful around Ladysmith, where the siege lines and static nature of Boer positions made them a potentially valuable reconnaissance asset. However, in terms of locating enemy guns, results were disappointing. Henry Rawlinson reported the difficulties associated with observing Boer guns from the air, noting that "[it is] difficult to spot guns from the Baloon [sic] as it rocks about so and keeps revolving round so much that one cannot keep ones glasses steady."[91] A further major problem was the inability of observation balloons to send rapid messages to friendly troops stationed below, with attempts to use heliographs from balloons proving a failure.[92] Although aerial reconnaissance had its uses in the Boer War, it did little to solve the problem of locating Boer guns.

For the British, the inability to deal with the outnumbered but concealed Boer artillery came as a profound shock. George White noted that at no point during his combat experience did he believe a Boer gun had been knocked out by counter battery work, commenting, "It has been a lesson to me that in modern warfare it is pretty hard to dismount an enemy's guns."[93] Even the most skillful gun crews had problems engaging hidden Boer guns. James Grierson remembered, "The Boers developed a truly marvellous skill in concealing the position of their guns; the officer who commanded the best-shooting battery at Okehampton in 1899 told me that, in all the actions up to occupation of Kroonstad [May 1900], he had never been able to range on a Boer gun, and at the passage of the Vet River one of our batteries was for hours under the fire from a long range gun which it could not locate."[94]

Although concealed Boer artillery fire often proved to be a source of indignation rather than injury for the British, the refusal of the Boers to fight in the open rendered the belief in the opening artillery duel a fallacy.[95] In combination with much longer artillery ranges, this represented a challenge to pre-war tactical ideas and training methods, which had anticipated a straightforward engagement over open sights at relatively short distances. Pre-war training had reflected this expectation, with artillery aiming for rapidity and accuracy at visible targets and achieving satisfactory results.[96] Indeed, the Royal Artillery, with the notable exception of the Royal Garrison Artillery, had taken a somewhat perverse pride in its unscientific methods toward gunnery and ranging, relying on the kind of dash demonstrated by the unfortunate Colonel Long to achieve results in battle.[97]

The Boer War shook faith in these concepts and caused a considerable degree of introspection among the gunners. A particular source of concern was that a contest between guns in the open and guns in cover was clearly an unequal one. Although the Boer guns had been hampered by poor ammunition, the threat to exposed British batteries was well recognized. At the Battle of Vaal Krantz, several batteries of British artillery deployed in the open and were enfiladed by a Boer Long Tom, with only faulty fuses saving the British guns from severe casualties.[98] Charles Callwell noted the changed circumstances of warfare meant that "A single well concealed hostile gun will wipe out a whole battery if this is brought into action in a bungling fashion; cases have occurred when even a pom-pom—not a formidable weapon—has given a battery in the open a lot of trouble."[99]

A fellow gunner echoed these sentiments in a blunter fashion, stating simply that to deploy in the open against hidden artillery was "little short of madness."[100] The idea of using cover and concealed positions also found favor outside the Royal Artillery. Lord Roberts cited training in concealment of guns as necessary for improvement of the arm as a whole, and his views were echoed by Ian Hamilton and Charles Warren.[101] Warren offered particularly strong opinions, noting, "Concealment of guns both on attack and defence is now a matter of primary importance, and in defence can be brought to such perfection that it is almost impossible to locate them."[102]

However, reversing the tactics of the previous thirty years was not a simple task. Although the idea of fighting from behind cover had been mooted prior to the Boer War, the difficulty in achieving accuracy from such positions had discouraged its use.[103] *Field Artillery Training* editions for 1904 and 1906 both emphasized the use of cover for guns, but translating this principle into training was more difficult and required devising new methods of delivering accurate, indirect fire. This work inevitably took time to bear fruit.[104] For example, in 1903 Lord Roberts noted at a post maneuvers conference, "I was disappointed to find the guns were so much exposed. There were exceptions, but on the whole there was practically little attempt at concealment."[105] In 1904, John French wrote in an Aldershot training memorandum, "We can all remember how splendidly the Boer guns were concealed and how it was often utterly impossible to locate them, at any rate for a long time. . . . I trust Artillery officers will give the matter their serious consideration."[106] Nevertheless, there were improvements over time, especially after the introduction of superior equipment in the form of new field and horse artillery guns. In 1906, Ian Hamilton had great praise for the artillery of Southern Command, writing, "So great has been the progress made during the past summer in the use of indirect laying and in the art of entrenching, that the methods of 1904 are already, to a great extent, obsolete."[107]

The Russo-Japanese War appeared to offer confirmation of the value of cover. The Japanese artillery was considered materially inferior to that of the Russians but was better trained and more willing to fight from concealed positions. Conversely, Russian gunners went to war with tactics similar to the pre–Boer War British, expecting to use their weapons at relatively close range and being prepared to sacrifice guns if necessary.[108] Against the Japanese this doctrine was costly and ineffective, with exposed Russian batteries being knocked out in short order. A British journalist saw a Russian battery attempt to redeploy across open ground at the Battle of the Yalu River (30 April–1 May 1904) only to be caught by Japanese fire after moving around two hundred yards. The journalist noted "the whole of the teams, men, guns, and everything else were all piled up at the end of that distance."[109]

Observers on both sides of the Manchurian conflict were shocked by the ferocity of artillery fire. A British attaché with the Russians reported to the Army Council that "The present shrapnel fire with Q.F. [quick-firing] guns is such that no troops can face it in the open nor can Artillery serve their guns under it. Indirect fire seemed to be the only practicable method."[110] A French officer noted that unless covered approaches were available, artillery generally only moved at night, commenting, "Invisibility has become an essential condition; this is the dominating fact of the whole war."[111] After the initial shock of combat, the Russians adapted methods of indirect fire, and, as in the Boer War, well-concealed guns proved "uncommonly difficult" to silence.[112] A British observer noted how on one occasion the Japanese had fired more than a thousand shells in an attempt to eliminate a hidden Russian battery, without success.[113] At another engagement, it was reported that the Japanese shelled Russian positions for fifteen hours prior to an attack, only for hidden Russian guns to unmask and overwhelm the infantry once they began their advance.[114]

The experience of the artillery in the Russo-Japanese War seemed largely to validate the lessons of concealment that the British had drawn from South Africa. However, even as the war in Manchuria was in progress, a movement against the use of concealed positions for artillery was beginning to gather force in Britain. The root of this reaction lay in the problem of achieving accuracy from a covered position. Reflecting prior prejudices against scientific gunnery, there was some disquiet among the artillery over the need to use several "strange appliances" to achieve effective indirect fire, and some felt the emphasis on technical matters threatened to overwhelm tactical considerations.[115]

The tactical conundrum that militated most against the use of concealed positions was the need to hit fleeting targets. Whereas the South African experience had shown the resilience of hidden guns, the conflict had also highlighted the fact that in battle against opponents who made the most of cover, opportunities for effective fire were likely to be brief and had to be seized immediately. Hence, of primary importance was having a skillful gun crew that was able to rapidly acquire the range and fire accurately. As with attempts to improve infantry musketry, training methods were revamped with moving and surprise targets introduced to test the gunners' reactions. Initially the results were somewhat farcical. When General Sir Evelyn Wood was asked in 1902 if surprise targets had made a difference in training, he replied, "So much so that this year within a month or so, I have seen an artillery officer so taken by surprise that he has said: '1,600 yards, 1,200 yards, 1,400 yards. As you were.' and the target escaped."[116]

However, the careful calculations and positioning required for delivering indirect fire seemed incompatible with seizing such fleeting opportunities. The paradox between taking covered positions to protect the guns and yet still being able to deliver sudden and effective fire when necessary was a serious problem. At Okehampton it was noted that time was a factor not considered enough in tactics, the camp commandant complaining, "A battery that comes into action under cover, and takes half an hour or more to open fire, with no certainty that it will be effective, when the G.O.C. [General Officer Commanding] requires artillery fire at once, does wrong."[117]

Reacting against the somewhat ponderous methods necessary for effective indirect fire, some officers began to denigrate the use of concealed positions, instead suggesting that rapid, direct fire was bound to be more damaging to the enemy than slow, deliberate indirect shooting. For example, artilleryman Major J. F. Cadell argued that the addition of shields to the latest field guns gave them great protection against enemy fire, allowing them to fight in the open once more.[118] Cadell's views were reminiscent of pre-war thinking, arguing the role of artillery was to help secure victory regardless of the cost: "To remain in action all day and fire off thousands of rounds over a hill is not an object in itself, even if you only lose three horses; what is required is a victory, even if obtained at some expense, by the artillery."[119]

Despite the examples of the Boer War and the Russo-Japanese War, such views found support. Indeed, the Russian adoption of indirect fire was held to have been greatly adverse to their fighting spirit, discouraging them from taking risks and thus leaving their

infantry unsupported at critical moments.[120] Even reformist officers such as Ian Hamilton expressed a certain degree of disquiet
over the way in which artillery in Manchuria had settled into semi-
permanent concealed positions. Hamilton commented that in the
latter stages of the war, the Japanese were spending so long concealing and positioning their field artillery that "they become almost as
immobile as guns of position. They take far too long in getting in
or out of their pits, and I think the habit of entrenching . . . is tending to lessen their initiative and audacity."[121] This loss of spirit was
seen as potentially damaging to the army as a whole. Infantry Captain P. A. Charrier ruminated, "The doctrine held by any Army of
avoiding losses, when carried too far, has invariably ended in defeat,
and it seems to me that the use of indirect fire, carried too far, can
only lead to the same result."[122] Similar views were also expressed at
higher levels, the inspector general of forces writing in 1906, "As the
reports of our attaches in Manchuria became available it soon made
itself apparent that protection was only one means to an end, and
that to attach too much importance to it would be disastrous to the
spirit of the arm; and Artillery officers have come to recognize, from
study of the subject and experience as to the limitations of indirect
fire, that its use is frequently incompatible with affording effective
support to the other arms and inflicting loss on the enemy."[123]

With the pendulum beginning to swing against the use of concealed positions, the attention of the Royal Artillery was drawn
toward the fire tactics of the French. In 1897, the French had introduced the famous 75 mm "Quick Firing" (QF) gun to their field
army, a weapon that possessed an unprecedented rate of fire attributable to a recoil-absorbing system that eliminated the need to run the
gun back into position after firing. As well as having an exceptionally stable firing platform, the gun also benefited from an automatic
fuse-setting machine that further increased the speed with which it
could be loaded and fired. Taking advantage of this rate of fire and
placing faith in their gun shields to keep them protected, the French
emphasized achieving annihilating fire effect at short to medium
range.[124] The culmination of French artillery tactics was the *rafale*,
a short but intense burst of fire that aimed to overwhelm the target
through ferocity and volume rather than precise accuracy.[125] British
observers were often favorably impressed with these tactics, which
stood in stark contrast to the slower, more deliberate methods of fire

in the Royal Artillery. Charles Repington wrote to Ian Hamilton on the subject, arguing that in the time it would take for a British battery to set up and acquire the target's range, a French battery could have wiped out an entire British infantry brigade.[126] Other officers echoed these opinions, feeling that the French had truly grasped the technical potential of QF guns, whereas the British emphasis on slow, precise methods did not take advantage of the vastly improved rate of fire now available to them.[127]

Interest in French fire tactics grew as the two nations forged greater military links in the pre–First World War period. By 1910, John French was expressing concerns that British artillery tactics were becoming out of date. German authorities were critical of British methods, and French himself noted, "My opinion is that our Artillery compared with the French is slow in ranging and in opening fire for effect, and that the ever-growing complication of our method is tending to surpass the capacity of the average battery commander and to become foreign to the atmosphere of the battlefield."[128]

In 1911, it was observed that some gunners who had attended maneuvers in France were organizing and training their batteries on French lines without official sanction.[129] There were also concerns that the reputation of the 75 mm was resulting in a tendency to denigrate the eighteen-pounder in comparison, leading to calls for a program of artillery rearmament to produce guns that could match the French weapons.[130] Ultimately, the growing disquiet with British tactics, as compared with French tactics, resulted in a series of trials in 1911 to ascertain if an adoption of French methods could improve the firepower of a British field battery. The French four-gun organization and methods of rapid ranging were tested, but the results were inconclusive and a unanimous decision on their practicality was not reached.[131] The main revelation of the tests was that the eighteen-pounder gun had a number of technical defects that prevented it replicating French methods effectively. A lack of steadiness in the carriage necessitated relaying the gun from round to round, and the need to set the fuse on each shell limited the ability to sustain very high rates of fire.[132] The chief of imperial general staff noted that the existence of these technical issues rendered the argument over the adoption of French methods largely irrelevant until they were corrected.[133] Financial considerations prevented the correction of these technical issues from occurring before the outbreak of the First World War, which meant that although French ideas were widely admired, they were difficult to put into actual practice.

The technical inability of the British guns to deliver the kind of fire that the French used meant that the Royal Artillery never became completely wedded to the idea of direct fire. Instead, throughout the period there was an ongoing debate on the value of indirect versus direct methods, with both camps enjoying periods of ascendency. As previously discussed, the British Army of the Edwardian period was very reluctant to adopt any official doctrine and instead preferred to place emphasis on tactical flexibility. This desire for flexibility was especially true of the field artillery. As early as 1907, the inspector general of forces had complained that there was an absence of uniformity in artillery training and had requested an official pronouncement from the General Staff regarding the merits of direct versus indirect fire.[134] However, little had been done by the following year, and it was noted that in some commands nothing but indirect fire was used, whereas in others the opposite was true.[135] At no point did the Royal Artillery officially declare itself dedicated to either method, and indeed on the eve of the First World War the emphasis remained on flexibility with regard to choice of position, with the French observing in 1914 that although British manuals were excellent, British doctrine was nonexistent.[136]

It was perhaps fortunate for the Royal Artillery that it did not completely adopt French methods. Although the 75 mm was a superb gun, the French belief that it could fire direct at relatively short range was anachronistic and proved to be a dangerous and costly tactic once war broke out. Conversely, the tactical lessons the Royal Artillery had learned in South Africa, and which had been confirmed by the Russo-Japanese War, were highly relevant to combat in 1914. Finding themselves outnumbered and outgunned by the Germans, the British understood the importance of adopting concealed positions to avoid being swept away by sheer weight of fire.

Unfortunately, while never abandoned, the importance of concealment had been somewhat diluted in the intervening years. Robert Scales has argued that the serious losses suffered by the Royal Artillery at the Battle of Le Cateau proves the weakness of British artillery tactics compared with those of the Germans, noting that a number of BEF batteries occupied open positions and were punished by concealed German guns.[137] However, of the three British divisions engaged—3rd, 4th, and 5th—it was the artillery of 5th Division who chose to occupy forward positions, ostensibly to inspire the infantry.[138] The artillery of 3rd and 4th Divisions chose to deploy farther back in more covered positions and suffered relatively minor casualties, with certain batteries eluding German attempts to locate them throughout the entire battle.[139] The fact that the artillery of the BEF divisions chose to adopt such distinct tactics at Le Cateau is more illustrative of the lack of formal artillery doctrine than inherent tactical weakness.

The Boer War had demonstrated the value of concealed positions, and although interest in such tactics waxed and waned, the use of cover remained an important part of Royal Artillery training throughout the period. The growing interest in French methods of direct fire from open positions was largely regressive, and if it had been adopted as a whole by the outnumbered artillery of the BEF, the results of early battles against the Germans could well have proved disastrous. Lack of formal doctrine on the type of position to use remained a consistent weakness, but emphasis on flexibility at least ensured the British were not wedded to a costly and ineffective tactical system such as the French.

The lessons of the Boer War had faded somewhat by 1914, but the experience of fighting against the numerically superior and more heavily armed German artillery soon highlighted the need to adopt the methods the Boers had made famous on the veldt. Fortunately for the British, although the popularity of concealment had declined to an extent, it had never been abandoned and was still considered an important element of training up to the eve of the First World War.[140] Although the gunners had much to learn about the new conditions of warfare, the lessons of concealment from the Boer War were an important element of future tactics and provided a valuable asset for future artillery development.

FIELD HOWITZERS

Although the delivery of indirect fire from concealed positions was difficult for guns designed to fire on a flat trajectory, the British Army possessed a weapon specifically designed to carry out this role: the howitzer. Modern field howitzers were a relatively new addition to the arsenal of the Royal Artillery, having only been introduced to the arm in 1896.[141] Prior to the Boer War they had seen action only during Kitchener's campaign in the Sudan, where their high-explosive shells had been used to bombard the Mahdi's tomb. The fearful destruction created by these lyddite shells had attracted favorable notice, and much was expected of them in the future.[142]

Unfortunately, lyddite proved to be a disappointment in the Boer War. Although it created spectacular explosions and large craters when it worked, it suffered from persistent malfunctions, with one gunner estimating that no more than 60 percent of his lyddite shells had detonated properly.[143] Furthermore, despite being visually impressive when it exploded, in terms of inflicting actual casualties its effects were noted as being "exceeding local."[144] Artillerymen brought up with the idea that the guns were primarily man-killers were especially critical of this apparent failure, one arguing shortly after the war that "I think lyddite [shells] are of so little value for heavy guns that I should myself be quite prepared to make them entirely auxiliary projectiles."[145]

Nevertheless, the Boer War had shown the need for an explosive shell to engage enemy earthworks, and a number of infantry officers at the Elgin Commission made reference to the potential value of common shell for dealing with trenches.[146] Common shell was an old-fashioned type of ammunition that was in some ways the forerunner of high explosive, but it had been largely phased out of the artillery because of its ineffectiveness. It had been found to lack a bursting charge large enough to damage hard targets and had failed to produce enough segments to cause heavy losses to troops in the open; thus, artillerymen were perplexed and frustrated by the call for its return.[147] However, in delivering a rebuttal to the common shell arguments, artilleryman G. H. Marshall unwittingly highlighted the key issue behind the revival of interest in the old ammunition when he noted, "I may say that the object of all field artillery ammunition is man-killing and not the damage of material. . . . We do not attempt it, and not only that, but we do not profess in the Artillery to kill people who get underground, with time shrapnel."[148]

In fact, howitzers and not common shell were the ideal solution to inflict damage upon a sheltering foe. Although lyddite fired from howitzers proved disappointing in South Africa, the combination of plunging fire and explosive detonation held the potential to scour trenches of their occupants as well as destroy emplacements and earthworks. Indeed, despite the limitations of the ammunition, where they had been well handled howitzers had proved extremely effective in this role. Some officers had much praise for the weapon, especially for its effect on enemy morale. Lord Methuen commented, "The lyddite shell did not come up to its reputation, but I always took one howitzer with me in the hills, as it terrified the enemy more than any other arm."[149] Charles Warren felt that the assertion made by several Boers that they had no fear of lyddite was bravado and "mere fiction," arguing that the effect had in fact been considerable.[150] The potency of effect was particularly true in Natal, where the British had been forced to hammer through a series of entrenched Boer positions in a campaign that loosely resembled the kind of trench warfare that would become common in Manchuria and on the Western Front. Here the howitzers had been so popular with the infantry that officers had often squabbled over who had authority over them, and the howitzers had proved vital in supporting difficult assaults.[151]

However, howitzers still emerged from the Boer War with something of a mixed reputation. Despite their success in Natal, they had achieved relatively little elsewhere, particularly during Lord Roberts's advance. Here, the wide-open spaces of Orange Free State and Transvaal made it possible to outflank the Boers rather than having to attack their trenches in a methodical manner. The best opportunity for the howitzers came during the Battle of Paardeberg, but their performance was disappointing against the cleverly constructed Boer entrenchments. James Grierson noted these contrasting experiences on his return from South Africa: "The 5-inch howitzer was a disappointment, but opinions differ as to its value. On the Natal side they swore by it and praised its effect, but on the force advancing from Bloemfontein, Lord Roberts left the brigade-division of howitzers behind, preferring to take heavier metal."[152]

Even after the war, the relative ineffectiveness of lyddite remained a contentious point, and there were calls for more shrapnel to be carried to increase the howitzer's utility as a man-killer.[153] Indeed, some went so far as to argue that high-angle shrapnel fire was the only solution to dealing with entrenchments owing to the failure of high explosive ammunition in South Africa.[154]

Furthermore, it was clear in the aftermath of the Boer War that the five-inch field howitzer had serious defects, including being too heavy for rapid movement during field operations and possessing an inadequate range to cope with long-range enemy artillery.[155] Unfortunately, design delays, financial parsimony, and manufacturing hold-ups meant that a new howitzer was extremely slow in forthcoming, with a replacement 4.5 inch field howitzer not entering British service until 1909. The slowness of rearmament was a source of great frustration to the artillerymen and helped contribute to a general lack of understanding of the weapon in the years following the Boer War. It was noted that although howitzers were well liked by the infantry for their ability to deliver plunging fire, their precise role as field artillery within the British Army remained poorly defined.[156] Lack of modern equipment was partially blamed for the cold attitude toward field howitzers, and they were also available only in limited numbers, with just three batteries per three infantry divisions in 1906.[157] Major C.B. Levita summed up the problems the weapon faced, writing, "Hitherto the official books, which fortify the mind of military readers, have presumed a discreet silence on the subject of Field Howitzers, or dismissed it with a few broad statements which have failed to excite commanders, at any rate at peace, to a study of their uses . . . [on maneuvers howitzers are] generally stowed away in the first hole available, out of touch with the infantry advance, and without a knowledge of the Q.F. gun's targets."[158]

J.B.A. Bailey has suggested that the Boer War caused howitzers to develop a bad name in the British Army and that they were neglected throughout the period, with just three batteries of six guns being assigned to each BEF infantry division in 1914, comparing unfavorably with 380 field howitzers available in the German Army, with each German corps possessing a further sixteen heavy howitzers.[159] However, this criticism is unfair. Although in numerical terms the provision of howitzers seems miserly when compared with the Germans, it must be remembered that a British division of 1914 possessed only seventy-two guns in total, and thus the howitzer brigade represented a full quarter of the total divisional artillery strength, a vast improvement from the pre-Boer War standard, where there had been just three howitzer batteries out of ninety-two field batteries. This represents a considerable proportion for a weapon that Bailey asserts had developed such a poor reputation. In addition, the British allocation was far larger than that of the French, who provided just six howitzers to each corps and did not incorporate them into maneuvers.[160]

Furthermore, despite its mixed performance in South Africa and the long delays before a new field howitzer was introduced, a number of artillery officers were favorably impressed with the weapon and saw a future for it in both European and colonial warfare.[161] The scale of entrenchment and the impressive performance of howitzers in the Russo-Japanese War confirmed these early ideas and emphasized their value in the field. Indeed, the employment of these weapons was selected as the first purely artillery subject ever to be discussed at a General Staff conference, with Colonel A. H. Hamilton-Gordon, a howitzer battery commander who had achieved distinction in Natal, as a key speaker.[162] Although lack of modern equipment hampered the development of the arm, once it had entered service the 4.5 inch howitzer proved to be an excellent weapon and was superior to continental rivals in the same class.[163] The new weapon proved popular among both artillerymen and infantry. For example, in 1909 the inspector general of forces complained that "Howitzer batteries are used almost too freely in all attacks" and warned that their limited ammunition should instead be conserved for critical moments.[164] There was perhaps an overemphasis on shrapnel from howitzers, with 75 percent of their ammunition being of this type, but in the early part of the First World War, this did not prove a weakness. Indeed, it has been suggested that shrapnel remained the most effective artillery ammunition throughout 1914.[165]

Although certain flaws remained, particularly the tendency in parts of the Royal Field Artillery to see howitzers as being highly specialized and technical, it is difficult to agree with Bailey's assertion that there was a lack of interest in the weapon.[166] Despite a somewhat mixed performance in South Africa, the success of the weapon in Natal showed its value against well-constructed earthworks, and the Russo-Japanese War confirmed the early faith many British artillerymen had in the gun. Bailey himself notes that the work of officers such as Hamilton-Gordon with howitzers in the pre-First World War period proved "invaluable" in 1914.[167] Although howitzers were not given the same level of prominence they received in the German Army, they remained an important and integral part of the BEF's artillery complement, and the Boer War played a large role in emphasizing their future value.

INFANTRY–ARTILLERY COOPERATION

Although the embarrassments and difficulties of fighting against modern enemy artillery had a profound effect on the Royal Artillery, arguably the most important issue to emerge from the Boer War was the need for far greater levels of infantry–artillery cooperation. As with many tactical considerations, pre-war manuals had seen artillery support for infantry attacks as a straightforward process.[168] After winning the artillery duel, it was expected that the guns would bombard the enemy position prior to the infantry advance, softening up the foe for the final assault. In the event of the attackers meeting stiff resistance, the gunners were expected to support as best they could, but suggested means by which this could be achieved were vague. A common maxim throughout the long arm during the period was, "The greater the difficulties of the infantry the closer should be the support of the artillery," but this was generally held to mean pushing guns up to short range, a tactic that brought Colonel Long to grief at Colenso.[169] The difficult matter of infantry support had received little clarification on the eve of the conflict, and training in cooperation prior to the Boer War was virtually nonexistent, with one gunner noting that the only result of peace maneuvers was to prove that as far as the subject went, "lamentable ignorance is very apparent."[170] These problems were to be brought into stark focus in South Africa. Modern small-arms fire vastly increased the difficulties of assault, and the infantry had greater need of artillery support than ever before. However, traditional methods of preliminary bombardment and close-range gun support were found wanting in the Boer War.

As previously discussed, one of the initial difficulties that faced the artillery in South Africa was the invisibility of enemy positions. Use of concealed trenches and smokeless powder made finding appropriate targets difficult, and inadequate reconnaissance failed to ease these burdens. These factors seriously reduced the effectiveness of any preliminary bombardment. At the battles of Colenso and Magersfontein, the artillery carried out heavy bombardments of presumed enemy entrenchments, when in fact they were shelling false positions that the Boers had left unmanned. A German writer offered a scathing description of the bombardment of Colenso, noting that "the fire of the guns was directed upon the opposite bank at random, the actual positions of the enemy being unknown, [and] the effect, as might have been anticipated, was nil."[171] At Magersfontein, an even greater bombardment was delivered during the late afternoon prior to the planned night advance. This artillery preparation was the heaviest bombardment delivered by British guns since the Crimean War. Lord Methuen noted in his official dispatch that "[with] the additional effect of lyddite I expected great destruction of life in their trenches, and a considerable demoralising effect on the enemy's nerves, thereby indirectly assisting the attack at daybreak."[172] However, as previously discussed, the correct location of the Boer trenches had not been ascertained, and the majority of the fire was delivered at unoccupied areas of the kopje. Furthermore, far from terrifying the burghers, the artillery preparation simply alerted them to the fact that an attack was imminent.

In addition to making such pre-battle bombardments largely ineffective, the relative invisibility of Boer positions also posed problems for the close-range tactics that had been favored in colonial wars. Guns that attempted to push forward to the infantry firing line and beyond, as Colonel Long did at Colenso, could find themselves in grave difficulties of their own if they blundered into previously unseen Boers. Furthermore, occupying a close-range position did not always ease the difficulties of locating invisible and fleeting targets. At the Battle of Modder River, British batteries managed to push forward to within 1,200 yards of the Boer line in an attempt to give renewed vigor to the stalled British attack. Although these guns drew praise for their efforts and had success in keeping down enemy artillery fire, they could avail little against the dug-in Boer riflemen and could not help the British infantry advance any farther.[173]

Overcoming well-constructed Boer defenses required more than ineffective preliminary bombardments, and no amount of close-range heroics could make up for a lack of thoroughness in preparation. The solution lay in better cooperation with the infantry, who by advancing could force the Boers to occupy their defenses and thus cause the burghers to reveal themselves as they rose to fire. Summing up this issue, one gunner noted that "Artillery preparation is essential, but a bombardment *followed by an attack* is futile."[174]

However, given the lack of pre-war training on the subject, achieving this level of cooperation posed considerable difficulties. The artillery had to ensure their fire was well-timed and accurate or else they risked hitting their own side, and the infantry required a means of signaling to their guns to change target or cease fire when necessary. Inevitably, there were errors in the heat of battle. At the Battle of Talana Hill, British guns continued to fire on the Boer position even after friendly infantry had seized it, causing such chaos that the hard-won hilltop was briefly abandoned.[175] At the Battle of Spion Kop, British infantry in the firing line lacked the means to communicate with the gunners as their heliographs had been smashed by bullets early on in the fighting and flag signals were difficult to read. Lacking information, the field artillery attempted in vain to try and silence invisible Boer guns, when their fire could have been more profitably directed on the riflemen who were engaging the British line.[176] When a battery of 4.7 inch guns opened an effective fire on the Boers from long range, Charles Warren, stationed at the bottom of the kopje and out of touch with the fighting there, sent an alarmed message for them to cease fire, stating, "We occupy the whole summit and I fear you are shelling us severely."[177] In fact, Warren was wrong and this valuable supporting fire was lost to the hard-pressed infantry.[178]

Nevertheless, the experience of combat began to improve the level of cooperation between the two arms. After the defeat at Spion Kop, artillery and infantry in Natal began to forge closer links and improve their tactical combinations. At the Battle of Vaal Krantz, heavy Boer fire from an unexpected quarter had deflected the infantry advance, but well-positioned artillery reacted quickly to suppress it and allow the infantry to continue forward.[179] During the fighting for control of the Tugela Heights later in the same month, Neville Lyttelton ordered his supporting artillery not to open fire until his infantry advance had compelled the Boers to man their positions, a policy noted as a "considerable tactical improvement" by Leo Amery.[180] These gradual improvements bore their greatest fruit at the culmination of the struggle for the Tugela heights, the Battle of Pieter's Hill (27 February 1900). Preparation for assault was exceptionally thorough, applying techniques normally reserved for sieges to a field battle. The British assembled around seventy-six guns along a four-and-a-half-mile front to support the infantry attack, and they had preregistered the ranges to important targets during the previous day. Describing the preparations, Lord Roberts noted, "Every sangar[181] and important point of the enemy's position had been given a name, the gun positions were connected by signallers, and special observers were posted at the principal points."[182] Specific instructions to the artillery of 5th Division stated, "Follow the infantry attacks up closely. When no longer safe to shoot at enemy's position, do not cease fire, but shoot over the enemy's trenches, "pitching them well up,' so as to make the enemy think he is still being shelled, and also catch him as he runs down the other side."[183]

The time spent in preparation was not wasted, and when the attack was delivered the artillery support proved decisive. Field guns firing shrapnel were forced to switch to firing over the Boer trenches as their infantry approached, but the howitzers and 4.7 inch guns continued their fire with lyddite and common shell until virtually the last moment. Lord Roberts reported the fire was maintained until the infantry were just fifteen yards from the Boer line.[184] Although some British troops were hit by their own artillery, it was generally considered by infantry officers that without such close supporting fire the attack would have failed.[185] The artillery preparation at Pieter's Hill was the most thorough of the war, and the British Natal Field Force demonstrated good levels of infantry–artillery cooperation at subsequent engagements such as Botha's Pass and Bergendal.[186]

The war in South Africa revealed several important issues with regard to supporting an infantry attack. Shrapnel from field guns was relatively harmless against entrenchments but had a suppressing effect that could keep down enemy rifle fire. High-angle fire from howitzers was more useful for inflicting damage on earthworks and could be continued longer with less fear of causing friendly casualties. In combination, the two weapons possessed synergy, with the shrapnel sweeping a wide area to prevent reinforcement or evacuation of the position, while howitzers searched the earthworks and caused chaos among the defenders. This effect was achieved at Pieter's Hill, where the Boers were noted as being "practically confined to their trenches by the severity of artillery fire."[187]

Unfortunately, in the aftermath of the conflict, the subject of cooperation in the attack received less attention than the value of long-range fire and the usage of concealed positions. Although a number of officers from both branches identified the fact that modern conditions made artillery support more critical than ever, little improvement in training was made in the years immediately following the war.[188] It is not entirely clear why the links that had been forged in South Africa were neglected in subsequent years, but several factors may have contributed to the decline. As previously discussed, the service branches of the British Army tended to learn within their own framework, and both infantry and artillery tended to focus on branch-specific issues in the years following the war. Artillery focused on long-range, accurate shooting at difficult targets, while infantry devoted attention to their own tactical reforms, such as extension and marksmanship; thus, the two arms drifted apart and forgot the lessons learned so painfully in Natal. Furthermore, an absence of suitable areas where combined training was possible limited the development of cooperative tactics.[189] When artillery and infantry did train together, infantry officers tended to leave all fire support decisions to the gunners, focusing solely on their own tactical problems. Artilleryman Major C.O. Head addressed the issue in a polemical article in 1904, writing, "An unfortunate idea has grown up in the Army that the use of field artillery is an obtuse science, to be understood only of a few, and beyond the intelligence of anyone not directly connected with it. . . . The ignorance of infantry officers on the employment of artillery is astounding, and it is only equalled by their misconceptions of its power."[190]

Voices were beginning to be raised regarding forging closer links between infantry and artillery by 1904, and this groundswell of interest coincided with reports from the outbreak of the Russo-Japanese War, with information from this conflict serving as a timely reminder of the importance of close cooperation between the two arms.[191] In Manchuria, artillery was noted as being more powerful than ever before, forcing infantry to dig themselves ever deeper underground and presenting problems for assaults.[192] Nevertheless, as in the Boer War, the artillery lacked the strength to shell determined troops out of their positions in preparatory bombardments, and instead combination in the attack was vital.[193] In terms of teaching cooperation, there was relatively little in the Russo-Japanese War that should have come as a surprise to veterans of the Natal campaign, but it had the valuable effect of revitalizing interest in the neglected subject and highlighting it as a critical element of future tactics. Interest steadily grew in the issue through the second half of the Edwardian period, although blunders could still occur in training. In 1907, Hubert Gough defeated John French during maneuvers at Aldershot, citing infantry and artillery cooperation as an important factor: "He [French] still talks of the artillery duel and artillery preparation, which are worse than useless. The preparation for the decisive struggle *must* be done by both Infantry and Artillery. The Infantry *must* advance and *threaten* assault to force the defenders to expose themselves to artillery fire."[194]

Although there was recognition of the need for cooperation, the problem for the infantry and artillery was how effective combination and support could best be achieved at a tactical level. The debate was further complicated by the continuing, unresolved arguments over whether artillery was best used from long range, concealed positions or at short range over open sights. Despite the unfortunate fate of Colonel Long's batteries at Colenso and the excellent example of carefully prepared artillery at longer range at Pieter's Hill, emphasis remained on getting guns close to the firing line during the decisive attack. *Combined Training 1905* emphasized the old pre-war mantra when it noted, "It should be borne in mind that the greater the difficulties of the infantry the closer should be the support of the artillery; this may necessitate some of the artillery being pushed forward to within decisive ranges during the final stages of the engagement."[195]

Officers from both branches supported the idea that guns needed to be deployed at close range to ensure attacks were successful. Long-range fire was held to increase the risk of friendly fire incidents and also was accused of failing to inflict sufficient damage or give the required moral support.[196] The need for fire to improve morale was considered especially important, as the extended formations adopted by infantry in the Edwardian period were viewed as requiring greater moral encouragement than the old close-order columns.[197] Although well-positioned, concealed guns were noted as having a distinct material effect on the enemy, some officers argued that this effect was not enough and suggested that the infantry needed to see their own guns to draw support from them. Undoubtedly, the sight of friendly artillery could be inspiring for hard-pressed infantry. For example, at a critical moment during the Battle of Elandslaagte, Ian Hamilton had ordered two guns to be brought up to the firing line "and was able to do some good by shouting out to the infantry that the guns were coming up to help them."[198] Building on this idea, artillery-man Captain B. Atkinson offered the opinion, "The sight of even a single gun shooting indifferently from an adjacent, exposed position will be far more morally valuable than a whole brigade under cover a mile away. . . . Moral support from the drawing-room never yet induced a frightened child to go upstairs alone in the dark."[199]

However, there were serious problems with this idea. The long ranges at which artillery initially deployed meant that moving them closer to the firing line would be a slower, more difficult process than many imagined. Infantry officers were heard at post-maneuver conferences offering to use their own men to man handle guns into the front line if the gunners would serve them, but artillerymen noted that this would be far harder in war than it appeared in train-ing.[200] Furthermore, as proved at Colenso and in the Russo-Japanese War, exposed batteries ran the risk of being knocked out by both infantry and artillery fire if they deployed in the open. The fate of artillery that attempted to cross open ground under fire in Manchu-ria had proved that to do so was "to court disaster," with one Rus-sian battery that tried such a deployment at the Battle of Liao-Yang (24 August–4 September 1904) suffering appalling casualties that included all its officers, fifty-six men, and fifteen horses.[201] A se-nior British artilleryman recognized the consequences of such losses in a rebuttal of close-range tactics: "The spectacle of a holocaust of men and horses in their immediate neighbourhood cannot but have a most unnerving effect on the best of infantry."[202] Conversely, guns operating from covered positions would be safer from incom-ing enemy fire and could continue firing with relative calm, which would be far more conducive to accuracy than occupying an open, bullet-swept crest.[203]

The debate continued throughout the pre-1914 period, with nei-ther side gaining official ascendency. As with the discussions over the value of cover, considerable freedom was allowed to individual artillery officers with regard to how they chose to fight with their guns. Although training and equipment allowed the use of accurate fire from concealed positions, the insinuation that artillery was not properly supporting their infantry comrades unless they were fight-ing their guns in the open touched raw nerves, and *Field Artillery Training* made mention of the need for batteries to be willing to sac-rifice themselves if necessary to support the attack.[204] Nevertheless, by 1914, the confusing and potentially misleading phrase "close support" had been dropped from British regulations, and although it was recommended to have guns at close hand to repel enemy counterattacks, the idea of pushing batteries up to decisive range during the attack was not to be found in *Field Service Regulations 1909*.[205] However, *Field Artillery Training 1914* offered a somewhat contradictory view, suggesting that "*To support infantry and to enable it to effect its purpose the artillery must willingly sacrifice itself.*"[206] This lack of official doctrine on how best to support the infantry prevented a systematic approach to cooperation and instead allowed a profusion of methods to exist, as revealed by the artillery deployments at the Battle of Le Cateau. The 5th Division's guns followed the line of *Field Artillery Training* and although offering strong support also suffered serious casualties, whereas 3rd Division's guns took the concealed route preferred by *Field Service Regulations* but missed certain opportunities to deliver effective fire.[207]

While the debate on close-range or long-range support continued, a problem common to both schools of thought was how to ensure effective communication between the infantry and artillery. In the Boer War, flag signals, heliographs, and even men fixing bayonets and waving their rifles over their heads had been used to communicate with the artillery, but even in the crystal-clear atmosphere of South Africa these methods had not always been reliable and communication had broken down on a number of occasions. In Manchuria, the Japanese used various methods, including carrying prominent flags in the firing line, but more important they had also experimented with the use of field telephones to link infantry and artillery.[208] However, the technology was still very much in its infancy and was bedeviled by a host of technical problems. Many British artillerymen saw a bright future for telephones, but few were prepared to place complete faith in them until the technology was more reliable.[209] Although telephones had value in connecting guns to observation posts, they were not yet sufficiently reliable to permit them being used in the firing line itself. This problem of communication between artillery and front-line infantry was one that affected all armies during the First World War and would not be adequately solved until the advent of portable wireless.[210]

In the absence of precise communications that could give the artillery an accurate picture of conditions in the firing line, a major tactical issue was how long the guns should continue firing during an assault. The risks of friendly fire were serious, but despite this concern the general opinion among both gunners and infantry was that fire should be continued until the very last moment, with one officer stating, "It is not sufficient, in the infantry attack, that the artillery support should be continued up to the last minute; it must be kept up to the last second."[211] The experience of South Africa was crucial in encouraging the idea that very close support was possible and demonstrating that friendly fire incidents were far less common than had been feared. The valuable experiences in Natal placed the British Army in advance of continental rivals, who expected to be forced to cease fire with the infantry around three hundred yards from the enemy line.[212] Conversely, British experience suggested fire could be continued for much longer, with one veteran of South Africa recalling that the last shells burst over the Boer trenches when his own men were less than fifty yards from the position and offering the opinion, "This is how it should be."[213] Nevertheless, the fear of causing friendly casualties was a real one for many artillery officers, and official regulations on the difficult issue were vague for much of the period.[214] No specific distance at which to cease fire was laid down in British regulations—the emphasis remained on flexibility and individual judgment. However, *Field Service Regulations 1909* effectively endorsed close support in the style that had been seen in South Africa, noting, "Artillery fire will be continued until it is impossible for the artillery to distinguish between its own and the enemy's infantry. The danger from shells bursting short is more than compensated for by the support afforded, if fire is maintained to the last moment."[215]

As theoretical interest in the difficult issue grew, improvements in cooperative training between the two arms followed. Calls for greater links between infantry and artillery had been raised at Aldershot in 1905, with John French noting that he believed close relations between the two "to be one of the great secrets of success on the modern battlefield."[216] Nevertheless, problems with achieving these laudable goals remained. There was little fraternization between infantry and artillery, and it was observed that these somewhat frosty relations reached the extent that artillery officers chose to mess with the Royal Engineers rather than the infantry if a battery mess was unavailable.[217] Ian Hamilton described relations and cooperation between the two arms as "one of the weakest, if not the weakest, spots in our system of training."[218] Various attempts to improve the situation and increase mutual understanding between the arms were made, with Ian Hamilton at Southern Command pioneering a successful policy of attaching infantry officers to artillery and vice versa.[219] Infantry officers were also encouraged to visit artillery practice camps to observe their methods, but by 1906 the inspector general of forces felt that encouragement was not enough, and he instead suggested that officers should be *ordered* to attend; the Army Council approved this policy.[220] Gradually, these initiatives began to improve the relationship between the two arms, but the process was slow, and relations between gunners and infantry could still prove somewhat bitter at post-maneuver conferences.[221] Nevertheless, the efforts had begun to bear fruit by the later part of the period. In 1913, Captain C. E. Budworth noted that discussions of cooperative tactics were "carried out to a much greater extent than before," while in the same year the inspector general reported, "There is a considerable improvement in the co-operation of Artillery and Infantry during training at all stations at which it can be arranged," although he felt still more could be done in this direction.[222]

Although the Royal Artillery had initially taken less interest in providing infantry support than in developing long-ranged and indirect fire, by the end of the period the issue was prominent and widely debated. The experience of combat in South Africa had shown the potential of close cooperation during infantry attacks, and Thomas Pakenham has suggested that the artillery tactics used in the latter stages of the Natal campaign were revolutionary, foreshadowing the creeping barrages that were used in the First World War.[223] Unfortunately, rearmament and the debate over cover and concealment meant the artillery lost sight of these valuable lessons for several years after the conflict, and it took the example of the Russo-Japanese War to renew interest in the subject. Although the artillery and infantry worked hard to improve their methods of cooperation, the flaws of existing communications technology and lack of clear doctrinal guidance on the best positions to occupy placed limitations on what could be achieved. British emphasis on flexibility meant that although close cooperation was seen as a crucial factor on the battlefield, the artillery had no systematic approach to providing fire support for infantry. This lack of a systematic approach led to some problems in 1914, particularly during the Battle of Aisne in September.[224] Although 1st Division achieved some success through close support from its artillery, for the most part the BEF struggled to coordinate infantry and artillery during this battle, leading in some cases to friendly fire incidents and limited progress against the German defenses.[225] Although the Royal Artillery acquitted itself reasonably well during 1914, ensuring cooperation on the vast battlefronts that emerged from 1915 took time, training, and bitter experience; it was not until 1917 that such methods were to become truly effective.[226]

CONCLUSIONS

Of all the combat arms in the British Army, the Royal Artillery faced the greatest challenge in the pre–First World War period, being forced to adapt to both new equipment and new tactics in a short space of time. Many long-held tactical ideas were found wanting in South Africa, and the debates on their potential replacements inevitably aroused controversy and argument.

The Boer War produced many important tactical ideas, including the need for accurate, long-range fire and the importance of close cooperation with infantry. The introduction of both the sixty-pound gun and the excellent 4.5 inch howitzer stemmed from the experience in South Africa, and although these weapons were in short supply, they provided a crucial platform for further development in the First World War. Equally, the ability of the Royal Artillery to engage from concealed positions and the attendant interest in more precise methods of fire were to serve it well on the Western Front. The flirtation with rapid but inaccurate French rafale tactics was fortunately abandoned, and it is significant to note that the French expressed considerable admiration for the close support and precision provided by the Royal Artillery in late 1914.[227]

The Russo-Japanese War provided a timely reminder of the growing importance of artillery and had the valuable effect of increasing interest in cooperative tactics. However, it offered relatively little that was new to the Royal Artillery. The use of howitzers to overcome earthworks, the dangers of deploying guns in the open, and the need for strong artillery support for infantry attacks had all been emphasized in South Africa, particularly in Natal. The Russo-Japanese War tended to confirm the lessons that had been demonstrated in the Boer War rather than offering anything that was entirely new, but it did have the valuable effect of increasing interest in and debate on the subject.

However, the great weakness of the artillery in this period was a failure to settle on any formal combat doctrine. Instead, a wide variety of tactical ideas were in circulation, with individual officers generally left to choose between them. Throughout the period, the popularity of certain tactical principles waxed and waned, with some briefly gaining ascendancy only to be abandoned soon after. The use of covered positions was never truly codified, with its reputation peaking after the Boer War, declining as the French rafale system gained popularity, and then enjoying resurgence as French methods were found to be impractical. In such an environment, much responsibility devolved onto the artillery commander for choosing how to fight with his guns. Although this situation ensured flexibility, it failed to create uniformity. In an army that was used to colonial campaigns with small numbers of troops in a variety of climatic conditions, such flexibility was an asset, but it became a source of weakness as the army underwent massive expansion from 1914 onward. The result was that for the early part of the First World War, the success of artillery was often dependent on the degree of enlightenment of the officers in charge, with higher command choosing not to enforce uniform fire plans.[228] This approach could achieve local successes but had serious flaws when used across large battlefronts.

Nevertheless, although flaws remained, the Boer War had the important effect of prompting a complete rearmament as well as forcing the Royal Artillery away from outdated ideas drawn from 1870–71 and into more practical tactics. In criticizing the British artillery performance in early part of the First World War, it is possible to lose sight of the level of development the branch underwent during the 1899–1914 period. In 1899, the artillery had been poorly equipped, wedded to outdated tactical ideas, and was lambasted for being outclassed by a handful of Boer guns, but by 1914 the British gunners were adept at fighting from concealed positions and were noted for their precision and accuracy by their allies. The ideas drawn from the Boer War and confirmed by the Russo-Japanese War proved a valuable basis for future development. The tactics of accurate long-range fire, concealment, and close co-operation with infantry were all essentially correct, and it was a lack of numbers and an absence of uniform doctrine that hampered the gunners in 1914 rather than inherent tactical flaws as in the case of the French. Although the reforms of the Royal Artillery were not as strikingly successful as those of the infantry, they nevertheless represented a substantial improvement in both tactics and equipment from those used in South Africa.

It has been suggested that the artillery went to war in 1914 "with a well-considered doctrine, which commanded confidence."[229] In fact, doctrine was notable by its absence from the Royal Artillery, but this problem was compensated to an extent by highly accurate gunnery and many good tactical ideas within the branch, even if they were not formally codified in the pre-war years. Building on the hard experience of the Boer War, the Royal Artillery was able to improve itself to the extent that it proved a determined foe for the numerically superior Germany artillery in the opening months of the First World War, providing crucial fire support to their infantry comrades.

A group of Boers armed with Mauser rifles. The range, smokeless powder, and rapid fire of these rifles posed unforeseen tactical difficulties for the British Army.

Boers posing with a heavy artillery piece. The mobility and range of these guns came as an unpleasant surprise for the British.

Mounted Boers on the march. The mobility of Boer forces posed unique problems for the British, especially as the war became a guerrilla conflict.

Boers in a defensive position. Direct attacks across open ground against positions such as these often proved costly undertakings. Credit: F. J. Waugh.

British troops fighting for control of a kopje. The effective use of cover and snap shooting was paramount in such actions. Credit: Frank Craig.

A dramatic representation of the Battle of Stormberg, 10 December 1899. Casualties among British officers in the early part of the war were so severe that visible indicators of rank, such as the carrying of swords, were rapidly abandoned.

A line of British infantry in extended formation. Such extended tactics were critical for allowing troops to cross the fire-swept zone. Credit: The Biograph Company.

British troops taking cover behind anthills and boulders. Use of cover was a controversial topic in the pre-war British Army, but combat experience soon showed its necessity.

Entrenched British infantry. Although the infantry were poorly trained in entrenchment methods, the experience of enemy fire meant that they soon learned the value of spadework.

A Maxim machine gun on a galloping carriage. A considerable number of British machine guns were mounted in this fashion. The bulky design made it a prime target for Boer fire. Credit: Gregory.

A 4.7-inch gun with naval crew. Although a hastily improvised weapon, the gun proved its value in South Africa. Credit: Cribb.

A dramatic portrayal of the charge of the lancers at the Battle of Elandslaagte, 21 October 1899. The most strikingly successful cold-steel charge of the war, it provided inspiration for those who argued in favor of the lance in the post-war years. Credit: J. Finnemore.

Dismounted British cavalry skirmishing in rocks. The small carbines carried by cavalry in the early part of the war proved inadequate in firefights with rifle-armed Boers. Credit: F. A. Stewart.

A lone rider ambushed by Boers. Cavalry scouts on weakened horses were easy targets for the Boers to ambush, prompting a reappraisal of reconnaissance tactics among some regiments.

Mounted infantry scouts. Hampered by rapid expansion and limited training, the mounted infantry branch came away with a mixed reputation from the South African war.

5

CAVALRY

Despite its preeminent social status, the cavalry of the British Army often played a relatively minor role in the colonial struggles of the late nineteenth century.[1] However, the war in South Africa proved to be a conflict in which mounted troops were to become the dominant arm. Initially, the cavalry were kept busy carrying out difficult reconnaissance against well-concealed foes and trying to cut off Boer retreats after British advances. Both these roles proved far more challenging than anticipated. Smokeless powder and long-range rifles made effective scouting exceptionally difficult, and the superior quality of Boer mounts and small numbers of British cavalry meant that the exhausted horsemen were often left trailing behind in pursuit, unable to turn local victories into decisive ones. After the fall of Bloemfontein and Pretoria and the beginning of the guerrilla war, the mobility of the Boers became even more pronounced. Fast-moving commandos were able to strike at exposed and vulnerable British formations with alarming success, before escaping the relatively slow-moving British pursuit columns.

To counter Boer mobility, the British deployed a vast number of mounted troops in South Africa, including regular formations of cavalry and mounted infantry as well as yeomanry from Britain and colonial volunteers from around the empire. Campaigning over the enormous geography of South Africa against a highly mobile foe made great demands on the British mounted forces. The varied duties included performing reconnaissance, screening, turning the flanks of fixed Boer positions, and finally charging and pursuing when the opportunity arose. The workload resulted in a staggering number of casualties among horses. Official figures noted that 347,007 animals were "expended" during the campaign—mainly as a result of exhaustion and disease—representing around 67 percent of the total number of horses sent to the theater.[2]

With such an important and prominent part to play, the British mounted forces' performance became a subject of scrutiny and criticism even while the war was still in progress. Critics argued that the cavalry had achieved precious little with sword or lance and had failed to effectively pursue the Boers and turn retreats into routs. However, supporters pointed to incidents such as the successful charge at Elandslaagte and the bold advance of the cavalry division at Klip Drift, suggesting that these examples had proven the viability of traditional cavalry on a fire-swept battlefield. The role of the mounted infantry also proved controversial, with some feeling that their ability to combine cavalry mobility with infantry firepower made them exceptionally valuable, whereas others argued their rudimentary riding skills and poor horse-mastery made them a liability that merely increased the number of horse casualties. The experiences of the Boer War set the stage for a heated debate that would rage throughout the pre–First World War period as to what tactical role cavalry would play in any future conflict. The crux of this discussion revolved around whether cavalry was better served focusing on a dismounted combat role or keeping the old shock-action traditions and aiming for a decisive charge. Fierce passions were aroused on both sides, and some of the most important soldiers of the British Army became involved in the debate, including the last commander in chief, Lord Roberts, and future BEF commanders John French and Douglas Haig.

This vociferous debate has caught the eye of historians, and the tactical development of cavalry in this period has received greater academic study than either infantry or artillery. Traditionally, views of cavalry have been largely negative, with historians seeing the arm as antiquated and reactionary and key officers like Haig as stubbornly wedded to obsolete ideas and ignorant of new technology.[3] However, in recent years a revisionist view has emerged to challenge the idea that cavalry was a military anachronism in the twentieth century. Historians such as Stephen Badsey and Gervase Phillips have argued that the British cavalry underwent important and valuable reforms prior to 1914, emerging as an effective battlefield force in the First World War during the more mobile periods of the conflict in 1914 and 1918, while also proving valuable in the Middle East.[4] The revisionists argue that far from being wedded to old-fashioned shock tactics, the British cavalry was considerably in advance of continental rivals in use of the rifle during the pre–First World War period, with tactics comprising an effective hybrid mixture of cold-steel charges and dismounted firepower.[5]

In this chapter I discuss the development of the regular army's mounted forces, tracing how the experiences of the Boer War produced a long-running debate that saw the cavalry develop considerably from the force that had struggled to cope with the Boers on the veldt. Although the focus is on experiences and reform of the regular cavalry, British mounted forces in South Africa were made up of a variety of different types of horsemen, including yeomanry, colonial formations, and local volunteers. It is difficult to disentangle these jumbled units. Passing reference is made to the nonregular forces, although the focus remains firmly fixed on the regular cavalry and mounted infantry. The chapter is structured around three important developments that came to prominence during the Boer War. The key part of the chapter centers on the long-running firepower versus shock debate that dominated discussion of virtually all aspects of cavalry reform until the outbreak of the First World War. I also examine the rise and fall of the popularity of mounted infantry as a distinct arm in the 1899–1914 period. Finally, I examine the importance and value of cavalry reconnaissance and its associated skill of horse-mastery. Using these divisions, I demonstrate in this chapter that the British cavalry underwent a difficult and controversial process of reform in the 1899–1914 period. At the end, although some weaknesses remained, the cavalry was able to acquit itself well in combat during 1914 using both firepower and cold steel.

THE FIREPOWER VERSUS COLD-STEEL DEBATE

On the eve of the Boer War, the cavalry of the British Army drew inspiration from a variety of different conflicts, including the American Civil War, the Franco-Prussian War, and various small-scale colonial operations. Although views from the continent emphasized the use of the shock charge, dismounted firepower had proved useful in colonial actions—particularly in Afghanistan and on the North-West Frontier—and the lack of formal doctrine in the British Army of the time meant that individual officers had considerable leeway to train their men in the use of the rifle if they saw fit. Indeed, the use of dismounted firepower was becoming fashionable among cavalry officers in the 1890s.[6] Nevertheless, this freedom also meant that reactionary colonels could choose to reject the ideas entirely, and official textbooks placed firm emphasis on the use of the mounted shock charge, with dismounted work being seen as strictly subsidiary.[7] Lord Wolseley was a particular critic of fighting on foot, arguing in 1891 that "The cavalry soldier is intended to fight on horseback. If you intend to make him fight on foot, well, you will make him into a very bad mongrel. . . . I think it would be prostitution of the finest part of our Service if for a moment you convert cavalry into men fighting on foot."[8]

However, although a variety of ideas were in vogue in the British cavalry prior to the war, the nature of combat in South Africa forced the arm in unexpected tactical directions. The Boers were peculiar opponents for the regular cavalry to face. The Boer commandos were an entirely mounted force but had little tradition of shock charges. Instead, the burghers typically engaged dismounted, taking advantage of the ability to deploy rapidly to seize good positions and then make the most of their rifles. Just as the Boers worked to avoid hand-to-hand struggles against British infantry, they also attempted to avoid mounted clashes with charging British cavalry. Using small, native ponies as their primary mounts, the Boer forces were faster and possessed greater endurance than the soldiers of the British cavalry, who were mounted on much larger animals that were often underfed and poorly acclimated. The result was that with a few important exceptions, the British horsemen were rarely able to catch the Boers to deliver an effective cold-steel charge, and were often forced to make much greater use of dismounted fire themselves.

The choice of tactical role to be adopted was complicated by the existence of several notable successes achieved in a traditional mounted role. At the Battle of Elandslaagte, two squadrons of cavalry had been able to launch a successful charge against disordered, retreating Boers, inflicting heavy casualties and creating a profound impression among participants on both sides. Douglas Haig recorded in a letter to his sister that "They [the Boers] are wild at the way the fugitives were killed with the lance! They say it is butchery not war."[9] A Boer who managed to escape the charge recalled after the war, "Revolvers were being promiscuously fired at us. . . . I could see their long assegais;[10] I could hear the snorting of their unwieldy horses, the clattering of their swords. These unpleasant combinations were enough to strike terror into the heart of any ordinary man."[11] Haig subsequently attributed the shock and fear created among the Boers as a key factor in allowing the bloodied British forces at Dundee to retreat unmolested despite their vulnerable condition.[12] The success of the charge also left a profound and lasting impression on John French, who subsequently recorded the anniversary of the battle in his diary for the rest of his life, the only action to which he afforded such an honor.[13]

A cavalry charge that was perhaps even more important was to take place some months later on 15 February 1900 at Klip Drift. Whereas the charge at Elandslaagte had involved just two squadrons of cavalry, at Klip Drift the entire British cavalry division was committed to rapidly break through the Boer lines and raise the siege of Kimberley. Around nine hundred Boers on a six-mile front, with some artillery support, opposed the advance, but despite having the British horsemen under a cross fire for a significant time, casualties were negligible and the cavalry broke through, relieving Kimberley as a result.[14] The advance was hailed as tremendous success by participants, including John French, Douglas Haig, Edmund Allenby, and Michael Rimington, but it was peculiar in the sense that it was not a "shock" charge in the style of Elandslaagte. Instead, the objective was a breakthrough rather than a direct collision with an enemy formation.[15] This factor made the charge somewhat unique and would prove a source of controversy, but, at the time, the ability for a mass of horsemen to successfully advance across open ground in the face of infantry fire was seen as highly significant.[16] Two days later, the cavalry division achieved further success by outmaneuvering the Boers who were retreating from Kimberley. French's cavalrymen were able to place themselves on the Boer line of retreat at Koodoosrand, holding the position using dismounted tactics and resisting attempts to dislodge them.[17] With British infantry pursuing the Boers and cavalry blocking their line of retreat, Boer leader Piet Cronjé made the fateful decision to dig in, ultimately leading to the Battle of Paardeberg and the eventual surrender of virtually his entire force.[18] However, cavalry actions such as Elandslaagte and Klip Drift were relatively rare, and the majority of the work undertaken by the arm in the Boer War involved fighting while dismounted.

Two related issues in South Africa made this type of fighting particularly demanding. First, as discussed in earlier chapters, the crystal-clear atmosphere of the veldt meant that targets could be spotted and engaged at incredibly long ranges, allowing the Boers to snipe at British troops from exceptional distances. Second, the Boers were armed with infantry rifles as compared with the carbines of the cavalry. The carbine was a small weapon that was easy to carry on a horse, but it was not designed for long-range shooting and was thus considerably outranged by the Boer Mausers. When the British were forced to engage at such unusual ranges in dismounted actions, the inadequacies of the weapon were soon exposed and a chorus of criticism followed. An officer of the 18th Hussars complained, "The carbine is useless as opposed to the modern pattern rifle, being completely outranged. . . . On many occasions during the present campaign, the men under my command have had to submit to a heavy rifle fire at ranges 2,500–3,000 yards, being quite unable to reply with the carbine."[19] Charles Warren identified similar problems, noting that although the carbine was accurate up to around 1,200 yards, "beyond that it rapidly tails off, and consequently the cavalry when armed with it were at a great disadvantage when meeting Boers. The Boers had only to keep at 2,000 yards from our cavalry in the hills, and they could shoot them down with impunity or surround them. . . . They [the cavalry] were practically useless in hilly country, and could not do the duties of cavalry or mounted infantry."[20] A handful of officers came to the defense of the carbine, but in the face of bitter combat experience, such views were in a distinct minority.[21]

With the carbine proving inadequate in combat and cavalry being outranged in dismounted firefights, it became necessary to seek a replacement weapon. Aside from keeping the carbine, the only option was to equip the cavalry with infantry rifles, which possessed the range and accuracy to compete with the Boer Mausers. However, the advantage of the carbine lay in its small size, allowing it to be carried without undue encumbrance, and although the rifle gave cavalry greater strength in dismounted combat, its large size was a problem for already overburdened horses. Moreover, the rifle proved awkward for the cavalryman to carry in addition to his cold-steel weapon. As the war moved into the guerrilla stage, the need for the cavalry to possess high levels of endurance and mobility became even greater, and the extra weight of equipment raised serious questions about the role of the mounted arm in South Africa. The Earl of Scarborough noted that the cavalrymen during this period "were working all day long to find the enemy, and acting practically as Mounted Infantry, attacking positions, and when the enemy did retire their horses were completely done up, so that they were not able to deliver any effective pursuit or to over-take them."[22]

With dismounted action the main employment for cavalry, even cavalry officers such as Douglas Haig had cause to doubt the value of the *arme blanche*.[23] Haig wrote soon after the war had begun, "It is a question whether the Dragoon-lancer is not a mistake! His lance hampers him."[24] In early 1900 Lord Roberts had toyed with the idea of removing steel weapons from the cavalry to improve their mobility and reduce encumbrance when fighting dismounted. However, the reaction from officers to the proposal was largely negative, and Roberts did not formally introduce the policy, instead leaving the decision to local commanders.[25] Nevertheless, the germ of the idea remained, and it returned to prominence following the fall of the Boer capitals. In the small-scale skirmishes and ambush actions that were typical of the early part of the guerrilla phase of the war, being able to dismount rapidly and take up effective positions was crucial to tactical success.[26] Conversely, the cavalry had few opportunities to deliver shock charges against small groups of scattered Boers in this stage of the war, and in combination with demands for ever-greater mobility to catch rapidly moving commandos, the balance between the value of rifle and cold steel seemed to tip in favor of firepower. In October 1900, lances and swords were officially withdrawn from regular cavalry regiments.[27] An order from Lord Kitchener's headquarters added that "The rifle will henceforth be considered the cavalry soldier's principal weapon," and Lord Methuen echoed similar sentiments on cavalry armament when he argued, "In this campaign I should say any weapons but a rifle is an incumberance [sic]."[28] The policy stirred up considerable controversy and was strongly opposed by John French, who sought and received permission to ignore the order for troops under his command.[29] Column commanders were also given a certain degree of flexibility on the armament of their cavalry, which allowed some units to retain edged weapons longer than others. For example, the 5th Lancers were still carrying their lances as late as June 1901, until their column commander Horace Smith-Dorrien informed them they could either keep the lance and remain in camp, or abandon the weapon and stay in action.[30]

Opponents of the decision to remove lances and swords, such as French and Haig, argued that removing the arme blanche seriously diminished cavalry spirit, suggesting horsemen armed only with a rifle lacked morale and fought in a timid manner. In May 1901 Haig bemoaned such an attitude, noting after a small action involving mounted forces that "Many men do not care to be shot at, and instead of pushing on, were satisfied at shooting off their rifles at 2,000 yards. This sort of thing will never end the war," and Michael Rimington felt that it caused the fighting to devolve into "fire at long distances and infinitely wearisome tactics."[31]

A further criticism of the policy was that the absence of close-combat weapons encouraged the Boers to approach to close range during attacks against the British, dismounting and making use of snap shooting to overwhelm the enemy or even launching mounted charges, firing from the saddle.[32] These methods were a striking change from the tactics used in the early stage of the war and could prove highly effective in the right circumstances. At Blood River Port on 17 September 1901, an advance guard of around two hundred and fifty mounted infantry was lured into a hasty attack on dismounted Boers, only to find themselves pinned by rifle fire to the front and charged from the right flank by mounted commandos, who killed or captured the entire force, including commanding officer Hubert Gough.[33] Similar results were achieved by the Boers at

Onverwacht on 4 January 1902, when a double envelopment was made by mounted commandos after dismounted Boers had acted as bait.[34] The skill of these Boer attacks often left British observers impressed. An assault on a supply convoy in Western Transvaal in October 1901 saw three commandos launch a combined charge, each forming up two or three lines deep and charging "like a regiment of European cavalry straight for the centre of the convoy."[35] Perhaps the greatest success achieved by a Boer assault came at Tweebosch on 7 March 1902, when a commando attacked and overwhelmed a British column, wounding and capturing Lord Methuen in the process. Methuen himself described the Boer rush as "a magnificent charge."[36] Although Boer mounted attacks could end in failure, such as at Rooiwal (11 April 1902), where the British stood firm and shot the Boers down as they charged, the experiences left a profound impression on the army. Explaining the success of these Boer charges was to remain a contentious issue for much of the period.

Following the end of the conflict, a number of officers cited the absence of edged weapons as encouraging the Boers to make such bold charges.[37] While British cavalry remained armed with cold steel, it was suggested that the Boers would not approach for fear of being countercharged, but once the weapons had been removed, the confidence of the Boers increased markedly. John French argued, "[I am] perfectly certain that on several occasions if we had stuck to our swords and lances, our men would not have been ridden down by the Boers with their rifles."[38] Although referring to his experiences in the yeomanry, one officer summed up the effect the removal of the lance apparently had on Boer tactics when he noted, "directly they found that we had not a lance, which they hold in mortal dread . . . then they said: 'Hello, here are these fellows, we can go at them,' and they came at us, and used to kick us from one end of the country to the other."[39]

However, not all officers felt that the removal of the arme blanche was to blame for encouraging Boer attacks. Firepower advocates such as Ian Hamilton argued that the veteran status of the surviving commandos made them more inclined toward bold tactics, and the poor shooting of irregular mounted formations such as the second contingent of yeomanry meant the Boers knew they could charge across the fire-swept zone with relatively minor losses.[40] Nevertheless, even some outside the cavalry branch wondered whether the complete removal of steel weapons had not ultimately been a step too far. For example, in early 1900 Sir Howard Vincent had confidently predicted "*the day of the sword is done* save as an emblem. It is doubtful if a sword in this campaign has ever inflicted a wound upon anyone save upon the hips and legs of the wearer, or the flanks of a horse."[41] However, by 1902 he had reversed his position and was expressing concern that the army had gone too far in turning cavalry into mounted infantry, citing the successful charge at Elandslaagte as "one of the few real lessons we have been able to drive home in blood to the enemy."[42]

For the cavalry, the experiences of the Boer War had been confusing and the lessons far from self-evident. Whereas the infantry could look toward improved marksmanship and extended formations as crucial lessons, the direction to take for future cavalry reform was less clear. The key tactical question that required resolution was whether firepower or shock action was to be the primary mode of engagement for cavalry. Dismounted action had been the principal tactic used for much of the war, and cold steel had achieved relatively little; however, the policy to remove edged weapons entirely had been distinctly unpopular and had arguably contributed to a number of small-scale British defeats. Furthermore, the success of the charges at Elandslaagte and during the Klip Drift operation showed the potential of more traditional cavalry methods, whereas the ability of the Boers to charge across fire-swept zones suggested that modern rifles were not as decisive at stopping mounted troops as firepower advocates such as Hamilton argued. Reconciling these views and solving the problem of future cavalry tactics was to produce a stormy debate that impeded effective reform for several years. The heart of the debate was between those who favored dismounted firepower as the principal tactic, championed by Lord Roberts, and those who preferred shock action, headed by John French. Although there were extreme views on the fringes of both camps, at its heart the debate was relatively narrow.[43] Both schools of thought emphasized flexibility of method and essentially advocated the creation of a hybrid soldier who could fight effectively both mounted and on foot.

Roberts and his core supporters wished to see cavalry reform based on the dismounted experiences of South Africa but had no wish to abolish shock action entirely. Speaking before the Elgin

Commission, Roberts summed up his views as follows: "Although it is very desirable that cavalry should be expert with their swords and trained for shock tactics, my belief is that in future wars shock tactics will be few and far between, and that cavalry will have to fight far more frequently on foot."[44] Ian Hamilton expressed stronger opinions, feeling that the sword and lance were "medieval toys" on a modern battlefield and that dismounted cavalry with good rifles would have a distinct advantage over troops attempting to force a mounted action.[45] Such opinions drew the ire of cavalrymen, Hamilton noting on his personal copy of the commission's report that "This infuriated Haig and French beyond measure," whereas future chief of the Imperial General Staff William Nicholson reportedly annotated his own copy with "This man has a tile loose!"[46] Nevertheless, Hamilton followed Roberts's line and expressed his support for the retention of the sword, albeit as a secondary weapon to the rifle.[47] The viewpoint offered by Roberts attracted support from a variety of sources. For example, Austro-Hungarian field marshal Gustav Ratzenhofer was impressed by British cavalry's dismounted work in South Africa, feeling it distinguished itself in the role and calling for a thorough study of the details to assist in future training in Austro-Hungary.[48] Even some cavalrymen supported Roberts's ideas, including successful Boer War commander Lord Dundonald, who felt the ideal cavalryman should be a first-class rifle shot above all other considerations.[49] Dundonald went on to embody his views in the Canadian edition of *Cavalry Training 1904*, arguing that cavalry who could "coolly dismount" in the face of a mounted charge could kill as many men in five minutes with their fire as could be killed in five hours by cold steel.[50] There were a few individuals at the periphery of the debate who called for the abolition of the arme blanche entirely, including Winston Churchill, who urged the cavalry to abandon "the sharp sticks and long irons" which were fit only for savage and medieval wars, but such views were in a minority.[51] Instead, the views offered by Roberts and his supporters were relatively moderate and represented a change of tactical emphasis toward dismounted work rather than a complete revolution. As part of this change, in the aftermath of the war, British cavalrymen were required to train to the same standard of musketry as the infantry.

Those who opposed the firepower school were primarily led by cavalrymen John French and Douglas Haig and were termed the "old school" by Lord Roberts.[52] Although their continued belief in the viability of shock action has been used as a means to criticize them as reactionary, in reality their viewpoint was not as divergent from Roberts and his supporters as it initially appeared.[53] For example, Haig had been impressed with the ability of the Boers to move rapidly to a flank, before dismounting and pouring enfilade fire into advancing infantry, suggesting that it could be imitated by British cavalry.[54] By the end of the conflict, although he remained critical of the withdrawal of steel weapons in South Africa, Haig argued that "The ideal cavalry is that which can fight on foot and attack on horseback"; nonetheless, he felt the morale advantages and potential for decisive success meant that shock action should take precedence in most circumstances.[55] French offered similar views, arguing that "no stone should be left unturned to make cavalry soldiers the best possible shots and thoroughly adept in all dismounted duties," but he cautioned that such tactics had a time and a place, and that overreliance on them would fatally erode cavalry morale and make them vulnerable to more aggressive enemy horsemen.[56] The old school pointed to Elandslaagte and Klip Drift as examples of traditional cavalry employment, arguing that the failure to carry out more successful charges was primarily due to the poor condition of the horses rather than any inherent tactical weaknesses.[57] Despite the limitations imposed by exhausted mounts, French argued that the cavalry had been able to drive away Boers on a number of occasions by advancing boldly against them, even if a physical charge was out of the question and the men had only been able to get their speed up by flogging their horses with the flat of the sword.[58] Although the old school had common ground with Roberts and his supporters in acknowledging the value of the firearm, French and his fellow cavalry officers argued strongly for the principal focus to remain on use of the arme blanche.[59]

However, the initially subtle difference in emphasis became a sore point that gradually forced the two camps farther apart. While these competing theories struggled for prominence throughout the period, it was initially Roberts and his new school that held the advantage. Roberts was in place as commander in chief of the British Army and had the prestige earned in South Africa to give weight to his policies. Emphasizing his belief in the value of dismounted firepower, Roberts had been considering the complete removal of the lance as a combat weapon in 1901 and made the policy official in March 1903, retaining it only for ceremonial duties and potentially for use against tribal foes.[60] Roberts acknowledged that the weapon had some positive attributes, including inducing terror in the enemy when used in pursuit such as at Elandslaagte, but he argued that unless the enemy was in an unprecedented state of disorder, any pursuing cavalry would be better served by cutting off the retreat with dismounted action as at Koodoosrand.[61] The lance was also held to offer some advantages in a charge against enemy cavalry, where it could potentially bring down the entire front rank on impact, but this was a theoretical aim that had never been achieved in actual warfare.[62] Conversely, Roberts argued that the lance was an easily spotted encumbrance when scouting and crucially was a positive hindrance when fighting in a dismounted action.[63] With opportunities for shock action likely to be limited in the future, Roberts saw no value in retaining the awkward weapon; the sword could be relied on instead should a charge become necessary.

Roberts also made clear that future cavalry tactics must depend on the rifle as their principal arm in *Cavalry Training 1904*, the first cavalry manual to be issued following the Boer War. The volume was relatively moderate in tone, approving of the use of both dismounted fire and shock charges. However, Lord Roberts was unsatisfied with the manual as it stood and took the unprecedented step of adding a preface expressing his own belief in the rifle and highlighting its importance in future tactics. Explaining what the improvements in rifle technology entailed for the cavalry, Roberts argued the following:

> The sword must henceforth be an adjunct to the rifle; and that cavalry soldiers must become expert rifle shots and be constantly trained to act dismounted. . . . I should consider that a leader who failed to take advantage of an opportunity for employing shock tactics when required to close with the enemy was unfit for his position. But I cannot agree with those military experts who hold that, in future wars, cavalry shock tactics will form as prominent a feature as heretofore. I think the improvement in firearms will give the victory to the side which can first dismount on ground less favourable to a charge than an open plain.[64]

The removal of the lance and insertion of the preface to *Cavalry Training 1904* marked the high-water mark of Roberts's influence and created a storm of controversy among the cavalry. The existence of the preface was highly irregular, with no other training manual possessing such an introduction. This anomaly caused the Army Council to have serious misgivings about its publication, only issuing it with the note that the manual was "provisional."[65] Many cavalrymen felt that the preface was a direct attack upon their arm, and the inspector general of forces noted that cavalry officers of all ranks were solidly united against the inclusion of the preface and wished to see it withdrawn.[66] Although Roberts rejected such critics as reactionary old school officers, they represented a broader consensus, including genuine cavalry reformers.[67]

Ironically, the creation of the controversial preface was to be one of the final acts of Lord Roberts in an official capacity. Soon after its issue, the recommendations of the Esher Committee unceremoniously swept the position of commander in chief away to be replaced with a General Staff headed by Neville Lyttelton. Removed from his position of authority, Lord Roberts saw his influence on the debate decline considerably, although for the rest of his life he remained vociferous on the need for the cavalry to improve its capacity to fight dismounted. However, his role in discussions of cavalry tactics was now marginal, and the controversial preface was dropped from a reprint of *Cavalry Training 1904* issued in January 1905. The removal of the preface also meant that the Army Council dropped the "provisional" tag from the reprinted manual.

Although the Roberts era was relatively short, its influence on the cavalry reform debate was considerable. Constant criticism from the press and the new school thinkers directed against regular army cavalry had caused considerable demoralization in the arm.[68] Declining morale among the cavalry was a matter of official concern, especially as it resulted in a large number of resignations and a consequent shortage of officers.[69] In April 1905, the inspector general of cavalry called for the creation of a journal for the cavalry branch, feeling that there was "special necessity for it at present owing to the feeling of discouragement which . . . exists at present amongst our cavalry officers."[70] In the same year, an Army Council discussion on the lack of cavalry officers noted unhappily that "There is a general agreement that the press and public opinion have disheartened cavalry officers by attacking and abusing them."[71] Even members of the new school, such as Ian Hamilton, expressed concerns over the demoralization that had been produced among the mounted troops, noting that cavalry in Southern Command in 1906 were showing a tendency to be overly cautious and reluctant to engage unless the opportunities were ideal. Hamilton called for a renewal of offensive cavalry spirit and made the suggestion that overemphasis in training on the casualties that would be suffered at the hands of rifle fire may have been the root cause.[72] Although tactical training at brigade level and below demonstrated considerable improvement over the period, the ongoing debate between Roberts and the old school had the effect of creating doubt about overall cavalry doctrine.[73] In 1905 the Duke of Connaught praised the professionalism and keenness of cavalry officers in both mounted and dismounted work but cautioned that an overall direction for training needed to be agreed upon, writing, "We have yet to learn the precise role of Cavalry under recent changes, and to what end to shape our training."[74]

The departure of Lord Roberts coincided with the outbreak of the Russo-Japanese War in the Far East and an opportunity to draw fresh examples to fuel the cavalry debate. In terms of mounted troops, the two opposing armies were somewhat unique. The Japanese had poor horse-breeding stock and thus deployed relatively few horsemen into the field, but the cavalry that they did use followed a German-inspired tactical model emphasizing shock action. Conversely, the Russians had a large number of Cossacks armed with carbines and ostensibly trained in dismounted work but possessed only a handful of regular army cavalry units that arrived late in the war. On paper therefore, the conflict seemed to provide a potential guide between the relative values of dismounted work against shock action. However, a variety of factors meant that drawing useful cavalry lessons proved more difficult than anticipated. The widespread use of entrenchments and obstacles and the difficult and often mountainous terrain combined to curtail the activities of the mounted arm. Despite their enormous numerical superiority, the Cossacks performed poorly and were universally condemned by critics.[75] One British observer summed them up as "pretty well useless for war purposes" and thought the cavalry of any European country were superior to them both mounted and dismounted.[76] Although the Cossacks were purportedly trained in dismounted work, critics pointed to the fact that their marksmanship was abysmal and seriously limited their ability to fight on foot.[77] Echoing the criticism of the Cossacks, senior British observer Ian Hamilton felt that the war in Manchuria had been full of opportunities for effective dismounted work but complained that they were rarely taken.[78] Conversely, those who favored shock tactics looked on the dismal performance of the Cossacks as proof that an overemphasis on dismounted firepower detracted from cavalry spirit and left the soldiers "emasculated."[79] Although the Japanese cavalry had achieved little of note, their preference for shock action and the fact they were on the winning side was offered as proof of the superiority of their tactics.[80]

The conflict provided few examples of successful cavalry actions from which to draw future lessons. Indeed, the tiny Japanese cavalry force was so peripheral to the main struggle that at the Battle of Liao-Ying in September 1904, Japanese cavalrymen were detailed to carry and cook rations for the infantry.[81] Overall, the Russo-Japanese War offered little fresh to the existing debates within the British cavalry and gave no clear direction for future reform. Lacking useful combat examples, participants in the debate tended to use the experience to confirm preexisting views. For example, Ian Hamilton confessed to feeling a "malicious satisfaction" that cavalry had achieved little success in shock action, feeling it helped prove the correctness of his earlier deductions from the Boer War, whereas Michael Rimington felt the conflict merely proved that the Russian cavalry had been "trained and organised for twenty years on wrong principles."[82]

Although the Russo-Japanese War offered few hints for future tactics, the need to decide on a tactical direction in the cavalry remained. A combination of factors, including the departure of Lord Roberts, continuing doubts about the use of mounted troops, and the declining morale of the arm all gave added impetus to old school theorists such as French and Haig. Both of these men held greater influence in the absence of Lord Roberts and could reshape cavalry along their own ideas, placing renewed emphasis on cold steel. French had never approved of the removal of the lance as a weapon, ignoring the order to discard it and turning a blind eye to its continued use at Aldershot. His continued support for the weapon ultimately led to the Army Council reinstating the lance for lancer regiments in 1909.[83] Perhaps more important, cavalry tactics were changed to reflect the ideas of the old school, and *Cavalry Training*

1907 therefore represented a departure from the 1904 edition, acknowledging dismounted work but placing much greater emphasis on the value of shock action and not even listing the word "rifle" in the index.[84] An infamous passage in the 1907 manual referred to the rifle being unable to match "the speed of the horse, the magnetism of the charge and the terror of cold steel," but as several historians have noted, taken within the context of the time this passage was not a desperate reaction against modern conditions but, in fact, was based on practical combat experience in South Africa and the desire to restore cavalry confidence.[85] In this latter respect, *Cavalry Training 1907* had some success. For example, in 1908 Ian Hamilton was pleased to find his cavalry had recovered much of the vigor they had lacked two years earlier, noting that they now "took their full share of the fighting."[86]

The exaltation of shock tactics found in the 1907 manual was not continued in later editions, lending weight to the idea that it represented something of a temporary expedient to provide direction to a confused and demoralized cavalry arm.[87] By the time of *Field Service Regulations 1909*, the tone was considerably more moderate, with emphasis being placed on tactical flexibility and the independence granted to cavalry by their rifle armament.[88] The trend was continued in *Cavalry Training 1912*, which saw opportunities for combining both fire and shock to good effect, drawing on the support of rifles, machine guns, and horse artillery where possible.[89] It was not dedication to either shock or fire but, rather, the idea of combining both tactics to create a hybrid approach that came to dominate the cavalry debate in the years prior to the First World War. Although *Cavalry Training 1907* favored shock as a means of restoring cavalry pride, at a tactical level there remained great interest in the use of firepower and dismounted work.

Few in Britain saw opportunities for charges against enemy infantry unless the foe was surprised or disordered, and instead the main target for shock attacks was to be enemy horsemen. Shock action was seen as being of primary importance during the opening of a European conflict, when there was an almost universal assumption, both in Britain and on the continent, that the war would begin with a vast cavalry engagement that would determine which side would hold the upper hand in reconnaissance.[90] This specific duty was seen as the most likely opportunity for shock action. Charles

Repington summed up the attitude in an article published in the first issue of the *Cavalry Journal* when he wrote, "Shock tactics in these days refer to the shock of cavalry against cavalry."[91]

For the job of destroying enemy cavalry, firepower was regarded as being too slow and potentially unreliable. Although in 1904 Lord Dundonald had felt dismounted troopers could kill far more enemy cavalry with the rifle than the sword, by 1912 ex-mounted infantry officer Henry DeLisle argued that such tactics would lead to indecisive long-distance shooting and a mutual standoff, preventing effective reconnaissance.[92] Indeed, some felt that the cavalry could achieve a tactical advantage if it were able to compel the enemy to dismount through either fire or maneuver, thus depriving it of its mobility.[93] Furthermore, electing to dismount against aggressive, mounted cavalry carried with it a risk of being swept away by an enemy charge before it could be stopped. The Boer War was cited as a potential example of this situation, particularly the fact that untrained burghers on small ponies had been able to cross fire-swept zones and deliver effective charges, with one officer noting that experiences in South Africa suggested that even his best marksmen were often intimidated by the sight of an enemy charging toward him, losing accuracy as a result.[94] Nevertheless, although shock action against cavalry was favored, emphasis remained on flexibility, particularly making the best use of the ground and immediate tactical situation. Following an inspection of the Cavalry Division in 1909, Douglas Haig complained that not enough attention was paid to the use of the ground in determining cavalry tactics, writing, "The principles which should determine the choice between mounted and dismounted action require to be more thoroughly considered . . . squadrons have been seen to remain mounted in enclosed country when under fire at close range from dismounted men."[95]

The flexible combination of both fire and shock was also emphasized in engaging enemy infantry. Although the initial priority was considered to be targeting enemy mounted troops, once the opposing horsemen had been defeated or at least driven off it was assumed the cavalry would have more tactical freedom to engage the infantry. Although officers saw the potential for successful charges against enemy infantry if conditions were favorable, it was recognized that such opportunities would be very rare.[96] To successfully charge enemy infantry, it was considered necessary either to achieve local surprise or for the enemy to be in a state of disorder and unable to resist effectively. Some officers thought that modern war made these circumstances more likely, with wide battlefronts giving the cavalry more room for maneuver, extended infantry formations lacking cohesion and discipline, and long, intense battles leaving troops exhausted and thus prone to panic at the sight of charging horsemen—a concept that was endorsed by *Cavalry Training 1907*.[97] Nevertheless, training exercises emphasized that cavalry should avoid reckless, headlong charges against infantry when dismounted action could serve them better.[98] This idea was highlighted in *Cavalry Training 1912*, with the focus resting on using dismounted fire and shock action in combination to overwhelm enemy formations; the manual argued that such tactics "present the greatest chance of success."[99] Senior officers also anticipated that British cavalry, armed with machine guns and horse artillery and possessing a high standard of individual musketry, could hold their own against enemy infantry formations, even to the point of concealing their "led horses" and deceiving the foe into thinking he was facing a genuine infantry formation.[100]

The hybrid cavalryman that emerged in the years preceding the First World War was a conciliatory yet practical solution to the New School versus Old School debate that had followed the Boer War. Dismounted training ensured the cavalry could fight effectively in difficult terrain, whereas retaining shock action meant it would be capable both of seizing sudden opportunities to charge, such as occurred at Elandslaagte, as well as of maintaining the morale and cavalry spirit that had been in decline during the Roberts era.

However, the hybrid concept did not draw universal admiration and was savaged in the notorious 1910 work *War and the Arme Blanche* by Erskine Childers. Childers was a civilian who had served as a volunteer artilleryman in the Boer War, but his criticisms were given considerable weight by the fact Lord Roberts provided a supportive preface. Childers argued that shock action "had been consigned to complete oblivion in South Africa," and Roberts supported the idea, suggesting the Klip Drift operation was not a genuine cavalry charge but instead "a rapid advance of fighting men."[101] The work called for the abolition of cold-steel weapons, feeling a true hybrid soldier skilled in both rifle and sword was an unattainable goal, and instead suggested that purely rifle-armed cavalry would be far more effective.[102]

Although Childers's work has drawn praise from some historians, several of his tactical suggestions were of dubious value.[103] For example, Childers still believed cavalry could charge, albeit using the rifle instead of the sword or lance. His work argued that rather than charging into contact with the enemy, the cavalry could rush forward and then dismount at close range, overwhelming the foe with firepower.[104] Although this technique had worked for the Boers in South Africa, particularly against low-quality troops such as later drafts of yeomanry, there were serious doubts about its value in a European conflict against regular soldiers. British officers were quick to point out that closing with the enemy and then trying to dismount invited a crushing countercharge from opposing cavalry using cold steel, as well as risking heavy casualties from enemy fire.[105]

While Childers stirred controversy with *War and the Arme Blanche* and a follow-up volume entitled *German Influence upon British Cavalry*, in reality his more moderate tactical views were not as divergent from the cavalry's own as first appeared. An article from the General Staff in response to the book argued that in many aspects, "the difference in opinion between Mr. Childers and our Training Manuals is by no means so great as he seems to think it is" and noted that both *War and the Arme Blanche* and British official works placed emphasis on mobility, firepower, and aggression as the keys to cavalry success.[106] In some ways, existing tactical thinking was more advanced. The General Staff criticized Childers for placing too much faith in the sheer speed of the horseman to cross fire-swept zones unharmed, arguing that for a successful charge it was instead imperative that the cavalry had the advantage of surprise, superior numbers, or local fire superiority.[107]

Although Roberts and Childers continued to complain the cavalry had regressed to pre-Boer War standards, by the later years of the period much of the heat had left the debate as both new school and old school became relatively reconciled in favor of the hybrid cavalry tactics discussed earlier. In 1908, firepower advocate Ian Hamilton expressed satisfaction that cavalry in Southern Command were demonstrating flexibility in both mounted and dismounted methods, and he noted, "There is reason, then, for hope that the heated controversies of the past few years as to the respective merits of

shock and fire tactics are at last cooling down into the sensible conclusion that there may be room on the battlefield for either or for
both."[108]

Cavalry officers expressed similar views on the usefulness of
the hybrid model and the value of a compromise tactical solution.
John French warned the debate on cavalry tactics risked producing
extreme solutions, noting, "One amateur Centaur would dash the
sword and lance entirely out of the cavalryman's hand. Another fa-
natic ('Beau Sabeur') would throw the horseman's splendid fire-arm
to the wind"; instead, he advocated a balanced approach.[109] Future
commander of the BEF cavalry division Edmund Allenby was char-
acteristically blunt with regard to cavalry tactics, stating, "We want
to kill. When we are in enclosed country we must use the rifle; if we
are in open country we ought to be able to use both the rifle and the
sword."[110] Although there was continued emphasis on the value of
shock action, it was moderated by the need to be highly proficient in
dismounted work. Michael Rimington argued that the cavalry ideal
should always be shock charges, but he tempered his arguments by
noting that fire action would be used nine times out of ten.[111] Perhaps the neatest summary of the attitude toward cavalry tactics following the departure of Lord Roberts was offered in 1910, when one
officer surmised, "The *desire* to use the sabre or lance should be predominant, but it must be held in restraint by a thorough knowledge
of the power of the firearm."[112]

The successful adoption of hybrid tactics put the cavalry of the
British Army considerably in advance of mounted forces on the continent. As part of the most formidable army of Europe, the German
cavalry had been a model to follow for most of the pre–Boer War
period. However, British and German cavalry methods became increasingly divergent in the Edwardian era, and although the determination of the German cavalry to charge home was admired, they had
little else to teach the horsemen of the future BEF. Drawing upon
conscripts with a limited period of enlistment rather than long-
service volunteers meant that continental forces lacked the time to
train their men effectively in both mounted and dismounted work,
and therefore focused on shock action to a greater extent than the
British.[113] There was some anxiety, particularly in Germany, that
modern warfare would require more dismounted work, but the limitations of training meant that little was done to make their cavalry

more effective in this regard. Instead, the Germans preferred to add
light infantry jäger battalions to their cavalry to provide firepower
when necessary, although there were concerns that the jägers would
not be able to keep up during fast-moving actions.[114] The cavalry of
France was even weaker when it came to dismounted action, taking
little interest in the subject and maintaining, in the words of one
British officer, a "robust and perhaps fanatical faith in the importance of shock tactics."[115] Attempts to reform the French mounted
arm achieved little in the pre-war period, despite the best efforts
of a few determined officers. In 1908, General de Negrier had lambasted the "dreaming" French cavalry in a searing article in *Revue
des deux Mondes*, laying out a full translation of the controversial
preface from *Cavalry Training 1904* as an example to follow.[116] However, these efforts produced few significant results, and the French
cavalry remained backward compared with the British and even the
German forces in terms of dismounted work. Both French and German cavalry continued to carry the carbine, weapons that were as
poor in comparison with the British rifle as the carbine had been to
the Mauser in South Africa.

The true test of the stormy period of cavalry reform came in the
opening months of 1914, when the outnumbered BEF cavalry division found itself operating against as many as five enemy cavalry
divisions, comprising German I and II Cavalry Corps.[117]

In addition to being outnumbered, the British cavalry division
also suffered from several serious operational problems, reflecting
the lack of doctrine and organization discussed in earlier chapters.
The formation was unusually large, consisting of four brigades
rather than the three preferred on the continent.[118] The division had
limited opportunities to train as a unit prior to the war, and its divisional staff was not permanently constituted. Furthermore, the
absence of operational doctrine within the British Army did nothing
to ensure unity of thought. The end result of these issues was that
when the cavalry division deployed to war, it essentially consisted
of four independent brigades directed by a divisional staff with almost no experience in handling such a formation.[119] Serious problems soon emerged: the division experienced difficulty coordinating
itself with infantry, and its commander, Edmund Allenby, struggled
to keep his brigades under central control. These problems almost
culminated in disaster before the Battle of Le Cateau, when one of

the key factors in persuading Smith-Dorrien to stand and fight was the fact that Allenby had informed him on the evening of 25 August that the scattered cavalry division would be unable to cover his retreat the following day.

However, despite the operational problems faced by the cavalry division, the quality of individual brigades and their ability to act comparatively independently proved a great asset. Aside from the breakdown prior to Le Cateau, the cavalry provided vital support for the infantry during the retreat from Mons.

The tactical qualities of the cavalry were critical in allowing them to perform this role. Although the 2 Cavalry Brigade launched a reckless and costly charge at Audregnies on 24 August 1914, this charge served the valuable purpose of covering the exposed flank of 5th Division, allowing the infantry to fall back.[120] Aside from this controversial incident, the majority of clashes with German pursuers ended with distinct tactical successes. The action at Cerizy (28 August 1914) represented an almost ideal combination of fire and shock, with dismounted fire from rifles and machine guns forcing German cavalry to dismount, shelling from horse artillery causing their led horses to stampede, and finally a cold-steel charge by the 12th Lancers sweeping into the enemy and routing them.[121] In the battles around Ypres in October 1914, British cavalry dismounted and held a portion of the line against the attacks of an entire German army corps, a clear testament to the quality of their pre-war training in this regard.[122] Conversely, German cavalry found their pre-war tactics were flawed on the western front. Unable to break through opposing cavalry, the cumulative effect of local defeats eroded the morale of the German horsemen, leaving them reluctant to engage; thus, they did not place any real pressure on the British during the retreat from Mons.[123] The weakness of German pre-war training was given expression in September 1914, when Eric von Falkenhayn announced that, "The dismounted cavalryman should be able to fight exactly as an infantryman; cavalry charges no longer play any part in warfare."[124] The cavalry of the BEF held clear advantages in these critical opening battles before trench deadlock stifled mobility, providing a testament to the effectiveness of their tactics and training.

The performance of the outnumbered British cavalry in the opening months of the First World War demonstrated that the difficult and controversial period of reform in the aftermath of the Boer War had not been in vain. The need for skill when fighting on foot and the use of rifles rather than carbines in South Africa gave the British cavalry a head start in future tactics. By 1914 the British cavalry possessed an extremely high standard of marksmanship and an ability to fight dismounted that was considerably in advance of continental armies, with the German army acknowledging the importance of such roles only after a month of fighting in the First World War. Shock charges remained a feature of British tactics, giving the cavalry the aggression and confidence that was in danger of being lost in 1904, but these methods were seen as being one part of a hybrid system that emphasized flexibility dependent on situation and terrain. Although the firepower versus steel debate produced strong opinions and controversial statements that sometimes bordered on the polemical, it resulted in reforms that ultimately produced a highly trained and tactically astute cavalry force that performed well in the critical opening battles of 1914.

MOUNTED INFANTRY

A curious adjunct to the firepower versus shock debate was the existence of the regular mounted infantry (sometimes abbreviated as MI). Composed of infantry temporarily mounted on horses, this arm showed some of the value of mobile troops who were able to fight dismounted. The British Army was unique among the major powers of Europe in maintaining mounted infantry as an adjunct to and sometimes replacement for the cavalry.[125] The mounted infantry owed their origins to the demands of colonial warfare. Small British forces stationed in distant corners of the Empire often had need of mounted troops but lacked local cavalry support. In circumstances such as these, mounted infantry were a handy, albeit improvised, solution. Although they were not trained to carry out shock charges, the mounted infantry were valuable in colonial warfare in scouting and screening roles, and their ability to fight dismounted as infantry made them useful mobile fire support for small forces. Furthermore, mounted infantry could provide dismounted support for cavalry, making use of their infantry rifles, which were superior to the cavalry carbines of the pre-Boer War era.

On paper it seemed as if the war in South Africa was an ideal theater for the mounted infantry to demonstrate their capabilities. The vast scale of the country, the mobility of the Boers, and the numerical weakness of British cavalry meant that there was a great need for mounted troops, with mounted infantry seeming to represent a perfect solution. In theory, these troops were a good match for the Boers, able to deploy rapidly and then dismount and take advantage of their infantry training and rifles to win the subsequent fire fight. With cavalry finding limited opportunities for shock action and dismounted fighting more common than expected, some felt that mounted infantry represented the tactics of the future. In 1900 Sir Howard Vincent commented that although the days of charging cavalry seemed to be over, there was still a great need for "mounted infantry, capable of quick movement on horse easy to mount, and of foot work in the fire zone."[126] Lord Roberts was a particular advocate of using mounted infantry in South Africa. Upon assuming command, Roberts ordered every British infantry battalion in or arriving in South Africa to muster one company of mounted infantry each in order to create eight new battalions consisting purely of mounted troops.[127]

Although there were some established MI formations that were considered elite, the unprecedented rate of expansion precluded effective training for much of the force.[128] Infantry detached to join the mounted infantry received rudimentary training in riding, often lasting three weeks or less, and were then rushed to the front.[129] Such troops were poorly trained in mounted work and almost entirely ignorant of horsemanship and care for the animals; thus, the early results were farcical. Artilleryman and author of the famous treatise *Small Wars* Charles Callwell remembered seeing mounted infantry in action during a small-scale engagement in Cape Colony. After a burst of firing, Callwell witnessed a crowd of riderless horses and men on foot running toward his guns and assumed that they had been driven back by a Boer attack with heavy casualties. Upon stopping one of the soldiers, the man related the cause of the apparent rout: "Them Boers they gets comin' nearer tho' we was shooting grand, and the Captain says 'Mount boys' and some as gets up they falls off, and some falls off as they gets up, and my d___ horse shoves up 'is d___ head."[130] Callwell went on to write of mounted infantry, "They do not fall off in the drill book, or if they do it does not say so."[131]

The mounted infantry's tactical handling was made difficult because of such poor horsemanship. For example, the day after the Klip Drift charge, an advancing column of mounted infantry inexplicably came to a halt in the open within rifle range of the Boers, giving the burghers time to bring up artillery and a pom-pom gun. The fire of these heavier pieces caused a large number of British horses to bolt, carrying the helpless riders with them, with many of the animals falling off a steep bank and ending up in the Modder River.[132]

As well as being vulnerable in battle, mounted infantry were appalling horse-masters because of their lack of experience and training. The attrition of horses in some MI formations was truly staggering. The 1st Mounted Infantry was completely re-horsed almost four times over the course of just fourteen months, yet of its total animal losses of 1,031, just fifty were killed in action.[133] Brief training had done little to teach the men the details of horse care. Michael Rimington recalled being asked by one of his troopers whether he should feed his horse beef or mutton, and William Robertson ruminated that, "No more unfortunate animal ever lived than the horse of the mounted infantryman during the early period of the march from the Modder to Pretoria."[134]

Nevertheless, despite their poor start, mounted infantry remained an important component of British forces in South Africa, especially in the guerrilla stage of the war when mobility was crucial. Experience in the field gradually improved the mounted infantry from its dismal early condition, and by the latter stages of the war both horse-mastery and tactics had improved.[135] In March 1902 an advance guard of mounted infantry pursuing a force under Boer leader Koos De La Rey marched thirty miles to reach the area and then chased the Boers "at speed" for around eight miles, a considerable improvement from the early actions of 1900.[136] The improved quality of the mounted infantry won the branch praise at the end of the war, with MI commander Edward Hutton feeling "the successful issue of the South African War was very largely due to the principles of mounted infantry being thoroughly recognised and carried into effect."[137]

A number of officers saw a key role for mounted infantry in the post-war British Army. A relatively common assumption existed in the years immediately following the Boer War that future conflicts would be dominated by mobility, suggesting the need for greater numbers of mounted troops.[138] For example, in a prize-winning essay published in 1901, Major E.G. Nicolls argued, "It does not then seem unreasonable to assume that war operations in the future will consist of a series of running fights, or minor actions, carried on by the mounted mobile troops on each side, and will culminate in one side being driven into a position where they must either fight a decisive action or surrender."[139]

Financial stringency meant that it was unlikely there would be enough cavalry to meet the potential demands of such a conflict; instead, a number of officers suggested that mounted infantry could provide a substitute on more mundane duties, such as screening and scouting, allowing cavalry to remain fresh for decisive battlefield action.[140] Developing on this idea, some officers felt the mounted infantry could provide dismounted fire support for the cavalry, allowing the cavalry to remain mounted and deliver shock charges when the opportunity arose.[141] A few supporters of mounted infantry went even further, most notably Erskine Childers, who felt that cavalry should become purely mounted riflemen inspired by the success of the Boers in South Africa, but such views were on the fringes of the debate.[142]

Although the debate about its precise usage continued, in the immediate aftermath of the Boer War the MI branch appeared to have a promising future ahead of it. In 1903, the Elgin Commission recommended the provision of "a considerable force of mounted riflemen" in addition to regular cavalry.[143] An inspection of mounted infantry at Aldershot in 1905 drew praise, with John French considering their performance "far beyond his expectations" and feeling "The importance of the part they have to play cannot be impressed too strongly upon MI officers of all ranks."[144]

However, the mounted infantry was far from universally popular within the British Army. Its risible performance in the early part of the Boer War had left many observers with a decidedly negative view of the arm. Opinions presented to the Elgin Commission were often highly critical of the mounted infantry. Michael Rimington felt that one cavalryman was worth three mounted infantrymen, and Lord Methuen lambasted the arm for being poor at reconnaissance and possessing horse-mastery that was "beneath contempt."[145] Douglas

Haig acknowledged that the mounted infantry had improved over time but still felt that "few ever became good enough riders to be fit for scouting work."[146] Furthermore, it had been noted that on several occasions during Boer War, mounted infantry had improvised a bladed weapon, usually by fixing a bayonet on the end of the rifle to create a makeshift lance, and then launched charges against Boers.[147] Rimington thought this was a "splendid thing," but other officers were concerned at the possibility that such examples would encourage mounted infantry to shed its infantry characteristics and become bad cavalry instead.[148]

There were also serious doubts about the capacity of mounted infantry to survive a battle against trained European horsemen. To fight effectively, mounted infantry needed to dismount and take up positions where they could use their rifles. However, there was a concern that if European cavalry caught mounted infantry while they were still mounted and launched a rapid charge, the mounted infantry would be unable to deploy in time to meet the attack. Some officers feared that if enemy cavalry was able to get among mounted infantry in this manner, the result would be a complete slaughter.[149] Given that many pro-MI officers saw the mounted infantry's ideal role as screening and scouting in place of cavalry—duties that would likely bring them into contact with enemy horsemen—this was a grave weakness. These flaws made it difficult to determine a doctrine for the future employment of the mounted infantry. Although they were still useful as an improvised force in colonial actions, doubts remained over their role and viability in a European conflict.[150]

Although these were valid criticisms, perhaps the greatest problem facing the mounted infantry was structural rather than tactical. The key problem was that mounted infantry had little permanent organization. Instead, infantry were detached from their own formations, given a brief course in riding and MI duties, and then returned to their parent battalions ready to be improvised as and when required. The perils of using such a system on a large scale had been starkly revealed in the early stages of the Boer War, when the ad hoc mounted infantry had performed very poorly; after the conflict, some suggested that the arm be established on a permanent basis.[151] However, this policy was rejected on grounds of cost and also because of the opposition of MI officers, who preferred to return to their original infantry formations rather than become a new and separate branch.[152] Edward Spiers has been critical of this attitude, accusing MI officers of "meek subservience" to the cavalry rather than pressing for independence, but as Stephen Badsey has argued, it seems more likely that these men simply wished to return to the familiar institutions of their home battalions.[153] The result was that the organization of the mounted infantry remained largely unchanged from the pre–Boer War structure. Infantry soldiers were taken from a parent battalion, trained for two months, and then returned to their original formation—a system that satisfied no one. The infantry battalion lost a company of men and officers, limiting its own training, whereas the mounted infantry themselves received brief and inadequate instruction.[154] Relative lack of interest from MI officers meant that the arm had no true patrons to argue its case for reform on more permanent lines, and so the inadequate organization continued unchecked.

A combination of unresolved tactical flaws and structural weaknesses led to the decline of the mounted infantry over the course of the Edwardian period. As the cavalry improved its dismounted skills and took firepower more seriously, the need for mounted infantry to carry out these duties declined, reducing their principal role. Under the Haldane reforms, the mounted infantry was instead given the duty of screening and reconnaissance for the BEF infantry divisions, but doubts about the ability of these loosely trained formations to face European cavalry remained. The ad hoc nature of the arm and the lack of interest from MI officers, who saw their posting as temporary, meant that addressing these tactical weaknesses proved nearly impossible. Although the arm still had potential value in colonial actions, the emergence of Germany as the principal threat to Britain meant that maintaining the force became harder to justify, especially as mounted infantry soldiers cost almost as much as regular cavalrymen but were considered tactically inferior.

In 1912, the return of cavalry regiments from overseas postings saw the final end of the mounted infantry, with the formation being disbanded and regular cavalry being substituted as divisional troops for the BEF infantry.[155] The process of successful cavalry reform based on firepower and shock action had sounded the effective death knell for the mounted infantry. Although the mounted infantry was barely changed from its pre–Boer War roots, the cavalry underwent considerable reform and emerged as a genuine and highly effective hybrid force. The mounted infantry had been a useful source of fire support to the cavalry in the days of the carbine, but by the eve of the First World War this role was far less important and it was difficult to justify their expense. Inadequately organized for European conflict, hampered by the tactical weaknesses that had been exposed in South Africa, and equaled in dismounted work by the cavalry it was intended to support, there was little reason to maintain the mounted infantry beyond this point, a fact recognized even by supporters of the arm.[156]

RECONNAISSANCE AND HORSE-MASTERY

Although the arguments over the relative merits of firepower as opposed to the arme blanche dominated much of the cavalry reform debate, the Boer War had also demonstrated the difficulty and the critical importance of effective reconnaissance on a modern battlefield. Smokeless powder, lack of cover, and serious horse attrition made the job of reconnaissance more challenging than ever before and placed great demands on the cavalry. Inadequate maps and the relative invisibility of Boer positions made the job still more difficult, but the consequences of insufficient reconnaissance were disastrous. Writing shortly before the outbreak of war, Robert Baden-Powell commented, "When acting against enemies armed with long-range weapons and smokeless powders that render his position invisible, we should be exposing our troops to absolute destruction were we to blunder them boldly against an enemy without knowing exactly how and in what strength he was posted etc."[157]

Unfortunately, on several occasions during the war, British forces failed to discover Boer positions until it was too late, stumbling into previously concealed fire zones and suffering heavy casualties as a result. Faulty reconnaissance played a critical role in the triple defeats of Black Week, particularly at Magersfontein and Colenso, where the true locations of the Boer trenches were revealed only after the burghers opened fire and took the British by surprise. These blunders contributed to humiliating defeats for the British, but there were also many smaller examples of poor scouting leading to feeble battlefield performance, with one anonymous officer ruminating, "Faulty reconnaissance has led us in this campaign into one mess after another."[158] Flawed scouting prior to the action at Zoutspans Drift (13 December 1899) caused Redvers Buller to lament, "I suppose our officers will learn the value of scouting in time, but in spite of all one can say, up to this point our men seem to blunder into the middle of the enemy and suffer accordingly."[159]

In addition to the difficult conditions imposed by smokeless weapons and the absence of useful maps, effective reconnaissance was hampered by the lack of training and interest that had been taken in the duty by the pre-war British cavalry. Even though scouting was of vital importance in colonial actions, such work was often undertaken by locally raised mounted troops led by intrepid officers, with regular cavalry only present in relatively small numbers, thus limiting opportunities to gain combat experience in the role.[160]

Although reconnaissance was regarded as an important duty, there was a dangerous assumption that it would not be possible until the enemy cavalry had been destroyed; this assumption caused practical training in scouting against active opposition to become neglected.[161] John French complained in 1895 that just three or four days a year were dedicated to reconnaissance work as compared with twenty-seven days in the French army, and an anonymous cavalryman bemoaned in 1899 that "the art of patrolling is almost unknown in our cavalry. *And yet patrolling is the most important service cavalry can render to its side in war.*"[162] Reconnaissance was not taken seriously at peacetime maneuvers, where the confined areas made true scouting difficult to practice and it was not uncommon "to see cavalry scouts approach openly to within five hundred yards of infantry firing at them, and often closer."[163] Training during the pre-war years instead focused on formation cohesion and riding ability, failing to nurture the level of individual initiative that was needed in hazardous reconnaissance missions in unfamiliar country.[164]

An additional restriction on scouting duties was the weak condition of cavalry horses throughout the campaign. The British selected cavalry horses on the basis of weight and strength, ensuring that the animal could carry a heavily equipped rider and also giving great impact in a shock charge. However, such animals were better suited for a short, intense charge than prolonged patrol work. In extended operations, the large size of the animals meant that they soon became exhausted and furthermore required a great amount of forage that often proved impossible to supply. Further exacerbating the problem of exhaustion was the fact that the average cavalry horse was expected to carry an enormous amount of weight. A fully loaded cavalry horse could be expected to carry as much as four hundred pounds in weight, including the rider, his weapons, and various other items of kit.[165] Adding to the woes of the horses, many were sent directly from a Northern Hemisphere winter to a Southern Hemisphere summer without being given adequate time to acclimatize, and thus went into battle still carrying their winter coats.

A combination of these factors posed serious health problems for the animals, and such difficulties were compounded by the poor horse-mastery prevalent among the cavalry. Lack of training meant that although the British cavalrymen were considered good riders, they were not accustomed to long-distance riding or extended operations in the field. Instead, rider and horse generally spent only a few hours per day together outside the stables, leading John French to admit after the war that "They [the cavalry] understood stable management better than the care of horses in the field," while Leo Amery was more scathing when he complained that the average British cavalryman was "hardly more conscious of their horse than of their boots."[166]

This lack of experience in horse-mastery meant that a number of bad habits were prevalent among the mounted forces, such as failing to allow a horse to graze when the opportunity arose and remaining mounted even when at a halt.[167] This latter error tired the horse needlessly and risked causing a sore back, making it impossible for the animal to wear a saddle and thus effectively rendering it a casualty. Michael Rimington, generally considered the best horse-master in the British Army, felt that remaining mounted unnecessarily was perhaps the greatest cause of horse losses in the entire war.[168] The problem was addressed in the "Notes for Guidance" issued by Lord Roberts upon assuming command in January 1900, urging that men should dismount whenever possible and even lead their horses on foot when the opportunity arose.[169] Strenuous efforts were also made to reduce the weight carried by the animal, with official memorandums urging the removal of unnecessary kit whenever possible.[170]

A further drain on the health of the horses was the difficulty of supplying forage. The length of British supply lines and their vulnerability to Boer raids meant that providing the vast quantity of forage required for the horses was a serious difficulty. Initially, horse rations were twelve pounds of oats a day, which would be reduced if hay or grazing was available.[171] By the time Lord Roberts took command in January 1900, the figure had dropped to ten pounds of oats a day, but in the midst of active operations this figure often proved impossible to provide. For example, during the advance to relieve Kimberley, the horses of the cavalry division went without feed for two days from 17 February to 19 February and then received just six pounds of oats per horse per day for the next four days.[172] These shortages were exacerbated by Lord Roberts's efforts to substantially increase numbers of mounted infantry, which placed still further demands on overburdened supply networks.[173] Adding to the difficulties was Roberts's controversial decision to reorganize transport arrangements while in the midst of launching a major offensive.[174] Desperately short of forage in the midst of a strenuous campaign, the cavalry division suffered terrible horse casualties, rendering the division virtually immobile for want of mounts by April 1900.[175]

Faced with dreadful horse attrition, the British made herculean efforts to bring replacement animals to South Africa, but the quality of these new horses varied enormously. In April 1900, Douglas Haig was infuriated to find that "only wretched beasts of Argentine ponies are arriving and very few of them."[176] Furthermore, the constant attrition of horses at the front line meant that there was no time to build up a reserve of fresh animals. New horses arriving in port were given little time to acclimatize to African conditions and were instead rushed to the front to replace losses. Michael Rimington described the process of bringing new animals to the front as "thirty days' voyage, followed by a five or six days' railway journey, then semi-starvation at the end of a line of communication, then some quick work followed by two or three days' total starvation, then more work, and so on."[177] In such circumstances, replacement horses rapidly became casualties, and the flawed procurement cycle continued.

As the British gained greater control over South Africa, the supply situation became more stable and the horses received a better supply of food; in addition, officers and men learned how to make

superior use of whatever forage was at hand.[178] However, the supply limitations during the campaign exacerbated the difficulties of
keeping horses fit and healthy in the unfamiliar climate of the veldt,
and the rate of horse attrition remained disturbingly high throughout the conflict.

The poor condition of mounts in South Africa imposed serious
limitations on cavalry tactics. Most obviously, weak horses were
unable to gain sufficient speed to carry out a shock charge, but the
state of the mounts also reduced the ability to reconnoiter effectively. The standard method of reconnaissance was the deployment
of detached patrols under the command of officers or NCOs, who
would range ahead of the rest of the squadron.[179] However, the feeble
condition of horses meant that these patrols were at risk of being
unable to escape if they were counterattacked by the Boers, who
benefitted from superior mounts that were native to the country.[180]
This risk caused the scouts to lose confidence and encouraged timid
movement, with the patrols reluctant to advance more than a quarter of a mile from the supporting squadron.[181] The poor results gar-
nered through traditional patrols meant that a number of regiments
abandoned the system in favor of forming a long line of scouts from
an entire squadron, spacing them out over several hundred yards and
performing a sweep of the countryside in force.[182] Although this process allowed the scouts to push farther forward and made it harder
for the Boers to isolate small groups, it was not an efficient system
for gathering information. The number of horsemen involved made
it highly conspicuous and also encouraged the men "to trust to their
neighbor instead of using their own eyes."[183] However, the worst
defect of this method was that unlike the system of officer patrols,
this large formation could not penetrate beyond the Boer pickets and
thus was often stalled by small Boer rear guards.[184]

Although some regiments favored the method of squadron-level
sweeps, the old system of small patrols was never entirely abandoned. As the war continued, combat experience among the men and
the gradual improvement of the horses' health meant that mounted
reconnaissance was beginning to show signs of improvement, with
scouts ranging farther and being able to report back more useful information. These improvements in reconnaissance led to several
successful surprise attacks on Boer laagers.[185] In addition, the controversial but widespread use of native guides and Boer deserters

alongside the scouts provided crucial local knowledge that had often been lacking in the early part of the conflict.[186] Ultimately, combat experience had rectified many of the flaws of reconnaissance by the later stages of the war, with scouts ranging farther and being able to report back more useful information.[187]

Despite these improvements, at the end of the conflict there was an almost universal call for improvements to be made in reconnaissance training and the related subject of horse-mastery.[188] Fortunately for the reformers, the issue of reconnaissance training was not caught up in the furious debate between the new school and old school, allowing quiet improvements in training and organization to develop. In the aftermath of the Boer War, several writers complained that cavalry had been "reduced" to scouting, and that this marked a perversion of the true combat role of the mounted arm.[189] However, these views were not accepted by the army as a whole, and throughout the Edwardian period reconnaissance was seen as a crucial duty. In 1903, Lord Roberts described scouting and reconnaissance as "two of the most important duties of the Cavalry soldier."[190]

In the aftermath of the war, a new organizational structure for scouting was introduced into the regular cavalry regiments. Under this system, promising men were taken from their squadrons to become trained scouts. The goal was to train at least four scouts per squadron, with a further twelve scouts at regimental level underneath a specially trained officer.[191] These men were trained in subjects such as direction finding, tracking, and observation.[192] Once trained, a scout held the position for eighteen months, at which point he had to qualify once again in competition with new applicants. This was the first time the cavalry had possessed an organization at regimental level for the purposes of reconnaissance, and although it took time to develop its full potential, it marked a distinct advance from the haphazard organization that had existed in the pre–Boer War army.[193] Supplementing the scouts was the institution of a group system, with a section of eight men under the command of an NCO becoming a permanent unit and encouraging "intelligence and initiative" when on detached and reconnaissance duties.[194]

Although these changes represented substantial improvements, there were calls for even more to be done. Initially, scoutmasters were noted to be highly enthusiastic but often lacking in practical knowledge, with one anonymous cavalryman complaining that they mainly consisted of 2nd Lieutenants who knew "little or nothing."[195] To address the problem, minor tactics in the art of reconnaissance became part of the Cavalry School syllabus in 1906. In addition, John French suggested assigning regimental scouts on a permanent basis rather than training them year by year, feeling that "Scouts should be made much of and given every reasonable privilege."[196] The process of reform was not without problems, and in 1910 Edmund Allenby commented severely on casual errors in reconnaissance that "ought by now to be impossible."[197] Nevertheless, reconnaissance training was beginning to bear fruit by the latter years of the Edwardian period, with superior use of the ground and all-around improvements noticeable.[198]

Allied to the reform of reconnaissance was a new emphasis on improving horse-mastery. Drawing from an ever more urbanized population, the cavalry could not count on prior knowledge of animal handling; as a consequence, efficient and realistic training in horse handling was important.[199] Long-distance riding was introduced into the training syllabus, alongside specific maneuver schemes that aimed to recreate service conditions by putting scouts into the field for extended periods against active opposition. These exercises were progressive, initially aiming to train individual scouts but later progressing to include the movement of friendly troops that were dependent on the reports received from the scouting forces.[200] The exercises were not without fault. It was noted that cavalry map-reading was poor, with the soldiers often having to ask for directions, and in one case, the "enemy" that was the target of the reconnaissance was carrying out a pre-planned ceremonial march with bands playing.[201] However, these schemes marked a distinct improvement in training for combat compared with prewar work. Whereas prior to the Boer War one cavalryman noted that the average cavalry horse spent twenty hours out of twenty-four in the stables, the new exercises lasted several days without interruption, forcing officers and men to handle supplies and horse care in a more realistic fashion.[202] Experience of horse care in the Boer War encouraged other simple reforms, such as dismounting and leading the animals whenever possible, removing excess weight, and using improved saddles.[203]

The British cavalry made steady and important improvements in reconnaissance and horse-mastery throughout the Edwardian period, although it was often overshadowed by the prominent and acrimonious fire versus sword debate. For example, Lord Roberts was still expressing concern in August 1914 that cavalrymen never chose to dismount unless ordered to do so, even though walking with the horses had been standard practice for several years.[204] In fact, by 1914 the British cavalry had emerged as perhaps the best horse-masters in Europe.

The value of the experience gained in South Africa was most clearly revealed in comparison with European cavalries of the era. For example, in the Russo-Japanese War, the Russian cavalry proved so abysmal in scouting duties in the early part of the war that even accurate reports were ignored by the time of the Battle of Mukden in February 1905, and reliance was instead placed on local spies.[205] In 1914 the superiority of British horse-mastery over that in the French and German armies was considerable, with BEF horses remaining fit even in the midst of active campaigning.[206] Conversely, German horses were overburdened and worked to the point of exhaustion, and the bad habit of staying mounted while marching on hard roads caused huge numbers of horses to become lame.[207] A British liaison officer found the French cavalry in an equally poor state, with many horses suffering from sore backs caused by the men remaining mounted at all times, noting that as a result the smell of some squadrons was "painful."[208]

When the anticipated clash of massed cavalry divisions failed to occur, the ability of the British cavalry to fight both mounted and dismounted gave them an edge in action against enemy screening forces. The British had long been expecting that the final stages of a reconnaissance would be carried out dismounted and were thus well-prepared for this role.[209] Conversely, German cavalry lacked any real training in dismounted tactics and relied on their jäger infantry to deal with stubborn rear guards. British cavalry were able exploit this weakness, often stalling German reconnaissance by delivering a burst of dismounted fire and thus forcing the cavalry to fall back onto its supporting infantry. This tactic could cause critical delays while stalled horsemen waited for their infantry to deploy to clear the position, at which point the British slipped away.[210]

Combined with rapidly rising horse attrition, such stalling tactics limited the German cavalry's potential to perform a reconnaissance role to the point where it has been suggested that it caused Alexander von Kluck, commander of German First Army, to operate in a "partial intelligence vacuum" in the opening months of the war.[211] Conversely, British cavalry reconnaissance had helped identify the looming threat of the powerful German advance prior to the Battle of Mons, albeit only to have it rejected by General Headquarters.[212] The cavalry also helped screen the retreat of the BEF after the battles of Mons and Le Cateau, keeping German cavalry at bay and ensuring a potentially hazardous withdrawal proceeded with relative safety. During the Battle of the Marne, British cavalry was able to maintain contact with retreating German forces and played an important role at the Battle of Ypres before trench deadlock brought mobile operations to a halt.

The reform of reconnaissance and horse-mastery in the 1902–1914 period was a quiet success story for the British cavalry. Because of the short period of mobile warfare in 1914, the value of this development has sometimes been overlooked in favor of a focus on the shock versus fire debate, but to do so is to neglect an important advance drawn from the painful experiences on the veldt. In the opening weeks of the First World War, German and French cavalry suffered from many of the same problems that had afflicted the British mounted arm in South Africa. Conversely, the British had learned from their experiences, maintaining healthy horses and thus retaining their mobility right up until trench deadlock set in during late 1914. Whereas prior to the Boer War such mundane duties as scouting and care of horses had received little attention, by the time of the First World War they were an integral and valuable part of training, giving the British cavalry a critical edge in the mobile operations of August and September 1914.

CONCLUSION

The tactical debates and reforms that surrounded the mounted arm in the pre–First World War British Army and the extent to which they changed the nature of the cavalry have long been a contentious and difficult subject. Looking back and surveying the trench deadlock of the western front, it is easy to be overly critical of what

Gervase Phillips has termed the "scapegoat arm."[213] Furthermore, the role of cavalrymen John French and Douglas Haig as commanders of the BEF has drawn much comment and criticism, with some historians using the fact they were cavalry officers to criticize the entire ethos of the arm itself.[214] With the benefit of hindsight, it is tempting to argue that any reform of the cavalry was essentially irrelevant in the face of modern weapons, but as recent scholarship has pointed out, cavalry did not become extinct in the First World War; indeed, they achieved a number of notable successes, particularly in the Middle East.[215]

The reform of the cavalry was a difficult process in which fierce passions were aroused and polemical positions were sometimes taken, both by the New School and the Old School. However, the two sides of the debate were ultimately reconciled with the creation of an effective blend of both mounted action and dismounted firepower, leading to the creation of a hybrid cavalryman capable of performing multiple roles. By the time of *Cavalry Training 1912*, the focus lay on tactical flexibility, using firepower, movement, and shock action in concert to overwhelm the enemy.[216] Emphasis remained on delivering the charge as the ultimate aim of any attack, but officers were almost unanimous in the view that dismounted action would comprise the vast majority of the cavalry's work. Furthermore, as Gervase Phillips has argued, there is a dangerous perception among military historians that a cavalry charge must inevitably be a tactically crude and anachronistic maneuver.[217] However, as demonstrated by *Cavalry Training 1912*, the British cavalry had a flexible and well-considered approach to delivering shock action, emphasizing surprise and fire support as prerequisites for anything other than small-scale actions.[218]

The vociferous and often public debate between new school and old school sometimes disguised the quiet work of reform that was progressing among the cavalry in terms of training, tactics, and equipment. Drawing on the hard lessons learned in South Africa, the cavalry undertook less glamorous reforms that have sometimes been ignored in favor of the prominent firepower versus shock debate. The complete overhaul of reconnaissance and horse-mastery training took time to bear fruit but ultimately proved its worth in the opening months of the First World War. The German and French horses suffered terrible attrition within a matter of weeks, often caused by simple and needless errors such as remaining mounted at all times, but the British cavalry had learned from their Boer War experience and were able to keep their animals fed and healthy for far longer.

Superior skills in dismounted action and improved training in reconnaissance also gave the British the edge over the German horsemen, who often found it difficult to break through British cavalry screens. Although not every action ended in automatic victory, the string of small-scale clashes between the British cavalry and German cavalry clearly demonstrated the tactical superiority of the BEF horsemen. Armed with the Lee-Enfield rifle and trained to the same high standard as the infantry in marksmanship, the British cavalry was indeed a "new element in tactics" as described by Douglas Haig, being far in advance of French, German, and Russian rivals. Although the ability of the cavalry to achieve success dismounted had been demonstrated in the Boer War in actions such as Koodoosrand, training in the pre–First World War period had built on these foundations and produced cavalry capable of improvising as infantry when necessary. This tactical flexibility stood in stark contrast to the German cavalry, which found itself being lambasted for its overreliance on mounted charges. Writing after the war, one German cavalry veteran paid tribute to British dismounted work, noting, "Owing to the advantage of long term service, as well as to the lesson learned in the South African War, the British Cavalry were indisputably far better trained for dismounted action than their Continental fellow horsemen."[219]

The British cavalry suffered from a number of serious operational weaknesses and was not immune to tactical errors, but for the most part the arm demonstrated its skill and flexibility in the opening months of 1914. Improvements in training, equipment, and tactics in the wake of the Boer War helped to create an elite force of mounted troops that was able to perform well despite being vastly outnumbered in the opening months of the conflict. Although the cavalry found itself short of opportunities once the trench deadlock began, during the mobile months of the war it demonstrated considerable tactical skill that was vital to the survival of the BEF as a whole.

CONCLUSION

The performance of the British Expeditionary Force during the desperate battles of 1914 has given the "Old Contemptibles" lasting fame.[1] Outnumbered and in a dangerous strategic position, the army demonstrated skill and tenacity in delaying the German advance and retreating in good order, before playing a vital role in stopping the great German offensive at Ypres. The early actions of 1914 stand in particular contrast to the opening of the Boer War in 1899, especially the triple defeats of Black Week, seeming to suggest that the British Army had developed a great deal in the intervening years. However, although historians have generally agreed that the BEF was particularly well trained, the importance of the Boer War in developing tactics and training in the intervening years has sometimes been neglected. For example, in a recent study of the BEF's performance in 1914, the importance of the South African experience in shaping tactical handling is only referred to in passing, and the force is criticized for remaining a "Victorian Army."[2]

As this work has demonstrated, though, the Boer War was the catalyst for a wide variety of tactical reforms that shaped the BEF of 1914. Not all of the lessons that emerged from the struggle proved useful, and some were neglected in the pre–First World War era, but the core training and tactics of the BEF were rooted in the experience of combat on the veldt. The improved tactics that were apparent among all service arms in 1914 were directly influenced by the experience of South Africa, not only in terms of providing combat examples for future use, but also in reforming attitudes toward training and the profession as a whole. Professionalism among the officer corps was encouraged, and the men were expected to demonstrate higher levels of skill and initiative rather than the simple obedience of earlier times. Even though social prejudice and budgetary constraints sometimes prevented the reforms being carried further, the dramatic change to the training ethos remained a huge step forward for the British Army. Not all the tactical lessons of the Boer War survived the process of reform; nonetheless, the overall impact of the conflict in changing training and tactics was fundamental to the success of the BEF in 1914. However, the unusual nature of the Boer War and the unique colonial policing duties of the British Army combined to create to a somewhat skewed process of development in the 1902–1914 period. The South African conflict held many useful tactical lessons that were to prove of value in 1914, but the short length of the conventional period of the war meant that it taught little about large-scale operational handling.

A common thread for many of the Boer War lessons related to the improvements in firepower within all combat arms. Infantry rifles were now longer ranged and more accurate than ever before, and cavalry carbines were found to be inadequate in comparison. In a similar manner, greater artillery firepower, in terms of both numbers of guns and weight of shell, was found to be crucial for suppressing enemy positions. The imperative to harness tactical firepower was a driving force behind many of the reforms of the Edwardian era. For the infantry, this imperative translated into training the men to handle their rifles with exceptional skill and rapidity. For the cavalry, it manifested in greater interest in dismounted work, the equipping of the troopers with rifles as opposed to carbines, and the institution of the same level of musketry training as was carried out within the infantry. At the same time, the artillery was reequipped with what were then the heaviest field guns of their class in the form of the eighteen-pounder, in addition to being provided a genuine heavy artillery piece for field service with the sixty-pounder.

Besides the improved tactical firepower of the army, there was also a greater respect for facing enemy fire. The second key component of British tactical reform in this period was a much greater appreciation of the difficulties of facing modern weaponry. To this end, tactical reform emphasized the need to use cover, approach by rushes, and avoid dense formations. The cavalry came to treat mounted charges as a more complex maneuver than had been the case in the nineteenth century, recognizing the general impossibility of charging formed infantry and regarding other mounted actions in terms of fire and steel in combination, rather than relying on a headlong rush to achieve the desired results. The artillery similarly saw the potential dangers in deploying guns in the open and instead came to appreciate the value of concealing their position and making use of indirect fire. Taken as a whole, these tactical changes gave the British Army an important grounding in the skills necessary for the conduct of modern warfare.

However, although it led to much improved tactics, the Boer War did not fundamentally change the role of the British Army. It remained a colonial force able to deploy rapidly around the empire to deal with various local threats, and in many ways it remained closely tied to small-war principles. Formal doctrine was rejected in preference for a flexible, problem-solving approach that was well suited to small-scale engagements in diverse environments but that was less appropriate for continental warfare on a mass scale. British service manuals were filled with useful ideas, but uniformity of training was only loosely enforced, with divisions, brigades, and even battalions finding their own preferred methods. As has been shown, despite the protestations of the inspector general of forces, such diversity of training received a degree of official sanction from the Army Council.[3]

This system of diversity harkened back to the Victorian era, when individual colonels had received considerable leeway to train their men as they saw fit, allowing antiquated methods to persist in certain regiments. Such vagueness of overall doctrine could have been disastrous. The French Army similarly lacked formal doctrinal direction and adopted the offensive a outrance to fill this gap. Lacking appropriate tactics for such an aggressive doctrine, the French suffered ruinous casualties in the opening weeks of the First World

War. Fortunately for the British, although the Boer War had not led to a formalized doctrine as such, it had instilled a new ethos within the British Army that informed the spirit of training throughout the period. This new ethos emphasized the need to harness tactical fire-power as well as pay due respect to that of the opposition. Although arguments over how best to fulfill these two related goals continued, with methods often differing from formation to formation, they provided an overriding ethos for training and thus remained the cornerstone of British tactical thought throughout the pre–First World War period. The Boer War provided key examples of how to achieve these aims, and although not all were carried through to the extent they could have been, the subsequent tactical and training reforms to inculcate these lessons to the army as a whole were generally successful.

Although the Boer War provided several crucial and lasting tactical lessons, the process of reform following the conflict was not entirely smooth. Some lessons faded from memory, whereas others were influenced and reshaped by other factors, such the Russo-Japanese War. Furthermore, despite their modern weapons, the Boers were unique opposition and South Africa was a peculiar theater of war, meaning that direct parallels between the Boer War and a European conflict were potentially misleading. For example, although the Boers possessed a handful of modern artillery pieces, they were massively outgunned by the Royal Artillery. With the exception of the Battle of Spion Kop, Boer artillery fire tended to be of nuisance value and taught the British little about the potential dangers of facing heavy shell fire. Inexperience in facing enemy artillery meant that in the early part of the First World War, British infantry tended to site their trenches with a view to acquiring the best possible field of rifle fire, neglecting the fact that this strategy often exposed the position to crushing German bombardments. In addition, although Boer trenches had been excellent and served as a model for the British in the years following the war, over time there was a distinct decline in interest in the subject. The tedium of digging trenches in peacetime and a fall in the number of veteran troops who appreciated their full value were important factors in the deterioration of entrenchment training. Thus, although entrenchment remained a key military skill, the quality of training in the subject fell noticeably in the years prior to the First World War.

The Boer War may have provided the catalyst for change in 1902, but it was not the only source of tactical ideas during the pre–First World War period: the influence of continental thought and the Russo-Japanese War became important factors in the latter years of the Edwardian era. The Manchurian conflict in particular caught the eye, with the British Army dispatching a record number of observers to study the war. The struggle between Japan and Russia seemed to offer certain contradictions to the tactical assumptions regarding firepower that had emerged during the Boer War. The Japanese success in pressing frontal attacks against entrenched Russian defenders posed a counterpoint to post–Boer War British ideas that direct attacks against modern weapons would be virtually impossible. The occurrence of bayonet fighting on a surprisingly regular basis in the Far East also suggested that firepower was not the only consideration in battle, and that courage and willpower could still carry the attackers into the enemy position. Such examples were particularly appealing to continental thinkers, who had generally been contemptuous of British tactics and combat performance in the Boer War, and who often saw Japanese successes as a vindication of their earlier ideas. Furthermore, the Russo-Japanese War was seen as being more relevant to European warfare than the South African war, being waged between two genuine powers with continental-style tactics and equipment. Although it is clear with the benefit of hindsight that the Russo-Japanese War showed the dominance of firepower and the value of entrenchment, at the time such conclusions were less common. Indeed, a virtual consensus emerged on the continent that the war demonstrated the continuing power of the attack over passive defense, and that although firepower had undoubtedly developed, courage and an acceptance of casualties would still ultimately ensure success.[4] Analysis of this consensus by subsequent historians has generally argued that because of the ambiguity surrounding some of the lessons of the war, European militaries tended to use them to confirm existing ideas rather than create new tactical concepts.[5]

Fortunately, in the case of the British Army, many of the more valuable examples that emerged from the Russo-Japanese War were already part of existing tactical thought developed from the Boer War. For example, the value of concealing field guns and the need for close cooperation between infantry and artillery were concepts that had been clearly demonstrated in South Africa, and their importance in Manchuria served as a timely reminder for the Royal Artillery. Although other lessons of the conflict contributed to ongoing debates within the service arms, their long-term influence was often limited. In common with other European armies, elements in Britain were impressed by Japanese assaults and felt they gave weight to arguments in favor of reducing infantry extensions in the attack. Allied to this idea, parts of the British Army rejected the cautious attitude that had been adopted toward the offensive in the aftermath of the Boer War, instead echoing European opinion and extolling the virtues of willpower in overcoming superior firepower. However, in contrast to European forces such as the French, these ideas were never entirely accepted by the British in the pre–First World War period. Though extensions were reduced from the scale used in the Boer War, they still remained wider than those used by the Japanese during the final stages of the Manchurian conflict. Likewise, the belief in the offensive grew in popularity but never became a cult for the British and had limited influence at the tactical level, despite the fact that the virtues of the offensive were often extolled at higher levels.[6]

In the most thorough analysis of the influence of the Russo-Japanese War upon the British Army, Phillip Towle has argued that although the war was an important influence on the Royal Artillery, its effect on infantry and cavalry was limited and temporary.[7] Instead, tactical ideas drawn from the Boer War remained the core principles of British training, with the Far Eastern struggle reinforcing the importance of such concepts as extension, concealment, and cooperation rather than proving their inefficiency. The Russo-Japanese War did not cause a fundamental overhaul of tactics in the way that the Boer War had done. Rather, it contributed to ongoing tactical debates that were still rooted in South African experience. The Manchurian conflict showed that many of the tactical lessons of the earlier war had been largely correct, but it offered comparatively little that was entirely new to British tactics. The Russo-Japanese War's most important influence on the British military was to encourage a greater belief in the offensive—an interpretation that seemed to run contrary to the tactical lessons of the war, but one that became popular at an operational level among armies across Europe, including Britain. However, in terms of driving tactical reform in the British Army, the Boer War was of greater importance than the Manchurian conflict.

Firmly based on the Boer War, but also shaped by the Russo-Japanese War and examples from continental thinkers, the learning process undertaken by the British Army in the 1902–1914 period was not straightforward. Rather, it was set against a background of political and economic shifts, with regular changes at the War Office causing confusion in the early part of the period, and the constant need to keep the army's costs low providing a limiting factor during the Haldane years. Although initially the tactical experiences of the Boer War were dominant in driving reform, their influence declined somewhat as the conflict faded from memory. The fact that not all the Boer War lessons prevailed by 1914 has been cited as evidence for the fact the war had limited tactical impact.[8] Even positive assessments of the army of the period have concluded that a number of the reforms introduced following the Boer War suffered from incomplete implementation.[9]

However, such negative interpretations are largely based on an analysis of the British Army at an operational rather than tactical level. The influences of the Boer War were felt most keenly at brigade level and below, where the lessons derived from combat experience could be put into practice. Conversely, the short duration of the conventional stage of the war meant that, despite the number of British and empire troops committed to South Africa, there was little to be learned about handling formations at divisional level and above in a continental-style war. In combination with the colonial policing role of the British Army, this fact contributed to an unusual developmental direction that emphasized tactical skill and high levels of flexibility while operational-level work was assigned a lower priority. Although detractors have articulated valid criticisms of the British Army's operational-level development, they marginalize the quality of low-level tactics that emerged following the Boer War. In the battles of 1914, the Germans were unable to destroy the BEF despite possessing a vast numerical advantage and a well-developed operational doctrine. In these clashes the quality of BEF's tactics proved to be critical to both survival and victory, and the operational weaknesses of the British Army would begin to be seriously exposed only when called upon to undertake demanding offensives in 1915.

The difficulties experienced by the British from 1915 onward have sometimes led to criticism of the BEF in 1914. Critics have often cited the small size of the British Army as being hopelessly inadequate for a European conflict.[10] Yet it is important to remember that European militaries and governments all anticipated a short, sharp war that would be over in a matter of months.[11] The British Army was expected to play a relatively minor role on the left flank of the French, while the decisive offensive blow fell on the right flank against Alsace-Lorraine. Based on the anticipation of a limited role in a short continental war, the BEF was by no means as ill-equipped as some critics have argued. Furthermore, despite its weaknesses, the flexibility and professionalism of the BEF meant that it was surprisingly well suited for the chaotic and hard-fought battles that marked the opening months of the war. Placed in the path of the German onslaught in 1914, the BEF proved its tactical adaptability. Although it suffered severe casualties, the BEF played a critical role in halting the offensive, particularly at the Battle of Ypres. The cost, however, was high and the old regular army was effectively destroyed by the end of 1914. Nevertheless, many of the tactical principles that were key notes of the regular BEF, particularly skillful infantry tactics, close artillery cooperation with infantry, and a respect for firepower, were to become crucial to the ultimate success of the British Army in the later stages of the First World War.

By the end of the 1902–1914 period, the armies of Europe had been forced to adapt themselves to a variety of technical and tactical changes. The success of this adaptation process would be revealed only in the acid test of combat. The BEF that deployed in the opening months of the First World War was a small colonial police force that stood in contrast to the mass armies of the continent. However, the British Army had benefited from the influence of the Boer War, which had been the predominant factor in the tactical reforms that led to the creation of the highly trained BEF. Not all of the lessons of the Boer War had endured, and some ideas were inapplicable to a European conflict, but key tactical principles learned on the veldt had prevailed in infantry, cavalry, and artillery, contributing to the creation of a small but skillful army. Combat experience against well-armed opponents in the Boer War gave the British a head start on numerous tactical problems that were to become apparent in 1914, including concealment, extensions, and use of firepower. The process of development had not been smooth, with the army struggling against continuous budget cuts and also a variety of duties that no other army in the world had to face. These factors contributed to a development path that largely ignored operational doctrine and did little to prepare the BEF for deployment in anything greater than divisional strength, but at the same time they encouraged flexibility and realistic tactics at low levels. Like all armies in the First World War, the British made both tactical and operational errors in the opening months of the conflict. However, despite its colonial background and operational limitations, it was able to win critical battles against a numerically superior army that was widely regarded as the finest in Europe. The success of the BEF in these early clashes was principally due to the fact that the British Army had been able to learn and absorb the combat lessons of the Boer War. Despite the existence of numerous competing ideas and examples, the South African experience remained the foundation of British tactical reform in the 1902–1914 period, giving the BEF the skills that proved so important in August 1914.

NOTES

INTRODUCTION

1. The paper strength of a British infantry division was 18,073 of all ranks, and the cavalry division was 9,269 all ranks. The full strength of the British Army in 1914 was approximately 247,000, but this figure included troops stationed in India and other parts of the globe. See Barnes, *British Army of 1914*, 76.

2. These divisions were held back to provide protection against a feared German naval landing on British shores. When this invasion did not materialize, the divisions were sent to join the main body of the B.E.F. as reinforcements. The 4th Division landed in France 22–23 August, and 6th Division landed 8–9 September. These units were formed into III Corps under the command of William Pulteney.

3. The original commander of II Corps was Lieutenant-General Sir James Grierson. Unfortunately, Grierson died of a sudden heart attack on 17 August 1914, and his place was taken by Horace Smith-Dorrien.

4. Ascoli, *Mons Star*, 8.

5. Edmonds, *Official History of the Great War*, 1:48–49.

6. Throughout this book, military units are designated by ordinals, Arabic numerals, or Roman numerals, according to the level of the unit, following traditional British military designations. For example, First Army, I Corps, 1st Division, 1 Brigade, 1st Black Watch.

7. Terraine, *Mons: The Retreat to Victory*, 76–77.

8. Quoted in Neillands, *Old Contemptibles*, 2. No copy of the Kaiser's order has ever been found, but the legend, and resulting nicknames, have endured.

9. Edmonds, *Official History*, 1:72.

10. Neillands, *Old Contemptibles*, 137.

11. Holmes, *Riding the Retreat*, 173; Antony Bird, *Stand and Fight*, 45–49.

12. Quoted in Ascoli, *Mons Star*, 97.

13. Ibid., 96–97; Antony Bird, *Stand and Fight*, 55–60.

14. Quoted in Ascoli, *Mons Star*, 140.

15. For a thorough examination of the battle, see Herwig, *Marne, 1914*.

16. Ascoli, *Mons Star*, 148

17. Neillands, *Old Contemptibles*, 235–36.

18. I, II, and III Corps consisted of two infantry divisions. IV Corps consisted of one infantry division and one cavalry division. The Cavalry Corps consisted of two cavalry divisions.

19. The Indian Corps was a force of native troops under the command of white officers drawn from the standing army of British India. It consisted of two infantry divisions and a cavalry brigade.

20. Although described as a single battle, it has been argued that Ypres consisted of four battles fought between October and November. See Edmonds, *Official History*, 2:125; and Neillands, *Old Contemptibles*, 261.

21. For a thorough account of the battle, see Beckett, *Ypres*.

22. G. C. W. [Graeme Chamley Wynne], *Ypres 1914*, 11.

23. Neillands, *Old Contemptibles*, 277.

24. Beckett, *Ypres*, 176–77, 182–84.

25. Ibid., 199.

26. Ibid., p. v.

27. Ibid., 198.

28. Neillands, *Old Contemptibles*, 299–300.

29. Ascoli, *Mons Star*, 13; G.C.W., *Ypres 1914*, 74–75.

30. A large number of German formations at Ypres were composed of reservists and volunteers. Both had received only limited training before being committed to combat. See Beckett, *Ypres*, 46–47.

31. Quoted in Sheldon, *German Army at Ypres 1914*, 105.

32. Edmonds, *Official History*, 2:466–67.

33. Ascoli, *Mons Star*, 244.

34. Ibid.

35. Lucy, *There's a Devil in the Drum*, 293.

36. For a discussion of this aspect of the 1918 campaign, see Philpott, *Bloody Victory*, 497–537.

37. Edmonds, *Official History*, 1:10.

38. From the poem "The Lesson" by Rudyard Kipling, first published in *The Times* in July 1901.

39. Teagarden, *Haldane at the War Office*; Tyler, *British Army and the Continent 1904–1914*; Poe, "British Army Reforms 1902–1914."

40. For example, Terraine, *Mons*.

41. Searle, *Quest for National Efficiency*, 50.

42. Neillands, *Old Contemptibles*, 100, 136, 138.

43. Badsey, *Doctrine and Reform*, 3.

44. Quoted in Newell, *Framework of Operational Warfare*, p. xi.

45. Ibid., 18–19.

46. Neilson, "That Dangerous and Difficult Enterprise," 31.

47. Sheffy, "Model Not to Follow," 262–64; Snyder, *Ideology of the Offensive*, 77–81.

48. Gardner, *Trial by Fire*, 236.

49. The official title of this committee was the Royal Commission on the War in South Africa. However, the body was commonly referred to as the Elgin Commission after its chairman, Victor Alexander, Earl of Elgin and Kincardine.

1. THE BOER WAR, 1899–1902

1. The word "Boer" translates as "farmer" in English.

2. The British had previously occupied Cape Town from 1795 to 1803 during the French Revolutionary War but had returned the colony to Dutch control at the end of this conflict.

3. Quoted in Millin, *General Smuts*, 58.

4. For a more detailed examination of the political build up to the war, see Pakenham, *Boer War*.

5. Although the substantial forces of the Indian Army were available to the British, the racial tensions inherent in using Indian troops against white Boers meant that their deployment was considered politically imprudent. Officially, the conflict was to be a "white man's war," although both sides unofficially employed black African volunteers.

6. Hall, *Hall Handbook of the Anglo-Boer War*, 187.

7. Amery, *Times History of the War in South Africa*, 2:9.

8. Wessels, *Lord Roberts and War in South Africa*, p. xiii.

9. Beckett, "South African War and Late Victorian Army," 33.

10. Falls, "Reconquest of Sudan," 299–301.

11. Moreman, "North West Frontier Warfare," 49.

12. Mead, "Notes on Musketry Training of Troops," 235.

13. Gatacre, "Few Notes on Hill Fighting," 1072.

14. Moreman, "Northwest Frontier Warfare," 52.

15. Evans, "From Drill to Doctrine," 36–39.

16. Quoted in Dunlop, *Development of the British Army*, 37.

17. Gooch, *Plans of War*, 27–28.

18. Grierson, *Scarlet into Khaki*, 173.

19. For criticism of pre–Boer War training, see Pollock, "Battle Drill of Infantry," 540, 554. For the impact of faulty tactics in the Boer War, see British Officer, *An Absent Minded War*, 8–9.

20. For a detailed study of the Afrikaner military system and the combat experience of the Boers, see Pretorius, *Life on Commando*.

21. Maurice, *History of the War in South Africa*, 1:81–84.

22. Ibid., 1:71.

23. Nasson, *South African War*, 67.

24. Maurice, *History of the War in South Africa*, 1:80.

25. Ibid.

26. Ibid., 1:86.

27. A traditional South Africa heavy whip, commonly used for driving cattle.

28. De Wet, *Three Years' War*, 294.

29. Literally, "bitter enders."

30. Quoted in Nasson, *South African War*, 69.

31. Military Notes on the Dutch Republics of South Africa, 49–52, The National Archives, Kew, War Office 33/154 (hereafter, citations to War Office records located at The National Archives, Kew, are cited as TNA WO, with the box or item number given).

32. Nasson, *South African War*, 55.

33. Boer forces in the field amounted to between 32,000 and 35,000 men in October 1899. For a detailed breakdown of Boer forces, see Hall, *Hall Handbook*, 4.

34. Pakenham, *Boer War*, 98.

35. Judd and Surridge, *Boer War*, 106.

36. Pakenham, *Boer War*, 98.

37. Ibid., 98, 107.

38. Maurice, *History of the War in South Africa*, 1:126–27.

39. Ibid., 126; Pakenham, *Boer War*, 108.

40. A precise figure for the number of Boers engaged is lacking. Maurice puts the numbers at 3,500 but acknowledges a number of individual Boers may have joined in the action. See Maurice, *History of the War in South Africa*, 1:127–28.

41. Ibid., 1:170–71.

42. Pakenham, *Boer War*, 168–69.

43. Ibid., 168–75.

44. Trew, *Boer War Generals*, 55.

45. Of five regiments operating in South Africa in the opening part of the war, four were trapped at Ladysmith.

46. Marquess of Anglesey, *History of the British Cavalry*, 69–70, 80, 85.

47. Maurice, *History of the War in South Africa*, 1:376; Pakenham, *Boer War*, 253.

48. Pakenham, *Boer War*, 257.

49. Maurice, *History of the War in South Africa*, 2:336.

50. Trew, *Boer War Generals*, 57.

51. Ibid., 61.

52. Maurice, *History of the War in South Africa*, 2:238–39.

53. Stephen Miller, *Volunteers on the Veld*, 166–68. However, Miller notes that although they were initially poorly trained, these volunteer formations often improved with combat experience.

54. Pakenham, *Boer War*, 392–94.

55. Ibid., 377.

56. Nasson, *South African War*, 220–24.

57. Pakenham, *Boer War*, 537.

58. Ibid., 549.

59. Hall, *Hall Handbook*, 176, 187, 217.

60. For a particularly damning critique of Colenso and Magersfontein, see Amery, *Times History*, 2:386–415 and 2:433–58, respectively.

61. "The Boer War Through German Glasses," no pagination, Lord Roberts Papers, TNA WO 105/40.

62. Gillings, *Battle of the Thukela Heights*, 34.

63. For example, Trimmel, "South African Campaign"; Ratzenhofer, "Retrospect of the War in South Africa"; von der Goltz, "What Can We Learn?"; and von Lindeau, "What Has the Boer War to Teach Us?," 48–56.

64. For a comprehensive study of this issue, see Searle, *Quest for National Efficiency*.

65. Quoted in Evans, "From Drill to Doctrine," 94.

2. DOCTRINE AND ETHOS

1. *Preliminary and Further Reports (with Appendices) of the Royal Commissioners appointed to Enquire into the Civil and Professional Administration of the Naval and Military Departments and the Relation of the those Departments to each other and to the Treasury*, pp. xxii–xxiii, TNA CAB (Cabinet) 37/27/28.

2. *Report of His Majesty's Commissioners* Q15973, 2:240 (hereafter cited as *Elgin Commission*).

3. For example, Samuels, *Command or Control?*, and Travers, *Killing Ground*.

4. Searle, *Quest for National Efficiency*, 50.

5. Ramsay, *Command and Cohesion*, 109.

6. Gatacre, "Few Notes on Hill-Fighting," 1066.

7. Quoted in Henderson, *Science of War*, 348–49.

8. For North-West Frontier experiences, see Gatacre, "Few Notes on Hill Fighting," 1076; for the weakness of pre-Boer War training, see Meinertzhagen, *Army Diary 1899–1926*, 15–16, and Pollock, "Battle Drill of Infantry," 540, 547.

9. Henderson, *Science of War*, 138–39.

10. Lord Methuen's Despatch on the Battle of Modder River, 1 December 1899, South Africa Despatches Nov. 1899–June 1900, TNA WO 108/237; Pakenham, *Boer War*, 312; and Symons, *Buller's Campaign*, 222.

11. Lord Methuen's Despatch on the Battle of Belmont, 30 December 1899, South Africa Despatches Nov. 1899–June 1900, TNA WO 108/237.

12. Notes for Guidance in South African Warfare, 5 February 1900, Lord Roberts Papers, TNA WO 105/40.

13. *Elgin Commission*, Q10447, 1:441.

14. Ibid., Q13247, 2:66.

15. Ibid., Q16481, 2:260.

16. Ibid., Q19688, 2:418.

17. Ibid., Q19189, 2:396.

18. Ibid., Q173, 1:7; and Q17620, 2:321.

19. Amery, *Times History*, 2:34–35.

20. Beedos, "Military Training," 78.

21. Garwood, "Realistic Targets," 935.

22. Balck, "Lessons of the Boer War," 1276.

23. Smith-Dorrien, *Forty-Eight Years' Service*, 141.

24. Pollock, "Tactical Inefficiency," 832.

25. Stellenbosch was a small South African town near Cape Town that was used as a remount station. Officers who had performed poorly in action were often banished here.

26. C. E. Howard Vincent, "Situation in South Africa," 15.

27. Smith-Dorrien, *Forty-Eight Years' Service*, 286.

28. For example, *Elgin Commission*, Q173, 1:7; Q174, 1:8; Q10320, 1:436; Q10442, 1:440; Q13145, 2:63; Q14193, 2:121; Q19299, 2:402.

29. MacDonald, "Infantry in a New Century," 243.

30. *Elgin Commission*, Q13941, 2:107–108.

31. Ibid., Q16772, 2:273.

32. Henderson, *Science of War*, 348; Ramsay, *Command and Cohesion*, 46.

33. MacDonald, "Infantry in a New Century," 251.

34. Inspector General of Forces (IGF) Report for 1904, p. 336, Army Council Minutes and IGF Annual Reports, TNA WO 163/10 (hereafter cited as "IGF Report," followed by the year of the report and item number from TNA WO).

35. Hamilton, "Training of Troops During 1906," 1522; Jay Stone and Schmidl, *Boer War and Military Reforms*, 117.

36. War Office, *Combined Training 1902*, 4.

37. Memorandum on Military Training 1905, 31 January 1905, Aldershot Command Papers, TNA WO 27/504; IGF Report for 1904, pp. 301, 321–22, TNA WO 163/10.

38. Jay Stone and Schmidl, *Boer War*, 117.

39. Ross, "Departments in War," 983–84; Memorandum on the Training of 1st Army Corps, 1905, Aldershot Command Papers, TNA WO 27/503.

40. Remarks on the Report of the Commandant, Practice Camp, Salisbury Plain, 26 October 1905, Aldershot Command Papers, TNA WO 27/504.

41. For steady progression in training, see IGF Report for 1904, pp. 321–22, TNA WO 163/10; IGF Report for 1905, pp. 155, 162, 199, 210, TNA WO 163/11; IGF Report for 1906, p. 36, TNA WO 163/12; and IGF Report for 1907, p. 5, TNA WO 163/13.

42. Army Manoeuvres 1904, p. 81. TNA WO 279/8.

43. IGF Report for 1907, p. 19, TNA WO 163/13.

44. Amery, *The Problem of the Army*, 182.

45. "Report on a Conference of General Staff Officers at the Staff College, 2–12 January 1906," p. 32, Joint Services Command and Staff College Library.

46. IGF Report for 1904, pp. 321–22, TNA WO 163/10.

47. IGF Report for 1912, p. 566, TNA WO 163/19.

48. Campbell, "Infantry in Battle," 353.

49. *Elgin Commission*, "Précis of Evidence by Lieut.-General Sir A. Hunter," 2:615.

50. IGF Report for 1906, pp. 73–74, TNA WO 163/12; Jay Stone and Schmidl, *Boer War*, 117.

51. In 1901, the minimum height requirement had been dropped from 5 feet 3 inches to 5 feet. See Judd and Surridge, *Boer War*, 60.

52. Quoted in ibid., 60.

53. Stephen Miller, *Volunteers on the Veld*, 154–55.

54. Ramsay, *Command and Cohesion*, 6, 56.

55. Grierson, Notes on Return from South Africa, TNA WO 108/184; Old Soldier, "Retrospect of a Successful Campaign," 79.

56. Hamilton, "Remarks on Training of Troops 1907," 93.

57. Red Coat, "Concerning Individuality," 66.

58. Army Council Comments on IGF Report for 1906, pp. 73–74, TNA WO 163/12.

59. Ibid.

60. Ramsay, *Command and Cohesion*, 56, 64.

61. Ibid., 64.

62. Bedan, "How Can Moral Qualities Best Be Developed," 132; Ramsay, *Command and Cohesion*, 64.

63. Ellis, *History of the Machine Gun*, 19.

64. Quoted in Arthur, *Forgotten Voices of the Great War*, 21.

65. Falls, *Official History of the Great War 1917*, 1, 554.

66. G. C. W. [Graeme Chamley Wynne], *Ypres 1914*, 17, 74.

67. Beckett, *Ypres*, 38; Ascoli, *Mons Star*, 8.

68. *Elgin Commission*, Q15502, 2:213.

69. Gooch, *Plans of War*, 20.

70. Amery, *Problem of the Army*, 4.

71. *Elgin Commission*, Q16235, 2:251; Maurice, comment on "Lessons of the War," by Vincent, 658–59.

72. IGF Report for 1908, pp. 159, 161, TNA WO 163/14.

73. Memorandum on Military Training, 31 January 1905, Aldershot Command Papers, TNA WO 27/504.

74. IGF Report for 1907, pp. 6–7, TNA WO 163/13.

75. IGF Report for 1911, p. 518, TNA WO 163/17.

76. "The irresistible urge to write."

77. Carter, "Our Failings in the Assault," 99.

78. War Office, *Infantry Training 1905*, 123.

79. *Combined Training 1905*, 99.

80. Ibid., 98.

81. War Office, *Field Service Regulations Part 1*, 14.

82. *Infantry Training 1905*, 135.

83. Luvaas, *Education of an Army*, 309; Barnett quoted in De Groot, *Douglas Haig 1861–1928*, 128.

84. Dunlop, *Development of the British Army*, 293.

85. *Field Service Regulations Part 1*, 13.

86. Ibid., 14 (emphasis in original).

87. IGF Report for 1912, pp. 566–68, TNA WO 163/18. The problems listed were employment of divisional cavalry (individual cavalry regiments

attached to infantry divisions), the use of advanced guards, deployment methods and use of reserves, and handling of encounter actions.

88. Ibid., 567–68.

89. Ibid., Army Council comment, 567–68.

90. Ibid., Army Council comment, 567.

91. Quoted in Morris, *Letters of Repington*, 109.

92. Gooch, *Plans of War*, 70–71, 82.

93. Bidwell and Graham, *Firepower*, 19.

94. IGF Report for 1907, p. 7, TNA WO 163/13. It is interesting to note that in his memoirs, Neville Lyttelton said little about his time as Chief of General Staff, never referring to it by its official title and instead categorizing it simply as "War Office work." See Lyttelton, *Eighty Years*, 270–75.

95. Samuels, *Command or Control?*, 58.

96. Army Council Comment on IGF Report for 1905, p. 212, TNA WO 163/11.

97. Quoted in Gooch, *Plans of War*, 118.

98. Rimington, *Our Cavalry*, 176 (emphasis in original).

99. Samuels, *Command or Control?*, 7–60. See also Travers, *Killing Ground*, 38–39, 41.

100. Travers, "The Offensive and Problem of Innovation," 539–40.

101. Ramsay, *Command and Cohesion*, 109.

102. Nasson, *South African War*, p. x.

103. Quoted in Ramsay, *Command and Cohesion*, 145.

104. Ibid., 145, 162.

105. For criticism of the operational handling of the BEF, see Gardner, *Trial by Fire*; for praise of the tactical skill of the army, see Terraine, *Mons*.

106. Bourne, *Britain and the Great War*, 28.

107. Bidwell and Graham, *Firepower*, 38.

108. Ramsay, *Command and Cohesion*, 162.

109. For sharply contrasting views on British attitudes toward firepower, see Leeson, "Playing at War," 460–61; Howard, "Men Against Fire," 43; and Ramsay, *Command and Cohesion*, 32.

110. Maurice, "Omdurman," 1054.

111. Henderson, *Science of War*, 339.

112. Amery, *Problem of the Army*, 405.

113. Smith-Dorrien, *Forty-Eight Years' Service*, 154.

114. Howard, "Men Against Fire," 46.

115. "The Boer War Through German Glasses," no pagination, Lord Roberts Papers, TNA WO 105/40.

116. Ibid.

117. Henderson, *Science of War*, 74.

118. *Elgin Commission*, Q13941, 2:108.

119. The elder brother of the famous Robert Baden-Powell.

120. Battine, "Offensive Versus Defensive," 655; Baden-Powell, B.F.S. *War in Practice*, 19–21.

121. Pakenham, *Boer War*, 168. In November 1899, many younger Boer leaders urged an offensive strategy but were held back by the hesitant Piet Joubert.

122. Battine, "Offensive Versus Defensive," 654.

123. War Office, *Infantry Training 1902*, 146–47.

124. Battine, "Offensive Versus Defensive," 663.

125. Ibid., 661.

126. Smith-Dorrien, *Forty-Eight Years' Service*, 337–38.

127. For example, see Ellis, *History of the Machine Gun*; Howard, "Men Against Fire," 44–57; Ramsay, *Command and Cohesion*; and Travers, *Killing Ground*.

128. Travers, "Technology, Tactics and Morale," 272–74.

129. Haig, "Army Training in India," 76.

130. Major Rooke, "Shielded Infantry," 772.

131. Howard, "Men Against Fire," 54.

132. Snyder, *Ideology of the Offensive*, 77–81.

133. Reports on Manchuria, p. 125, TNA WO 33/350.

134. Hamilton, *Staff Officer's Scrap Book*, 1:151.

135. Heath, "Field Engineering," 314–16. Japanese Pioneer units that led assaults were reported as suffering 75 percent casualties on one occasion.

136. Craster, "Attack of Entrenched Positions," 342.

137. Snyder, *Ideology of the Offensive*, 78.

138. Sheffy, "Model Not to Follow," 263–64.

139. Snyder, *Ideology of the Offensive*, 80.

140. Kuropatkin, *Russian Army and the Japanese War*, 2:80.

141. Quoted in Barret, "Lessons Learned from the Russo-Japanese War," 813.

142. Kowner, "Between a Colonial Clash and World War Zero," 12–13.

143. Travers, *Killing Ground*, 43.

144. Quoted in ibid., 44.

145. *Field Service Regulations Part I*, 13.

146. *Combined Training 1905*, 100; *Field Service Regulations Part I*, 144.

147. Travers, "Technology, Tactics and Morale," 275.

148. "Report on a Conference of General Staff Officers at the Staff College, 17–20 January, 1910," p. 28, Joint Services Command and Staff College Library.

149. Samuels, *Command or Control?*, 102.

150. General Staff Conference 1910, p. 28, Joint Services Command and Staff College Library.

151. "Report on a Conference of General Staff Officers at the Royal Military College, 12–15 January, 1914," p. 73, Joint Services Command and Staff College Library; Ramsay, *Command and Cohesion*, 109.

152. W. D. Bird, "Some Notes on Modern Tactics," 492.

153. "Report on a Conference of General Staff Officers at the Staff College, 9–12 January 1911," pp. 11–13, 28; and General Staff Conference 1914, pp. 75–76, 95, both in Joint Services Command and Staff College Library.

154. May, "Freedom of Manoeuvre," 445.

155. Rooke, "Shielded Infantry," 773.

156. Travers, "Technology, Tactics and Morale," 277.

157. Ramsay, *Command and Cohesion*, 109.

158. Samuels, *Command or Control?*, 124–58, 230–70.

159. Cox, "Of Aphorisms, Lessons, and Paradigms," 397–98.

160. Gudmundsson, *Stormtroop Tactics*, 13; Jackman, "Shoulder to Shoulder," 103–104.

161. Terraine, *Mons*, 83; Beckett, *Ypres*, 48–49.

162. Porch, *March to the Marne*, 214–15.

163. Ibid., 215.

164. Ibid., 216–17.

165. Report on French Manoeuvres 1912, p. 20, Report on Foreign Manoeuvres, TNA WO 33/618.

166. Edmonds, *Official History of the Great War* 1:465.

167. Cave and Sheldon, *Le Cateau*, 13–14.

168. Ibid., 11–19.

3. INFANTRY

1. *Elgin Commission*, Q4104, 1:173; Q16235, 2:251.

2. Spiers, "Reforming Infantry of the Line," 94.

3. Van Creveld, *Technology and War*, 171–74.

4. Quoted in Amery, *Times History*, 2:59.

5. Pollock, "Smokeless Powder and Entrenchments," 806.

6. For example, see *Elgin Commission*, Q15483, 2:212, and Q16594, 2:264, for views that British shooting was better than that of the Boers.

7. Not A Staff Officer, "Some Remarks on Recent Changes," 47.

8. *Elgin Commission*, Q12441, 2:19.

9. Quoted in Amery, *Times History*, 2:164.

10. L. M. Phillips, *With Rimington*, 8.

11. Also known as the Battle of Graspan.

12. A formation of volunteers drawn from the Royal Marines and Royal Navy. Although sometimes referred to as the "Bluejacket Brigade," they were dressed and equipped as per regular infantry.

13. Lord Methuen's Despatch, 26 November 1899, South Africa Despatches Nov. 1899–June 1900, TNA WO 108/237.

14. Amery, *Times History*, 2:338–39, suggests 44 percent casualties. Maurice, *History of the War in South Africa*, 1:242, suggests 47 percent.

15. Pakenham, *Boer War*, 225; Maurice, *History of the War in South Africa*, 1:353–57.

16. Conan Doyle, *Great Boer War*, 93.

17. Quoted in Pakenham, *Boer War*, 232.

18. For example, see Gunter, "German View of British Tactics," 801–802.

19. Meinertzhagen, *Army Diary 1899–1926*, 15–16.

20. Maurice, *History of the War in South Africa*, 1:131.

21. See for example Hamilton, *Fighting of the Future*.

22. Lee, *A Soldier's Life*, 49; Amery, *Times History*, 2:184.

23. "Notes for Guidance in South African Warfare," 26 January 1900, Lord Roberts Papers, TNA WO 105/40.

24. *Elgin Commission*, Q13247, 2:66; Q16772, 2:273.

25. Gatacre, "Few Notes on Hill Fighting," 1072.

26. Quoted in Ram, "Observations on the War in South Africa," 50.

27. "Notes for Guidance in South African Warfare," 26 January 1900, Lord Roberts Papers, TNA WO 105/40.

28. *Elgin Commission*, Q16974, 2:286.

29. Ibid., Q15694, 2:226.

30. Ibid., Q17468, 2:313.

31. Lyttelton, *Eighty Years*, 220.

32. Ram, "Observation on the War in South Africa," 50.

33. "Military Observations of the War in South Africa," 357.

34. Ibid.; Gunter, "German View of British Tactics," 804.

35. *Elgin Commission*, Q16772, 2:273.

36. Pakenham, *Boer War*, 312; Symons, *Buller's Campaign*, 222.

37. Pakenham, *Boer War*, 151.

38. Ratzenhofer, "Retrospect of the War in South Africa," 41.

39. C. E. Howard Vincent, "Lessons of the War," 635.

40. Pakenham, *Boer War*, 312; Symons, *Buller's Campaign*, 222.

41. 3rd Division Inspection, 24–29 July 1905, Aldershot Command Papers, TNA WO 27/502.

42. "Tactical Points" (n.d.), Aldershot Command Papers, TNA WO 27/504; Memorandum on the Training of I Army Corps 1905, 31 January 1905, Aldershot Command Papers, TNA WO 27/503.

43. 1st Division Defensive Work, 27 June 1904, Aldershot Command Papers, TNA WO 27/501.

44. Amery, *Problem of the Army*, 46.

45. *Elgin Commission*, Q16974, 2:288.

46. Lord Roberts comments on "The Boer War Through German Glasses," Lord Roberts Papers, TNA WO 105/40; Battine, "Offensive Versus Defensive," 668.

47. Maude, "Continental Versus South African Tactics," 324.

48. Lord Roberts comments on "The Boer War Through German Glasses," Lord Roberts Papers, TNA WO 105/40.

49. British musketry regulations defined 1,400 yards as the limit of effective fire, with fire beyond that considered "long" (1,400–2,000 yards) or "distant" (2,500–2,800 yards). See War Office, *Combined Training 1905*, 100.

50. "Some Considerations Connected with formations of Infantry in Attack and Defence," p. 7, Aldershot Command Papers, TNA WO 27/505.

51. War Office, *Combined Training 1905*, 100–101.

52. W. D. Bird, "Infantry Fire Tactics," 1176.

53. Reports on Manchuria, p. 73, TNA WO 33/350.

54. De Negrier, "Some Lessons of the Russo-Japanese War," 912.

55. Hamilton, *Staff Officer's Scrap Book*, 1:307.

56. Mitake, "Infantry Battlefront," 329–30.

57. Barret, "Lessons Learned from the Russo-Japanese War," 815–16.

58. Neilsen, "Dangerous and Difficult Enterprise," 31.

59. Reports on Foreign Militaries: The Japanese Army, Reports on Foreign Militaries, TNA WO 33/425.

60. Army Council Précis 1908, Précis 385, pp. 6, 73–74, Army Council Minutes and IGF Annual Report, TNA WO 163/13.

61. Hamilton, "Training of Troops During 1906," 1522.

62. IGF Report for 1907, p. 80, TNA WO 163/13.

63. IGF Report for 1908, p. 169, TNA WO 163/14.

64. F. C. Carter, "Our Failings in 'The Assault,'" 99.

65. Ibid., 104.

66. Turner, "Corps Manoeuvres of the German XIV," 629.

67. Rooke, "Shielded Infantry," 771–73.

68. Solando, "The Decisive Range," 296.

69. Towle, "Influence of the Russo-Japanese War," 17–18.

70. Hamilton, "Remarks on the Training of Troops 1907," 89–90.

71. Remarks by Lieutenant-General Sir C. W. Douglas on the Training of Troops in the Command During 1909, p. 4, Southern Command Training 1909, TNA WO 279/524.

72. IGF Report for 1913, p. 334, TNA WO 163/20.

73. Army Council Comment on IGF Report, p. 334, TNA WO 163/20.

74. War Office, *Infantry Training 1911*, 111–15.

75. War Office, *Notes from the Front, Part II*, 3.

76. Gough memorandum, 27 September 1914, War Diary, I Corps, August–October 1914, TNA WO 95/588.

77. Quoted in Arthur, *Forgotten Voices of the Great War*, 35.

78. Ibid., 35.

79. De Thomasson, "British Army Exercise of 1913," 149.

80. Lyttelton, *Eighty Years*, 212.

81. Mead, "Notes on Musketry Training," 250–51.

82. Ibid., 250. The captain of each company received forty rounds, and the battalion colonel received forty-one. The lazy attitude of many officers toward musketry training incensed reformists. See Bailes, "Technology and Tactics," 42–43.

83. For example, see Colleton, "Training of a Battalion in the Attack," 140; Swanton, "Collective Practices," 923.

84. Jackson, *Record of a Regiment of the Line*, 21.

85. "Military Observations of the War in South Africa," 356.

86. *Elgin Commission*, Q6859, 1:294.

87. Murray, "Musketry and Tactics," 653; Grierson, *Scarlet into Khaki*, 137.

88. "Lessons of South African and Chinese Wars," 292.

89. Gunter, "German View of British Tactics," 803–804.

90. *Elgin Commission*, Q16772, 2:72.

91. *Elgin Commission*, Q15483, 2:212; Forbes, "Experiences in South Africa," 1389.

92. *Elgin Commission*, Q15697, 2:226.

93. Quoted in Balck, "Lessons of the Boer War," 1276.

94. Ibid., 1276.

95. Wessels, *Lord Roberts and War in South Africa*, 203–204.

96. Lyttelton, *Eighty Years*, 238–39.

97. Jay Stone and Schmidl, *Boer War and Military Reforms*, 80.

98. *Elgin Commission*, Q13941, 2:108.

99. Ibid.

100. Baillie-Grohman, "Marksmanship, Old and New," 756–57.

101. Extracts from Reports of Officers Commanding Units in South Africa 1899–1901: Rifles, Carbines and Small Arm Ammunition, Rifle reports, report no. 102, TNA WO 108/272.

102. *Elgin Commission*, Q6859, 1:294.

103. Army Order, 1 September 1902, R/122/4/325, Lord Roberts Papers, National Army Museum.

104. *Combined Training 1905*, 100.

105. *Elgin Commission*, Q10426, 2:439.

106. Army Council 1904, Précis 113, p. 281, Army Council Minutes and IGF Annual Report, TNA WO 163/9.

107. Ibid.

108. War Office, *Musketry Regulations Part 1, 1909*, 254–55.

109. Army Council 1907, Précis 359, p. 154, Army Council Minutes and IGF Annual Report TNA WO 163/12.

110. Ibid., 154–55. The only general officer commanding who did not dissent was G.O.C North China.

111. Stewart, "Hythe and its School of Musketry," 484.

112. "K," "Suggestions for Improvement of Course of Musketry," 300.

113. Van Emden, *Tickled to Death to Go*, 23–24.

114. Gordon, comment on "Notes on Musketry Training of Troops," 254.

115. Smith-Dorrien, *Memories of Forty-Eight Years' Service*, 359.

116. Ibid.

117. War Office, *Musketry Regulations Part 1, 1909*, 258–61.

118. Ibid.

119. Ibid., 56, 122, 191.

120. Ibid., 260.

121. Van Emden, *Tickled to Death*, 24; Pridham, *Superiority of Fire*, 56–57.

122. Pridham, *Superiority of Fire*, 57.

123. *Musketry Regulations 1909*, 200–204.

124. Comments on the Training Season 1913, p. 11, Aldershot Command Papers, TNA WO 279/32.

125. Ibid., p.12.

126. The official name for the rifle was the "Short, Magazine, Lee-Enfield," usually abbreviated to SMLE.

127. Hogg and Weeks, *Military Small Arms*, 101.

128. Pridham, *Superiority of Fire*, 54; "Report on a Conference of General Staff Officers at the Staff College, 17–20 January 1910," pp. 25–28, Joint Services Command and Staff College Library.

129. Quoted in Pridham, *Superiority of Fire*, 56.

130. Edmonds, *Official History of the Great War*, 2:463.

131. Samuels, *Command or Control?*, 102–103; Travers, *Killing Ground*, 67.

132. Edmonds's writing on the topic has been bluntly described as "disinformation." See Graham, "British Expeditionary Force in 1914," 192.

133. "Report on a Conference of General Staff Officers at the Staff College, 2–11 January 1906," p. 118, Joint Services Command and Staff College Library.

134. *Combined Training 1905*, 100.

135. W. D. Bird, "Infantry Fire Tactics," 1177.

136. "Infantry Combat in Russo-Japanese War," 1169–75.

137. "Report on a Conference of General Staff Officers at the Staff College, 17–20 January 1910," p. 26, Joint Services Command and Staff College Library.

138. Tudor, "Collective Fire," 1023.

139. *Combined Training 1905*, p.100; War Office, *Field Service Regulations Part 1: Operations 1909*, 144.

140. Samuels, *Command or Control?*, 102; Travers, *Killing Ground*, 67.

141. General Staff Conference 1910, p. 26, Minutes of pre-1914 General Staff meetings, Joint Services Command and Staff College Library.

142. IGF Report for 1907, p. 84, TNA WO 163/13.

143. IGF Report for 1910, pp. 247–48, TNA WO 163/16.

144. IGF Report for 1911, pp. 513–14, TNA WO 163/17.

145. IGF Report for 1913, p. 384, TNA WO 163/20; "Report on a Conference of General Staff Officers at the Royal Military College, 12–15 January 1914," p. 73, Joint Services Command and Staff College Library.

146. For the higher figures, see Ascoli, *Mons Star*, 73; and Holmes, *Riding the Retreat*, 130. For the lower figure, see Zuber, *Mons Myth*, 167.

147. von Kluck, *March on Paris*, 48.

148. For reconsideration of the casualties on both sides at Le Cateau, see Cave and Sheldon, *Le Cateau*, 9; for an alternative viewpoint, see Antony Bird, *Stand and Fight*, 145–53.

149. Quoted in Holmes, *Riding the Retreat*, 128.

150. Quoted in Adcock, *In the Firing Lines*, 24–25.

151. Quoted in Cave and Sheldon, *Le Cateau*, 159.

152. Quoted in Zuber, *Mons Myth*, 250–51.

153. Bloem, *Advance from Mons 1914*, 43.

154. Quoted in Zuber, *Mons Myth*, 229.

155. Terraine, *Mons*, 83, 85.

156. *Notes from the Front*, 2; Bidwell and Graham, *Firepower*, 67.

157. G. C. W. [Graeme Chamley Wynne], *Ypres 1914*, pp. x–xi, xvi, 17, 74; Edmonds, *Official History of the Great War*, 2:462–63.

158. G. C. W. [Graeme Chamley Wynne], *Ypres 1914*, 17.

159. Ellis, *History of the Machine Gun*, 16–17; Samuels, *Command or Control?*, 100–101; Travers, *Killing Ground*, 62–65.

160. Extracts from Reports of Officers Commanding Units in South Africa 1899–1901: Machine Guns, Mounted Infantry report no.1, TNA WO 108/267.

161. The 37 mm Maxim-Nordernfelt gun, better known as the pom-pom, was the first modern example of an autocannon. It was capable of firing 1-pound explosive shells at a rate of up to 200 rounds a minute. The pom-pom name was derived from the distinctive sound of the gun firing. Although manufactured in Britain, the British Army had rejected the chance to purchase any of the guns prior to the war. Conversely, the Boers had imported a number of pom-pom guns, and these weapons caused a considerable stir in the early battles of the war.

162. Infantry report no. 50, Reports from South Africa on machine guns, TNA WO 108/267.

163. Infantry report no. 92, in ibid.

164. R. G. Clarke, "Machine Guns," 99.

165. See Reports from South Africa on machine guns, TNA WO 108/267. For example: Mounted Infantry reports no. 8 and no. 14; Infantry reports no. 6, no. 49, no. 87.

166. Infantry report no. 32, Reports from South Africa on machine guns, TNA WO 108/267.

167. Infantry report no. 75, in ibid.

168. W. D. Bird, "Russian Machine Guns at Liao-Yang," 1502–503.

169. Takenouchii, "Tactical Employment of Machine Guns," 452–53.

170. Applin, "Machine Gun Tactics," 41–45.

171. Evans, "From Drill to Doctrine," 129.

172. Committee on Pom-Poms and Machine Guns, TNA WO 32/9029.

173. Congreve, Comment on "Machine Gun Tactics," 63.

174. Ibid. Although the article was published in 1910, it was a transcript of a lecture given in the previous year.

175. IGF report for 1910, p. 246, TNA WO 163/16; IGF Report for 1911, p. 516, TNA WO 163/18; IGF Report for 1912, p. 624, TNA WO 163/19.

176. Ellis, *History of the Machine Gun*, 70.

177. Bidwell and Dominick, *Firepower*, 53–56.

178. J. E. Carter, "From Enslin to Bloemfontein," 146.

179. Wessels, *Lord Roberts and War in South Africa*, 59.

180. Duxbury, *Battle of Magersfontein*, 2.

181. Ibid., 7.

182. Maurice, *History of the War in South Africa*, 1:316–18.

183. Amery, *Times History*, 2:386–87; Duxbury, *Battle of Magersfontein*, 2.

184. Grierson, *Scarlet into Khaki*, 166–67.

185. *Elgin Commission*, Q16003, 2:242; Q20215, 2:444.

186. Maurice, comment on "Lessons of the War," 657.

187. *Elgin Commission*, Q17888, 2:331.

188. Ibid., Q15972, 2:238–239.

189. Ibid., Q16003, 2:242.

190. Ibid., Q16004, 2:242.

191. Ibid., Q18010, 2:337.

192. Quoted in C. E. Howard Vincent, "Lessons of the War," 657.

193. Quoted in *Elgin Commission*, Q17888, 2:331.

194. Swinton, *Defence of Duffer's Drift*, 165.

195. *Elgin Commission*, Q16600, 2:264; Q16924, 2:282.

196. Ibid., Q17888, 2:331.

197. Ibid., Q16635, 2:267.

198. Ibid., Q18010, 2:337.

199. Notes by Colonel J. M. Grierson R. A. on Return from South Africa, TNA WO 108/184.

200. *Elgin Commission*, Q13941, 2:107.

201. IGF Report 1905, p. 214, TNA WO 163/11.

202. *Infantry Training 1911*, 175–76.

203. Inspection of 1st Division, 27 June 1904, Aldershot Command Papers, TNA WO 27/501.

204. Inspection of 2nd Division 10 August 1905, Aldershot Command Papers, TNA WO 27/502.

205. Memorandum on the Training of I Army Corps 1905, 31 January 1905, Aldershot Command Papers, TNA WO 27/503.

206. IGF Report for 1908, p. 219, TNA WO 163/14.

207. IGF Report for 1910, p. 221, TNA WO 163/16.

208. See variously, IGF Report for 1910, p. 243, TNA WO 163/16; IGF Report for 1911, pp. 476, 514–15, TNA WO 163/17; IGF Report for 1912, p. 627, TNA WO 163/18.

209. IGF Report for 1913, p. 383, TNA WO 163/20.

210. Hamilton, "Remarks on Training of Troops 1908," 1557.

211. Ascoli, *Mons Star*, 8.

212. "Report on a Conference of General Staff Officers, 15–18 January 1912," p. 57, Joint Services Command and Staff College Library.

213. Report on Army Manoeuvres 1909, p. 112, TNA WO279/31.

214. Report on Army Manoeuvres 1910, p. 152, TNA WO 279/39.

215. "Report on a Conference of General Staff Officers, 15–18 January 1912," p. 74, Joint Services Command and Staff College Library.

216. *Field Service Regulations Part I: 1909*, 146. This line was reiterated in *Infantry Training 1911*, 132–33. Emphasis in the original.

217. Quoted in Adcock, *In the Firing Lines*, 24.

218. Anthony Bird, *Stand and Fight*, 58.

219. Ibid., 83.

220. For example, *Notes from the Front*, 2.

4. ARTILLERY

1. Bidwell and Graham, *Firepower*, 11–12, 19.

2. Scales, "Artillery in Small Wars," 314.

3. Spiers, "Rearming the Edwardian Artillery," 176.

4. *Elgin Commission*, Q1673, 1:79.

5. Ibid.

6. Ibid.

7. Amery, *Times History*, 2:81.

8. N. F. Gordon, "Experience of War in South Africa," 258.

9. Buller's Despatch on Colenso, 17 December 1899, South Africa Despatches, Nov. 1899–June 1900, TNA WO 108/237.

10. Quoted in Powell, *Buller: A Scapegoat?*, 150.

11. Pakenham, *Boer War*, 231.

12. Headlam, *History of the Royal Artillery*, 3:377–80.

13. Powell, *Buller: A Scapegoat?*, 150.

14. Diary of Major H. de Montmorency, no date, p. 62, TNA WO 108/185.

15. Headlam, *History of the Royal Artillery*, 3:340.

16. "Notes for Guidance in South African Warfare," 26 January 1900, Lord Roberts Papers, TNA WO 105/40.

17. Amery, *Times History*, 2:182; Headlam, *History of the Royal Artillery*, 3:514.

18. Pakenham, *Boer War*, 41.

19. Bailes, "Military Aspects of the War," 70; Nasson, *South African War*, 59.

20. *Elgin Commission*, Q1680, 1:80–81.

21. N. F. Gordon, "Experience of War in South Africa," 251.

22. *Elgin Commission*, Q10569, 1:448; Reports on Artillery Equipment in South Africa: Heavy Artillery, p. 17, TNA WO 108/266.

23. Morrison, "Lessons Derived from South Africa," 797.

24. *Elgin Commission*, Q1682, 1:82.

25. Ibid., Q19192, 2:388.

26. Ibid., Q1680, 1:82.

27. Reports on Artillery Equipment in South Africa: Heavy Artillery, p. 21, TNA 108/266; Headlam, *History of the Royal Artillery*, 3:394.

28. Reports on Heavy Artillery, see pp. 1–3, responses to question (a), TNA 108/266.

29. *Elgin Commission*, Q14657, 2:142.

30. Owen, comment on "Lessons of the War," 641–42.

31. Reports on Heavy Artillery, p. 103, TNA 108/266.

32. *Elgin Commission*, Q15471, 2:211; Q15850, 2:233.

33. For example: Dawson, "Modern Artillery," 462; Morrison, "Lessons Derived from South Africa," 798.

34. *Elgin Commission*, Q14654, 2:141.

35. Ibid., Q18562, 2:364.

36. Ibid., Q1674, 1:79–81.

37. War Office, *Combined Training 1905*, 100.

38. *Elgin Commission*, Q1674, 1:79.

39. Headlam, *History of the Royal Artillery*, 2:52–53.

40. Army Council Précis 1904–Précis 77, p. 199, Army Council Minutes and Inspector General of Forces Annual Report, TNA WO 163/9.

41. *Elgin Commission*, Q13941, 2:111.

42. Ibid., Q17932, 2:333.

43. Army Council Précis 1904–Précis 77, p. 188, Army Council Minutes and Inspector General of Forces Annual Report, TNA WO 163/9.

44. Ibid., p. 193.

45. Ibid., pp. 206–207.

46. Ibid., pp. 188–207.

47. Quoted in Headlam, *History of the Royal Artillery*, 2:82.

48. Ibid. Although it was considered obsolete following the Boer War, the 4.7 inch gun remained in service with the heavy batteries of the Territorial Divisions, and the guns served in World War 1 on the Western Front until April 1917. A handful remained in service in other theaters of war until the very end of the conflict.

49. Scales, "Artillery in Small Wars," 259.

50. McHardy, "On Heavy Artillery," 54.

51. Scales, "Artillery in Small Wars," 259.

52. Inglefield, "Remarks on the Royal Artillery," 505–508.

53. Nicolls, "Training, Organisation and Equipment," 102.

54. Nicolls, "Type of Guns," 227.

55. Churchill, "Impressions of War in South Africa," 839; see also McHardy, "On Heavy Artillery," 59–60.

56. Ducrot, "Guns in South Africa," 204.

57. Wynter, "Experience of War in South Africa," 270.

58. Stone, "Employment of Heavy Artillery in the Field," 2–3.

59. Bethell, "Experience of War in South Africa," 137.

60. School of Gunnery Reports 1905–1913, pp. 7, 12, Royal Artillery Museum.

61. Burney, "Role of Heavy Artillery," 503. Heavy artillery pieces were known as "cow guns" because of the practice of using oxen to drag them in South Africa.

62. Ibid., 503; Stone, "Employment of Heavy Artillery," 14.

63. Callwell, "Use of Heavy Guns," 5.

64. *Combined Training 1905*, 117.

65. Stone, "Employment of Heavy Artillery," 11–12.

66. Ibid., 7–8; Weber, "A Plea for the Artillery Arm," 248–52.

67. Belfield, comment on "Employment of Heavy Artillery," 16.

68. Burney, "Role of Heavy Artillery," 503.

69. General Staff Translation, "Russo-Japanese War: Opinions and Criticisms," 789.

70. Scales, "Artillery in Small Wars," 262–63.

71. McHardy, "Heavy Artillery," 54. Interestingly, the French Army speculated that the large allocation of German heavy artillery was a direct response to the superiority of the French 75 mm field gun at close to medium range. See Ripperger, "Development of French Artillery," 602, 605.

72. Terraine, *Mons*, 28.

73. Becke, *Royal Regiment of Artillery*, 60, 62.

74. Ibid., 38.

75. Farndale, *History of Royal Regiment of Artillery*, 385.

76. Callwell, "Use of Heavy Guns," 5. However, at Le Cateau the heavy batteries appeared to have been deployed as a whole.

77. War Office, *Field Service Regulations Part 1*, 17.

78. Bailey, *Field Artillery and Firepower*, 229.

79. Ibid., 232.

80. Ripperger, "Development of French Artillery," 599–605.

81. General Staff, *Report on Foreign Manoeuvres in 1912*, 28.

82. Ripperger, "Development of French Artillery," 606.

83. Quoted in Porch, *March to the Marne*, 236.

84. Ibid., p. vii.

85. Ibid., 233.

86. Ibid., 242.

87. Ibid., 218–19.

88. *Elgin Commission*, Q18522, 2:362.

89. van Heister, "Orange Free State Artillery," 189.

90. "Further Notes for Guidance in South African Warfare," 5 February 1900, Lord Roberts Papers, TNA WO 105/40.

91. Quoted in Carver, *National Army Museum Book of Boer War*, 22.

92. Ibid., 23.

93. *Elgin Commission*, Q14817, 2:153.

94. Notes by Colonel J. M. Grierson R. A. on Return from South Africa, TNA WO 108/184.

95. Wynter, "Experience of War in South Africa," 275.

96. *Elgin Commission*, Q17928, 2:333.

97. Bailey, *Field Artillery*, 213.

98. Callwell, "Artillery Notes from the Veld," 286.

99. Ibid., 286.

100. Wynter, "Experience of War in South Africa," 277.

101. *Elgin Commission*, Q13247, 2:66; Q13941, 2:111; Q15850, 2:233.

102. Ibid., Q15850, 2:233.

103. Headlam, *History of the Royal Artillery*, 3:515. For further discussion on the topic, see Gillings, "Indirect Artillery Fire," 182–83.

104. Ibid., 2:61, 2:154–55.

105. Quoted in DuCane, "Cover and Co-Operation," 358.

106. Memorandum on the Training of the I Army Corps, 28 September 1904, Aldershot Command Papers, TNA WO 27/503.

107. Hamilton, "Training of Troops 1906," 1519.

108. Reports on the Campaign in Manchuria, 11–12, TNA WO 33/350.

109. Kirton, "With the Japanese on the Yalu," 277.

110. Lieutenant-General Sir M. Gerard to Army Council, 9 September 1904, Reports from the Russian Army in Manchuria, TNA WO 106/39.

111. De Negrier, "Lessons of Russo-Japanese War," 805.

112. Reports on the Campaign in Manchuria, p. 15, TNA WO 33/350.

113. Ibid., 13–14.

114. De Negrier, "Lessons of Russo-Japanese War," 808.

115. Headlam, *History of the Royal Artillery*, 2:61.

116. *Elgin Commission*, Q4346, 1:185.

117. School of Gunnery Reports 1905–1913, p. 9, Royal Artillery Museum.

118. Cadell, "Best Position for Quick-Firing Artillery," 1478.

119. Ibid., 1489.

120. Ibid., 1479–80.

121. Hamilton, *Staff Officer's Scrap Book*, 1:225.

122. Carrier, "Correspondence Re: Best Position," 109.

123. IGF Report for 1906, p. 30, TNA WO 163/12.

124. Headlam, *History of the Royal Artillery*, 2:193n.

125. "Rafale" literally translates to "squall" in English, but in French it implies sudden, violent winds.

126. Charles Repington to Ian Hamilton, 1 November 1910, Hamilton Papers 7/3/14/4, Liddell Hart Centre for Military Archives.

127. For example, Holmes Wilson, "QF Artillery in the Field," 192–98.

128. IGF Report for 1910, p. 224, TNA WO 163/16.

129. IGF Report for 1911, pp. 495–96, TNA WO 163/17.

130. Ibid., p. 498; IGF Report for 1912, p. 587, TNA WO 163/18.

131. Report of a Committee appointed to carry out certain Field Artillery trials on Salisbury Plain, pp. 47–65, Army Council Minutes and IGF Annual Reports, TNA WO 163/17.

132. Ibid., p. 51.

133. Ibid., p. 45.

134. IGF Report for 1907, pp. 79–80, TNA WO 163/13.

135. IGF Report for 1908, pp. 159–160, TNA WO 163/14.

136. Bidwell and Graham, *Firepower*, 15.

137. Scales, "Artillery in Small Wars," 323.

138. Holmes, *Riding the Retreat*, 179.

139. Becke, *Royal Regiment of Artillery*, 53, 83–84.

140. IGF Report for 1913, pp. 346–47, TNA WO 163/20.

141. Wynter, "Experience of War in South Africa," 267.

142. Headlam, *History of the Royal Artillery*, 3:243, 498.

143. "Detonation of Lyddite"—Major C. E Callwell's answer, p. 10, Reports from South Africa on heavy artillery, TNA WO 108/266.

144. Inglefield, "Remarks on Royal Artillery," 506.

145. Nicolls, comment on "Remarks on Royal Artillery," 521.

146. For example, *Elgin Commission*, Q15850 2:233; Q16313, 2:254; Q16520, 2:261.

147. See ibid., Q18533, 2:362, for a rebuttal of the common shell argument.

148. Ibid., Q18529, 2:362.

149. Ibid., Q14341, 2:128.

150. Ibid., Q15850, 1:233.

151. Hamilton-Gordon, "Fourteen Days' Howitzer Work," 351.

152. Notes by Colonel J. M. Grierson R. A. on Return from South Africa, TNA WO 108/184.

153. IGF Report for 1905, 176–77, Army Council Minutes and IGF Annual Reports, TNA WO 163/11.

154. Hezlet, "Role of Field Howitzers," 55.

155. Notes by Colonel J. M. Grierson R. A. on Return from South Africa, TNA WO 108/184.

156. Wade, "Tactical role of Field Howitzer," 409.

157. Levita, "Plea for Connection between Infantry and Field Howitzers," 37.

158. Ibid., 38–39.

159. Bailey, *Field Artillery*, 221.

160. Ibid., 221.

161. For example, Nicolls, "Type of Guns," 364.

162. Headlam, *History of the Royal Artillery*, 2:179.

163. Scales, "Artillery in Small Wars," 302.

164. IGF Report for 1909, p. 298, TNA WO 163/15.

165. Bailey, *Field Artillery*, 233.

166. For example, see IGF Report for 1912, p. 587, TNA WO 163/18.

167. Bailey, *Field Artillery*, 221n72.

168. Headlam, *History of the Royal Artillery*, 2:43.

169. Ibid., 3:382.

170. Head, "Desirability of Acquirement," 1176.

171. "Heavy Artillery at River Crossings," 166.

172. Lord Methuen's Despatch, 15 February 1900, South Africa Despatches Nov. 1899–June 1900, TNA WO 108/237.

173. Duxbury, *Battle of Modder River*, 2–3.

174. N. F. Gordon, "Future of Q.F. Field Artillery," 187. Emphasis in the original.

175. Amery, *Times History*, 2:165–66.

176. Ibid., 3:256.

177. Quoted in Gore-Browne, "Best Methods," 306.

178. Ibid., 306.

179. Weber, "Employment of Divisional Artillery," 358–59.

180. Amery, *Times History*, 3:502.

181. An improvised defensive position built from rocks and stones.

182. Lord Roberts's Despatch, 28 March 1900, South Africa Despatches Nov. 1899–June 1900, TNA WO 108/237.

183. Quoted in Maurice, *History of the War in South Africa*, 2:509.

184. Lord Roberts Despatch, 28 March 1900, South Africa Despatches Nov. 1899–June 1900, TNA WO 108/237.

185. Dawnay, "Artillery and Infantry," 55. See also "Correspondence—Artillery Support of Infantry," 665.

186. Maurice, *History of the War in South Africa*, 3:398–99.

187. Lord Roberts Despatch, 28 March 1900, South Africa Despatches Nov. 1899–June 1900, TNA WO 108/237.

188. *Elgin Commission*, Q16924, 2:282.

189. IGF Report for 1904, pp. 306–307, TNA WO 163/10.

190. Head, "Desirability of Acquirement," 1173–74.

191. Spiers, "Rearming the Edwardian Artillery," 172.

192. For example, De Negrier, "Lessons of the Russo-Japanese War," 805.

193. "Combination in the Attack," 1198.

194. Quoted in Badsey, *Doctrine and Reform*, 200.

195. *Combined Training 1905*, 118.

196. Molyneux, "Artillery Support of Infantry," 1457; Knapp, "Tactical Employment of Pack Artillery, 722.

197. Atkinson, "Co-operation in Action between Artillery and Infantry," 334.

198. School of Gunnery Reports 1905–1913, p. 16, Royal Artillery Museum.

199. Atkinson, "Co-operation in Action," 334.

200. Crowe, "Artillery from Infantry Point of View," 78.

201. Outsider, "Artillery Training," 228.

202. DuCane, "Co-Operation of Field Artillery with Infantry," 104.

203. Ibid., 109.

204. Bidwell and Graham, *Firepower*, 56–57; Crookenden, "Co-Operation between Infantry and Artillery," 122.

205. *Field Service Regulations Part I: 1909*, 143.

206. War Office, *Field Artillery Training 1914*, 232 (emphasis in the original).

207. Bidwell and Graham, *Firepower*, 68.

208. Hamilton, *Staff Officer's Scrap Book*, 1:180–81. Hamilton was rather unimpressed with the use of telephone lines, feeling they would be cut by an aggressive, resourceful foe.

209. For example, Burney, "Role of Heavy Artillery," 500; Molyneux, "Artillery Support of Infantry," 1461–62.

210. Bryson, "Once and Future Army," 28–29.

211. Molyneux, "Artillery Support of Infantry," 1465.

212. Bailey, *Field Artillery*, 229.

213. Quoted in Dawnay, "Artillery and Infantry," 53.

214. Ibid., 49

215. *Field Service Regulations Part I: 1909*, 143.

216. Memorandum on the Training of I Army Corps 1905, 31 January 1905, Aldershot Command Papers, TNA WO 27/503.

217. Atkinson, "Co-operation in Action," 331.

218. Hamilton, "Remarks on Training of Troops 1908," 1152.

219. Hamilton, "Training of Troops 1906," 1525.

220. IGF Report for 1906 and Army Council comment, p. 58, TNA WO 163/12.

221. Gore-Browne, "Best Methods," 310.

222. Budworth, "Training and Action Necessary," 68; IGF Report for 1913, pp. 328–29, TNA WO 163/20.

223. Pakenham, *Boer War*, 361–62.

224. Bidwell and Graham, *Firepower*, 67–68.

225. Gardner, *Trial by Fire*, 86–88.

226. Bailey, *Field Artillery*, 246.

227. Beckett, *Ypres*, 135; Bidwell and Graham, *Firepower*, 83–84.

228. Bidwell and Graham, *Firepower*, 82.

229. Quoted in Spiers, "Rearming the Edwardian Artillery," 176.

5. CAVALRY

1. Difficulties imposed by local terrain and the high cost of keeping cavalry in the field militated against their large-scale deployment. Nevertheless, they were considered especially useful for reconnaissance and pursuit roles during colonial warfare. For example, see Gall, *Modern Tactics*, 132.

2. *Elgin Commission*, 4:97.

3. De Groot, *Douglas Haig 1861–1928*, 109; De Groot, "Educated Soldier or Cavalry Officer?," 65; Spiers, "British Cavalry, 1902–1914," 79; Ellis, *History of the Machine Gun*, 54–55.

4. Badsey, *Doctrine and Reform*, 229; Badsey, "Boer War and British Cavalry," 76; Gervase Phillips, "Obsolescence of the *Arme Blanche*," 39–41; Gervase Phillips, "Scapegoat Arm," 38.

5. Badsey, "Boer War and British Cavalry," 76.

6. Badsey, *Doctrine and Reform*, 77.

7. Spiers, *Late Victorian Army*, 260; Grierson, *Scarlet into Khaki*, 146.

8. Quoted in Bethune, "Uses of Cavalry and Mounted Infantry," 628.

9. Quoted in Scott, *Douglas Haig*, 132.

10. "Assegai" was a common name for the spears used by various native tribes throughout Africa and here refers to the lances of the British.

11. Viljoen, *Reminiscences of the Anglo–Boer War*, 34.

12. Scott, *Douglas Haig*, 131.

13. Holmes, *Little Field Marshal*, 14, 67.

14. Badsey, *Doctrine and Reform*, 103–104.

15. Amery, *Times History*, 3:393–95.

16. Ibid., 394–95.

17. Anglesey, *History of the British Cavalry*, 140–42.

18. Ibid., 142.

19. Extracts from Reports of Officers Commanding Units in South Africa 1899–1901: Rifles, Carbines and Bayonets, "Carbine General Serviceability"—Response no. 191, TNA WO 108/272.

20. *Elgin Commission*, Q15850, 2:233.

21. Defenders of the weapon included Redvers Buller and Michael Rimington. See "Carbine Accuracy"—Response no. 1, Reports from South Africa on rifles, carbines, ammunition and bayonets, TNA WO 108/272; and *Elgin Commission*, Q12687, 2:29, respectively.

22. *Elgin Commission*, Q7308, 1:311.

23. *Arme blanche* translates as "white weapon" and refers to edged and bladed weapons. The name is derived from the pale color of metallic weapons and from the white appearance that can be created when sunlight reflects on the surface of a blade. The phrase was popular in European armies of the early twentieth century. Arguably the closest equivalent in the English language is "cold steel."

24. Quoted in Cooper, *Haig*, 1:379.

25. "Opinions as to the Arming of the Cavalry with the Long Rifle," Lord Roberts Papers, TNA WO 105/29.

26. Vaughan, "Cavalry Notes," 452.

27. Anglesey, *History of the British Cavalry*, 4:236.

28. Ibid.; Extracts from Reports of Officers Commanding Units in South Africa 1899–1901: Swords and Lances: "Lance"—response no. 2, Reports from South Africa on swords, lances and pistols, TNA WO 108/273.

29. Anglesey, *History of the British Cavalry*, 4:236.

30. Smith-Dorrien, *Memories of Forty-Eight Years' Service*, 260–61.

31. Quoted in Scott, *Douglas Haig*, 189; Rimington, *Our Cavalry*, 74–75.

32. Anglesey, *History of the British Cavalry*, 4:264.

33. Amery, *Times History*, 5:338–41.

34. Anglesey, *History of the British Cavalry*, 4:266.

35. Quoted in ibid., 4:267.

36. Stephen Miller, *Lord Methuen and the British Army*, 229.

37. *Elgin Commission*, Q6780, 1:290; Q6843, 1:294; Q7044, 1:300–301.

38. Ibid., Q6780, 1:290.

39. Ibid., Q6843, 1:292.

40. Ibid., Q13886, 2:105.

41. C.E. Howard Vincent, "Lessons of the War," 634 (emphasis in original).

42. C.E. Howard Vincent, "Situation in South Africa," 182.

43. Badsey, *Doctrine and Reform*, 151.

44. *Elgin Commission*, Q13247, 2:66. See Lord Roberts's response in Q10409, 1:439, for similar views.

45. *Elgin Commission*, Q13941, 2:109.

46. Lee, *Soldier's Life*, 75.

47. *Elgin Commission*, Q13941, 2:109.

48. Ratzenhofer,"Retrospect of War in South Africa," 42.

49. Webber, "Army Reform," 389.

50. Quoted in Rimington, *Our Cavalry*, 55.

51. Quoted in Anglesey, *History of the British Cavalry*, 4:391; Badsey, *Doctrine and Reform*, 151.

52. Angelsey, *History of the British Cavalry*, 4:389.

53. For criticism, see De Groot, "Educated Soldier or Cavalry Officer?," 5.

54. Cooper, *Haig*, 1:378–79.

55. *Elgin Commission*, Q19299, 1:403.

56. "Report to the Army Council on the Role of the Cavalry by the Commander of the I Army Corps," 7 March 1904, pp. 120 –22, Army Council Minutes and IGF Annual Reports, TNA WO 163/10.

57. Rimington, *Our Cavalry*, 82.

58. "Report to the Army Council on the Role of the Cavalry by the Commander of the I Army Corps," 7 March 1904, p. 122, Army Council Minutes and IGF Annual Reports, TNA WO 163/10.

59. Ibid., p. 120.

60. Wessels, *Lord Roberts and War in South Africa*, 80–81; "Circular Memo on Cavalry Role and Armament," 10 March 1903, p. 123, Army Council Minutes and IGF Annual Reports, TNA WO 163/10.

61. "Circular Memo on Cavalry Role and Armament," 10 March 1903, p. 127, Army Council Minutes and IGF Annual Reports, TNA WO 163/10.

62. Ibid., p. 126; Von Czerlieu, "Lance as Weapon of Cavalry," 40–41.

63. "Circular Memo on Cavalry Role and Armament," 10 March 1903, p. 127, Army Council Minutes and IGF Annual Reports, TNA WO 163/10.

64. War Office, *Cavalry Training 1904 (Provisional)*, p. v.

65. Angelsey, *History of the British Cavalry*, 4:395–96.

66. IGF Report for 1904, p. 302, TNA WO 163/10.

67. Badsey, *Doctrine and Reform*, 183.

68. Ibid., 188–89.

69. Ibid., 188.

70. Army Council Précis: Précis 216—Establishment of a Cavalry Journal, p. 373, Army Council Minutes and IGF Reports, TNA WO 163/10.

71. Army Council Précis: Précis 248—Cavalry Officer Shortage, p. 470, Army Council Minutes and IGF Reports, TNA WO 163/10.

72. Hamilton, "Training of Troops 1906," 1518.

73. IGF Report for 1904, pp. 301–304, TNA WO 163/10; IGF Report for 1905, pp. 155–56, 162, TNA WO 163/11.

74. IGF Report for 1905, p. 163, TNA WO 163/11.

75. For scathing criticism of Russian cavalry, see the military attaché reports contained in TNA WO 33/350, WO 106/181, and WO 33/618.

76. Reports from Manchuria, pp. 40, 42, TNA WO 33/350.

77. De Negrier, "Lessons of the Russo-Japanese War," 688–89.

78. Hamilton, *Staff Officer's Scrap Book*, 1:278–79.

79. Quoted in Bond, "Doctrine and Training in British Cavalry," 114.

80. Angelsey, *History of the British Cavalry*, 4:405.

81. Battine, "Use of the Horse Soldier," 309.

82. Hamilton, *Staff Officer's Scrap Book*, 1:197; Rimington, *Our Cavalry*, 75.

83. Army Council Précis: Précis 419, p. 71, Army Council Minutes and IGF Annual Reports, TNA WO 163/14.

84. Angelsey, *History of the British Cavalry*, 4:398.

85. Holmes, *Riding the Retreat*, 61–63; Badsey, *Doctrine and Reform*, 210.

86. Hamilton, "Remarks on Training of Troops 1907," 83–84.

87. Badsey, *Doctrine and Reform*, 210.

88. War Office, *Field Service Regulations Part I: 1909*, 12.

89. War Office, *Cavalry Training 1912*, 268–71.

90. For example, "German Ideas on Cavalry," 947; W.D. Bird, "Some Notes on Modern Tactics," 493; DeLisle, "Strategical Action of Cavalry," 788.

91. Special Correspondent [Charles Repington], "Cavalry Lessons of the War," 58.

92. DeLisle, "Strategical Action of Cavalry," 788; see also W.D. Bird, "Some Notes on Modern Tactics," 493.

93. Applin, "Machine Gun Tactics," 50.

94. *Elgin Commission*, Q6827, 1:109.

95. Quoted in Rimington, *Our Cavalry*, 51.

96. For example, Mayne, "Lance as Cavalry Weapon," 120–21; Rimington, "Spirit of Cavalry," 1235.

97. Rimington, "Spirit of Cavalry," 1235; Battine, "Use of the Horse Soldier," 314–15; *Cavalry Training 1907*, 186.

98. See IGF Report for 1910, p. 224, TNA WO 163/16; IGF Report for 1912, p. 576, TNA WO 163/18.

99. *Cavalry Training 1912*, 268–70. In particular, see the diagram illustrating an ideal combined action on p. 270.

100. Badsey, *Doctrine and Reform*, 230; IGF Report for 1909, p. 293, TNA WO 163/15.

101. Childers, *War and the Arme Blanche*, pp. x, 4.

102. Ibid., 243.

103. Bond, "Doctrine and Training in British Cavalry," 109.

104. Childers, *War and the Arme Blanche*, 245.

105. General Staff, "War and the Arme Blanche: General Staff's Views," 1061.

106. Ibid., 1060.

107. Ibid., 1062.

108. Hamilton, "Training of Troops 1907," 84.

109. French, comment on "Uses of Cavalry and Mounted Infantry," 633.

110. Allenby, comment on "Proposed Changes in Cavalry Tactics," 1444.

111. Rimington, *Our Cavalry*, 22, 52. *Cavalry Training 1912* also emphasized this idea.

112. Quoted in Holmes, *Riding the Retreat*, 63.

113. "German Ideas on Cavalry," 949–50.

114. von Pelet-Narbonne, "Primary Conditions for Success of Cavalry," 333.

115. Quoted in Badsey, *Doctrine and Reform*, 215.

116. Childers, *War and the Arme Blanche*, 353.

117. Badsey, *Doctrine and Reform*, 243. Fortunately for the British, clumsy operational handling by the Germans meant that their cavalry strength was often wasted or misdirected. See Martin, "Cavalry in the Great War," 131–37, 437–48.

118. The reason for this unusual size is disputed. Stephen Badsey has attributed it to financial considerations, whereas Nikolas Gardner has argued it was due to the greater weight it possessed in the charge. See Badsey, "Cavalry and Development of Breakthrough Doctrine," 147; Gardner, "Command Control," 35.

119. Gardner, "Command Control," 36.

120. Ibid., 43.

121. Holmes, *Riding the Retreat*, 213–19.

122. Beckett, *Ypres*, 100, 158–59.

123. Badsey, *Doctrine and Reform*, 243.

124. Quoted in ibid., 243.

125. Mounted infantry was used by some of the smaller Balkan states, such as Montenegro.

126. Vincent, "Lessons of the War," 634.

127. Maurice, *History of the War in South Africa*, 1:414–15.

128. Robinson, "Search for Mobility," 143; Robertson, *Private to Field Marshal*, 105.

129. Robertson, *Private to Field Marshal*, 105.

130. Callwell, "Looking Back," 261.

131. Ibid.

132. Johnstone, *History of Tactics*, 195.

133. Angelsey, *History of the British Cavalry*, 4:323.

134. *Elgin Commission*, Q12729, 2:31; Robertson, *Private to Field Marshal*, 105.

135. *Elgin Commission*, Q19299, 2:399.

136. Angelsey, *History of the British Cavalry*, 4:271.

137. Comment on "Uses of Cavalry and Mounted Infantry," 629.

138. Amery, *Times History*, 2:96.

139. Nicolls, "Training, Organisation and Equipment," 100.

140. Morrison, "Lessons Derived from South Africa," 816; Battine, "Proposed Changes in Cavalry Tactics," 1431.

141. Bethune, "Uses of Cavalry and Mounted Infantry," 623; Godley, "Mounted Infantry," 143–44.

142. Childers, *War and the Arme Blanche*, 4–7.

143. *Elgin Commission*, 4:49. Although not specifically stated, these "mounted riflemen" included yeomanry and volunteer formations from the Dominions and colonies, as well as mounted infantry. See Badsey, *Doctrine and Reform*, 170.

144. Mounted Infantry Inspection, 30 June 1905, Aldershot Command Papers, TNA WO 27/502.

145. *Elgin Commission*, Q12729, 2:31; Q16595, 2:264.

146. Ibid., Q19299, 2:402.

147. Ibid., Q12485, 2:21; Q12703, 2:29–30.

148. *Elgin Commission*, 4:52.

149. Rimington, "Spirit of Cavalry," 1222; Dilke, comment on "Use of the Horse Soldier," 320.

150. IGF Report for 1905, p. 204, TNA WO 163/11.

151. *Elgin Commission Report*, 4:52.

152. Précis 160, pp. 78–80, Army Council Minutes and IGF Annual Reports, TNA WO 163/10.

153. Spiers, "British Cavalry 1902–1914," 78; Badsey, *Doctrine and Reform*, 217.

154. Report on Troops and Defences in South Africa, January and February 1907, Inspector General of Forces Reports, TNA WO 27/510.

155. Badsey, *Doctrine and Reform*, 217.

156. Ikona, "Passing of the Old M.I.," 210–11.

157. R.S.S. Baden-Powell, *Aids to Scouting for NCOs and Men*, 12.

158. British Officer [Cairnes], *An Absent Minded War*, 27.

159. Quoted in R.S.S. Baden-Powell, *Aids to Scouting*, n.p.

160. For a detailed discussion of methods used to gather intelligence in colonial actions, particularly the Sudan campaign, see Spiers, "Intelligence

and Command," 661–81. For the limited role of regular cavalry in colonial scouting, see Badsey, *Doctrine and Reform*, 54–55.

161. French, "Cavalry Manoeuvres," 565.

162. Ibid., 565–66; Cavalry Officer, "British Cavalry," 453. Emphasis in original.

163. Morrison, "Lessons Derived from South Africa," 816.

164. *Elgin Commission*, Q14242, 2:109; Q15695, 2:226.

165. Jay Stone and Schimdl, *Boer War and Military Reforms*, 93.

166. *Elgin Commission*, Q17129, 2:301; Amery, *Times History*, 2:75.

167. *Elgin Commission*, Q12652, 2:27.

168. Ibid., Q12652, Q12653, 2:27.

169. Notes for Guidance in South African Warfare, 26 January 1900, Lord Roberts Papers, TNA WO 105/40.

170. Circular Memo No. 8, 5 February 1900, Lord Roberts Papers, TNA WO 105/40.

171. Smith, *Veterinary History of War in South Africa*, 14–15.

172. Badsey, *Doctrine and Reform*, 105.

173. Ibid., 98–99.

174. Ibid., 99.

175. Ibid., 113–14.

176. Scott, *Douglas Haig*, 167.

177. Rimington, *Our Cavalry*, 82.

178. *Elgin Commission*, Q17129, 2:301.

179. Vaughan, "Cavalry Notes," 449.

180. Ibid.

181. Jay Stone and Schimdl, *Boer War and Military Reforms*, 94.

182. Vaughan, "Cavalry Notes," 449.

183. Ibid., 450.

184. De Wet, *Three Years' War*, 213.

185. Ibid., 263–64; Jay Stone and Schimdl, *Boer War and Military Reforms*, 94.

186. Pilcher, *Some Lessons from the Boer War*, 90–91; De Wet, *Three Years' War*, 18.

187. Vaughan, "Cavalry Notes," 448; Jay Stone and Schimdl, *Boer War and Military Reforms*, 94.

188. For example, *Elgin Commission*, Q173, 1:7; Q4161, 1:176; Q6969, 1:298; Q13941, 2:109; Q17129, 2:301.

189. Notes by Colonel J.M. Grierson R.A. on Return from South Africa, TNA WO 108/184; Johnstone, *History of Tactics*, 191.

190. Combined Manoeuvres 1903, p. 4, TNA WO 279/7.

191. IGF Report for 1904, p. 301, TNA WO 163/10.

192. For a detailed list of subjects for scout training, see War Office, *Cavalry Training 1912*, 215.

193. Ibid., 301.

194. Ibid., 301–302.

195. Another Cavalryman, "Squadron System," 171.

196. IGF Report for 1908, p. 15, TNA WO 163/13.

197. Comments on Staff Tour, IGF Report for 1910, pp. 264–65, TNA WO 163/16.

198. IGF Report for 1913, pp. 330, 338, TNA WO 163/20.

199. Rimington, *Our Cavalry*, 18. Rimington estimated that only 15 percent of cavalry recruits had any prior experience with horses.

200. Cavalry Training: The Ulster and Wicklow Schemes, pp. 1, 11, Aldershot Command Papers, TNA WO 27/503.

201. Comments on the Ulster Scheme, p. 3, in ibid.

202. Webber, "Army Reform," 388; Comments on the Wicklow Scheme, p. 1, Aldershot Command Papers, TNA WO 27/503.

203. Angelsey, *History of the British Cavalry*, 448–49; Holmes, *Riding the Retreat*, 65.

204. Badsey, *Doctrine and Reform*, 239.

205. Barret, "Lessons Learned from the Russo-Japanese War," 801; Reports from Manchuria, pp. 40–41, TNA WO 33/350.

206. Badsey, *Doctrine and Reform*, 246.

207. Cave and Sheldon, *Le Cateau*, 14.

208. Spears, *Liaison 1914*, 101.

209. Ormsby-Johnson, "Reconnaissance as a Fine Art," 1210.

210. Darling, *20th Hussars in the Great War*, 26–27, 32; Cave and Sheldon, *Le Cateau*, 14.

211. Cave and Sheldon, *Le Cateau*, 14–15.

212. Badsey, *Doctrine and Reform*, 244.

213. Gervase Phillips, "Scapegoat Arm," 38.

214. De Groot, "Educated Soldier or Cavalry Officer?," 60–61.

215. Gervase Phillips, "Obsolescence of the *Arme Blanche*," 39–40.

216. *Cavalry Training 1912*, 268–71.

217. Gervase Phillips, "Obsolescence of the *Arme Blanche*," 49.

218. *Cavalry Training 1912*, 268–71.

219. Martin, "Cavalry in the Great War," 447.

CONCLUSION

1. For example, see Holmes, *Riding the Retreat*, 26–42.

2. Neillands, *Old Contemptibles*, 100, 136, 138.

3. IGF Report for 1912 and Army Council Comments, 567–68, TNA WO 163/18.

4. Sheffy, "A Model Not to Follow," 262–64.

5. Ibid., 263–64; Snyder, *Ideology of the Offensive*, 77–81.

6. Travers, "Technology, Tactics and Morale," 277.

7. Towle, "Influence of the Russo-Japanese War," 1.

8. Beckett, "South African War and the Late Victorian Army," 32; Searle, *Quest for National Efficiency*, 50.

9. Ramsay, *Command and Cohesion*, 145.

10. Neillands, *Old Contemptibles*, 3, 78.

11. Joll, *Europe Since 1870*, 193.

ESSAY ON
HISTORIOGRAPHY

In terms of existing literature on the subject, the historiography of the Boer War and the period of development within the British Army that followed can be seen as having two distinct phases. The earliest views on the war emerged during and immediately after the conflict, providing the basis for orthodox interpretations of the war that would endure for more than fifty years. In later years, the First World War inevitably came to overshadow the Boer War, and writing on the earlier conflict declined as a result. Compared with the colossal bloodletting of 1914–18, the struggle in South Africa seemed trifling and, in military terms, largely irrelevant. The cultural legacy of the war, especially in South Africa, ensured its remembrance, but among historians the conflict merited little work of note until a growth in interest in the study of the late Victorian army began in the late 1960s and early 1970s. The era marked the passing of the last few veterans of the wars of the nineteenth century, including survivors of the Boer War, prompting a resurgence in studies of the period. This second phase of interest saw a number of searching academic analyses that challenged the orthodox views that had emerged in the immediate aftermath of the conflict, offering a more positive analysis of the Victorian army and its performance in South Africa.

Debate between orthodox and revisionist historians continues, but in more recent years studies have tended to focus on previously neglected aspects of the war, such as the combat experience of the Boers (e.g., Fransjohan Pretorius, *Life on Commando*) and the role of colonial contingents (e.g., Carman Miller, *Painting the Map Red*). Furthermore, the recent centennial of the Boer War produced a flood of fresh work on the subject, showing that the topic still holds considerable interest for both historians and the public. In addition, it is important to note that the study of the Boer War has assumed some political aspects in post-apartheid South Africa. Transvaal ceased to exist and the Orange Free State lost its distinctive Dutch "Orange" in 1994; other Boer towns have received new post-colonial African names in the last ten years. The desire to preserve Afrikaner identity through remembrance and commemoration of the war has produced substantial writing in South Africa, work that at times sits uneasily with the new political agendas of the Rainbow Nation. In the twenty-first century the example of this war as a struggle for Afrikaner freedom from the oppressive British government carries connotations that have allowed certain radical white groups in the country to use it as a rallying cry against black rule.

The first, orthodox interpretation of the Boer War emerged while the conflict was still in progress. The struggle produced voluminous literature, with the war proving immensely controversial and prompting numerous authors and journalists to weigh in with their opinions. An explosion of literature emerged both during and after the war, with more than a hundred books on various aspects of the conflict being produced in 1903 alone. Britain printed two multivolume histories soon after the conflict, namely the seven-volume *Times History of the War in South Africa* (hereafter *Times History*), principally edited by Leo Amery, and the seven-volume *History of the War in South Africa* edited by Major-General Sir Fredrick Maurice and others. The German General Staff also chose to produce a history of the conflict, devoted almost entirely to the early, conventional stage of the war, with the guerrilla phase meriting just a single paragraph in a two-volume work (translated by Walter). In addition to these official works, numerous other books and articles appeared on the causes of the war, its course, and particularly on the perceived failures of the British Army in its immediate aftermath. It was not until the Russo-Japanese War of 1904–1905 that army and public attention was drawn away from the experience of battle on the veldt.

The two key printed sources for study of the military aspects of the Boer War are the *Times History* and the *History of the War in South Africa*. The *Times History* had a complex origin. It was originally planned as a rapid cash-in to seize on public interest in the war and to head off the possibility of the numerous *Times* correspondents each producing his own individual book, thereby depriving the newspaper of a source of income. The first volume, on the origins of the war, was rushed out in December 1900. However, the attitude began to change in the following months, with Leo Amery expressing his desire to create a more accurate and rigorous account in keeping with the traditions of the *Times* newspaper. However, with the vast majority of paperwork from the war still classified, it was necessary for Amery to approach the army directly to assist him with information.

This process inevitably brought Amery into contact with Lord Roberts. The two were on already on friendly terms, and, crucially, both were supportive of army reform. Amery had written a number of critical pieces on the state of the army in the *Times* prior to and during the war, later publishing some of them in book form as *The Problem of the Army* in 1903. In the creation of the *Times History*, the two shared a common goal of producing a work that would ensure future army reform. Roberts was to prove an enormous source of assistance to Amery in the preparation of his work. Although Roberts stopped short of providing certain classified documents, he provided information, commented on draft chapters, and even deputed a member of his staff to deal with some of Amery's queries.

In pursuing the agenda of army reform, the *Times History* savaged the pre-war Victorian army as being ineffective in combat against anyone other than the most primitive foes, and commanders who came to grief on the veldt, especially Redvers Buller, Charles Warren, and Lord Methuen, are the subject of severe criticism. Amery singled out the early parts of Buller's Natal campaign for particular attention, casting the general as little more than a bumbling incompetent representing all that was wrong with pre-war army thinking. Conversely, Lord Roberts received considerable praise for his largely successful invasion of the Boer Republics, standing in contrast to the slow progress and repeated defeats of Buller's army in Natal.

By portraying the early-war British Army as incompetent and the reformist Lord Roberts as the savior of the campaign, Amery's work presented a powerful message in favor of military reform under the leadership of the new commander in chief.

Later in his life, Amery admitted that his work on the history was "essentially propagandist" (quoted in Beckett, "Historiography of Small Wars," 287). However, benefitting from the strength of the *Times* name, the cooperation of senior officers, and a lucid writing style, Amery's work was influential in shaping views of the Boer War. The harsh criticisms leveled by Amery toward the British Army and its combat performance essentially set the tone for academic study of the war for decades.

Amery's work may have been less influential had the *History of the War in South Africa* provided a useful counterpoint. This work was edited by the military and provides a far dryer account of the war than the popular *Times History*. Original editor and forward thinker G. F. R. Henderson died while the work was at an early stage, and it was passed on to Major-General Frederick Maurice. Numerous problems emerged during production of the work, including repeated delays imposed by the parsimonious allocations of funds and staff by the Treasury. Originally planned as a searching and unbiased work on the war, official interference and censorship stripped the teeth from the writers. For example, in the interests of reconciliation with South Africa, political aspects of the war were to be avoided where possible. Furthermore, the work suffered from being produced by men who were reluctant to criticize their fellow officers or the army as a whole. As such, the account is flat and offers little in the way of judgment or analysis, instead presenting bald facts and typically steering well away from criticism or comment upon the actual conduct of the war. Crippled by censorship and delayed through lack of resources, the work was far from the in-depth analysis of the conflict that had been planned when it was originally commissioned. Lack of comment combined with lifeless prose caused the *History of the War in South Africa* to become neglected in preference to the more readable *Times History*.

In the immediate aftermath, and even sometimes while the war was still in progress, several histories charting the course of the conflict were published to take advantage of widespread public interest in the struggle. Several notable figures, including Arthur

Conan Doyle, Alfred Thayer Mahan, and Winston Churchill, published their own accounts of the war. The quality of these works varies enormously, from picture book histories to more academic studies, although a weakness common to many of them is their date of publication. Public interest and enthusiasm for the war surged in the aftermath of British reverses during Black Week in December 1899, reaching a peak with the invasion of the Boer Republics in early 1900. Many works were published to take advantage of this interest and were written on the assumption that the fall of the Transvaal and Orange Free State capitals marked the end of the war. With the Boxer Rebellion in China capturing the public imagination in late 1900, interest in the Boer War waned. In addition, the subsequent guerrilla phase of the war lacked the grand sweep or glamour of the conventional phase and thus was largely neglected in works intended for popular consumption.

After the initial surge of publishing in the immediate aftermath of the Boer War, the topic faded from public interest and received little fresh historical analysis. Historians still periodically returned to explore the subject in the decades that followed, but the influence of Leo Amery remained paramount in these early studies; historians did little to challenge his interpretations and in some cases saw no reason to do so. For example, *Buller's Campaign* by Julian Symons openly acknowledged the influence of Amery, arguing that the analysis of Redvers Buller offered by the *Times History* was essentially correct and in no need of revision. The work ends with Ladysmith relieved but devotes the majority of its prose to the defeats at Colenso and Spion Kop, offering little analysis of the victories on the Tulega Heights that ultimately broke the siege.

Indeed, it was not until the 1970s that Amery's interpretation of the war was subject to serious academic challenge. Interest in the Boer War and the late Victorian army enjoyed resurgence during this period, and the considerable number of works produced during this era reflects this change. A critical work of this period is Thomas Pakenham's major revisionist study *The Boer War*. Pakenham's work consciously attempted to break free from the influence of Amery's *Times History* and instead offered a reinterpretation of the performance of Redvers Buller. Pakenham argues that during early defeats Buller was a victim of circumstances beyond his control, concluding that after the initial setbacks, it was Buller's army that developed new, modern tactics that allowed the British to achieve final victory. Conversely, Lord Roberts is criticized for his neglect of logistics, failure to deal the Boers a crushing blow in battle, and mistaken belief the war would end with the capture of the Boer capitals. However, Pakenham's attempt to rehabilitate Redvers Buller is not always entirely convincing. Although some of the criticism leveled at Buller in the aftermath of the war may have been unfair and ignored the difficulty of the situation, his feeble performance as a strategist during the Natal campaign and as a battlefield commander at Colenso, Spion Kop, and Vaal Krantz are difficult to excuse. Furthermore, in attempting to improve Buller's reputation, Pakenham is sometimes overly critical of other officers, such as Lord Roberts, John French, and Ian Hamilton. Yet, despite these flaws, Pakenham's work challenged the existing historiography of the Boer War, forcing future historians to go beyond Leo Amery's early interpretation. Subsequent works have continued the efforts to rehabilitate commanders castigated by Amery, including revisionist studies of Buller (*Buller: A Scapegoat?*) by Geoffrey Powell and of Lord Methuen (*Lord Methuen and the British Army*) by Stephen Miller.

Allied to the reinterpretation of British combat performance in South Africa, the army in the Victorian era has also received greater academic study since the 1970s. Brian Bond's *The Victorian Army and the Staff College 1854–1914* was the first of these works and remains one of the most important for exploring the course and nature of staff officer training during the nineteenth and early twentieth centuries. The work was ground-breaking when first published and remains a key component for understanding attitudes toward training and leadership within the officer class throughout this era. Bond touches on numerous tactical issues and illustrates how a gradual move toward professionalism from the 1890s onwards began to reshape the nature of the British Army. However, the work also argues that this process remained painfully slow, and that tradition and obstinacy hampered reform work right up until the First World War. Complementing Bond's work is Edward Spiers's *The Late Victorian Army 1868–1902*, offering an overview of the history of the armed forces in this period. The work is wide ranging, covering the War Office and civil–military relations as well as the nature of the fighting forces themselves. Spiers argues that the army, although often criticized for being hidebound and retrograde in its thinking, was in fact effective at the roles it was expected to play within the navy-dominated Victorian military. Reforms were gradually introduced over the period as the army gained prominence, but Spiers acknowledges that they were rather limited in their impact. Concluding the era in question, the Boer War shook the army and illustrated that it still had much to learn, but the army's ability to expand to eventually win the war demonstrated a considerable degree of flexibility.

Building on these ideas, Howard Bailes in his article "Patterns of Thought in the Late Victorian Army" has suggested that the British Army in the years prior to the Boer War was not the reactionary and antiquated institution that some of the more vociferous critics of its combat performance tried to suggest. He identifies several schools of thought within the late Victorian army that were both highly educated and fully aware of continental and technological developments. Subsequently, he has argued that British tactical thought in the era was moving toward flexibility throughout the 1890s and that early defeats in the Boer War were due to a failure to act in line with accepted British doctrine, although he does acknowledge that these ideas were at an early stage. Building on the idea that tactical thought within the British Army prior to the war was more advanced than commonly believed is the work of Tim Moreman, in particular his article "The British and Indian Armies and North West Frontier Warfare." Decades of combat against local tribes, often well armed, in difficult terrain had taught the British a number of valuable lessons. However, Moreman argues that a failure to disseminate these important ideas outside of a small number of regiments regularly deployed on the frontier meant that other units were forced to learn through bitter experience. Although Bailes and Moreman offer interesting arguments, both historians seem to suggest that although there were strands of advanced tactical thinking within the army, they had not achieved large-scale acceptance by the time of the Boer War. More recently, D. M. Leeson has rejected the positive assessments of the pre-Boer War army in his article "Playing at War: The British Military Manoeuvres of 1898," using the example of the 1898 maneuvers to argue that the army was operationally and tactically backward. Although Leeson uses a rather narrow range of sources to argue his case, the work shows that the debate around the quality of the pre-Boer War army is by no means over.

However, although the Boer War itself and the Victorian-era army have benefitted from greater historical study and revisionism in recent years, the pre–First World War army has received less attention. Study of the pre-1914 army has focused on the strategic and organizational reforms that created the General Staff, the BEF, and the Territorial Army. The classic account of this reorganization and reformation is *The Development of the British Army 1899–1914* by Colonel John Dunlop. The book provides a wide-ranging and detailed study of the work of various defense secretaries to reform the British Army as the risk of war on the continent loomed, with a natural emphasis on the critical Haldane years (1905–1912) when the 1914 army took its final shape. As an account of the reorganization of this era, the work is an excellent starting point, but it does not delve into the realms of tactics or post–Boer War army doctrine except in the briefest terms, preferring instead to focus on the reforms at the highest levels of the army structure. Another work produced during the 1930s, J. E. Tyler's *The British Army and the Continent 1904–1914*, complements Dunlop's account. This work again focuses on reorganization at higher levels, although the main thrust of the book is a discussion of British strategy with regard to continental commitments in the years preceding the First World War. Although useful in charting the change in British Army thinking away from another colonial war toward fighting against Germany, the work lacks any discussion of alterations in tactics or operational thinking that accompanied the overall change in strategic direction. Subsequent work on the origins of the First World War has shown the surprising extent to which British planning was based on assumption and reaction to events; nevertheless, these two works give an important overview of events taking place in the higher reaches of the British Army structure and the effect these events would have on the army by the time it was committed to war in 1914.

A number of studies have analyzed the impact of organizational changes on the BEF, but the tactical development of the army in the pre–First World War years has remained comparatively neglected. Edward Spiers offered an early analysis of infantry, cavalry, and artillery tactics in the years before the First World War in a series of articles published in the *Journal of the Society for Army Historical Research*. Offering a an overview of the vital tactical reforms in this period, Spiers is generally positive in his analysis of Edwardian infantry and artillery reorganization, concluding that in particular the infantry had reached a peak in their training that made them the best in Europe. Conversely, the cavalry are singled out for much criticism. Spiers argues that an initial impulse toward tactical reform after the Boer War was lost and that, in contrast to infantry and artillery, cavalry was tactically regressing throughout much of the pre-1914 period. Although acknowledging that some improvements were being made from 1912 onward, Spiers damningly concludes that the British cavalry in 1914 was no more tactically advanced than it had been on the eve of the Boer War in 1899. Spiers's articles provide a useful starting point for study of the question, but they are relatively brief and thus inevitably offer only a general overview of the progress of tactical reform.

Treading similar ground to Edward Spiers is *The Boer War and Military Reforms* by Jay Stone and Erwin A. Schmidl. Split into two separate parts, the book deals with responses from British and Austro-Hungarian armies to the Boer War. Much of the study of the British Army in this regard deals with reorganization and military reforms that were undertaken while the war was still in progress and that were introduced as immediate countermeasures to Boer tactics. Stone argues the ability of the British to reform in the midst of active operations was crucial in winning the eventual victory over the Boer Republics. However, while this work convincingly demonstrates the ability of the British Army to learn in-theater, there is relatively little analysis given to whether these new tactical ideas endured beyond the end of the conflict. Post-war organizational reforms are discussed at some length, but tactical reforms are dealt with only in general terms; in addition, there is no real analysis of the extent to which the BEF of 1914 benefitted from the Boer War experience. The second half of the book studies the reports of the Austro-Hungarian military attaché and his attempts to convince his army that the Boer War indicated the need for tactical reform. This work offers a unique study of how the military of a major continental power regarded this far-flung colonial war, and the different way in which British and Austro-Hungarian armies regarded the war provides an interesting contrast. However, the long-term influence of the Boer War on both the nations in question is given comparatively little attention. Thus, although the work is valuable for its illustration of in-theater learning, it is of less value in tracing the overall development of the British Army in the post-war years.

There has been relatively little work dealing with the army as a whole, but there have been more specific works focusing on individual service branches. Of the three combat arms, cavalry has received the most attention from historians for the crucial 1902–1914 timeframe. The role and future tactics of cavalry were in considerable dispute during this period, as evidenced by works such as those of Douglas Haig (*Cavalry Studies*) and Erskine Childers (*War and the Arme Blanche*). More recent historians have examined the debate in considerable detail, including Stephen Badsey, Gerard De Groot, Gervase Phillips, and Jean Bou. A historical consensus on the quality of British cavalry in this period has yet to emerge, although even critical writers such as Edward Spiers conclude that, compared with continental cavalry forces, the British were tactically advanced, especially in terms of their ability to fight dismounted. The Marquess of Anglesey, whose multivolume work *History of the British Cavalry* treats the subject with unmatched detail, has produced the most comprehensive study of British cavalry in this era. The author traces the complex factors influencing the cavalry during this period and argues that although the cavalry retrenched with determination immediately after the Boer War, as the years advanced even hardliners gradually reformed their views. Although the nature of cavalry tactics continues to divide historians, the reformist viewpoint put forward by the Marquess of Anglesey, Stephen Badsey, and Gervase Phillips appears to be gaining increased acceptance.

As the most technical and least glamorous of the three arms, British artillery in this era has received relatively little attention. The standard work on the arm in this period remains John Headlam's three-volume *History of the Royal Artillery 1860–1914*, originally written in the 1930s. The first two volumes cover the organizational, tactical, and technical development of the artillery, whereas the third details the numerous "small wars" in which the gunners fought during the period in question. As a technical history the works retain a great deal of value and chart a period in which the artillery was assuming an unprecedented level of importance.

Jonathan Bailey and Sanders Marble have touched on the subject of artillery in more general works, whereas Edward Spiers and R. H.

Scales have carried out more specific studies of the post–Boer War period. However, in most of these studies the immense importance of artillery in the First World War tends to overshadow its comparatively small-scale development in the 1902–1914 period. The most detailed study of the artillery in the post–Boer War period has been undertaken by R. H. Scales, who paints a negative picture of the arm, particularly as compared with that of Germany. Though Scales has valid criticisms, there is an overemphasis on doctrine that is not well-suited for an analysis of the British Army in this period. Subsequently, his views have been challenged by Shelford Bidwell and Dominick Graham's *Firepower: The British Army Weapons and Theories of War 1904–1945*. This work argues that on the eve of the First World War, the British artillery was caught between the technical capacity to deliver indirect fire and the tactical impulse, following French methods, to scorn such techniques and instead to fight in a traditional, old-fashioned, direct-fire role. Although there were officers within the Royal Artillery who were in favor of a more technical approach toward artillery fighting, their views were undermined by budget restrictions and many traditional thinkers who held that the only true way to support infantry was with medium-range direct fire. Although brief, Bidwell and Graham's analysis remains valuable as an introduction to the issues facing the Royal Artillery in the pre–First World War period.

Although tactics in the British Army have received relatively little analysis, there have been several important works on operational-level thinking in the 1902–1918 period. Tim Travers has written several pieces on this subject, most notably *The Killing Ground: The British Army, the Western Front and the Emergence of Modern War 1900–1918*. Although mainly concerned with combat in the First World War, Travers discusses the continuity of ideas that ran through the Edwardian army and the cult of the offensive that apparently gripped much of the senior leadership. The book is generally critical of Douglas Haig, identifying his pre-war training at the Staff College as creating an erroneous and inflexible idea of strategy that was to cost the British Army in the First World War. Although Travers acknowledges that there were strands of advanced thought within the army, he concludes that in the face of anti-intellectual bias and Victorian attitudes, they were unable to make much impact on operational-level thinking. A work that covers similar ground is

Martin Samuels's *Command or Control? Command, Training and Tactics in the British and German Armies 1888–1918*. Despite the title, the majority of the work deals with combat in the First World War, and although some interesting points are raised, the work suffers from an overemphasis on German tactical and operational brilliance contrasted against bumbling British incompetence, illustrated through the highly selective case studies of the first day of the Battle of the Somme 1916 and the opening of the German spring 1918 offensive. Samuels touches on some of the points raised by Travers's earlier work, particularly regarding concepts of structured battles within the British high command, and he offers a damning assessment of British military thought in the Edwardian period and the First World War itself.

A convincing challenge to Travers and Samuels has been provided by M. A. Ramsay in his work *Command and Cohesion: The Citizen Soldier and Minor Tactics in the British Army, 1870–1918*. In particular, Ramsay argues that Travers's interpretation is overly narrow, and he suggests that tactics at lower levels were realistic and advanced. While acknowledging that the British Army was struggling with growing problems presented by mass warfare and modern firepower, Ramsay suggests that it made steady progress prior to and during the First World War in adapting to these issues. The work is particularly concerned with morale and motivation in a citizen army and provides an important counterpoint to the generally negative assessments of Travers and Samuels.

Despite the wide variety of literature published on the Boer War and the era that followed it, gaps in the historiography still remain and the wide range of interpretation of events reveal that much of the history remains contested. The gaps in the historiography regarding the influence of the Boer War on the tactical development of the BEF become particularly apparent when studying works focusing on British combat experience in 1914. Standard works on this topic include studies by John Terraine, David Ascoli, and Robin Neillands. These works offer praise for the British Army in the opening weeks of the First World War, particularly its training and professionalism. However, in all cases the links between the skill of the BEF in 1914 and the lessons derived from the Boer War are either ignored or casually asserted.

BIBLIOGRAPHY

ARCHIVAL SOURCES

Joint Services Command and Staff College Library, Shrivenham, England
   Minutes of pre-1914 General Staff Meetings.
   Papers for officer promotion exams 1900–1914.
   Syllabuses for officer education 1900–1914.

Liddell Hart Centre for Military Archives, King's College, London, England
   Hamilton, Ian. Papers.

The National Archives (TNA), Kew, London, England
   Aldershot Command 1913, WO 279/53.
   Aldershot Command Papers, War Office (WO) 27/501–506.
   Army Council Minutes and Inspector General of Forces Annual Report,
      WO 163/9–20.
   Army Manoeuvres 1904, WO 279/8.
   Army Manoeuvres 1909, WO 279/31.
   Army Manoeuvres 1910, WO 279/39.
   Army Manoeuvres 1912, WO 279/47.
   Boer War Correspondence, WO 108/405.
   Chief of Staff Papers, WO 105/115–117.
   Combined Manoeuvres 1903, WO 279/7.
   Committee on Pom-Poms and Machine Guns, WO 32/9029.
   De Montmorency, Major H., Diary. WO 108/185.
   Grierson, Colonel J. M., Notes. WO 108/184.

Inspector General of Forces Reports, WO 27/508–10.
Irish Command Manoeuvres 1910, WO 279/40.
Lessons of the Russo-Japanese War, WO 106/181.
Military Notes on the Dutch Republics of South Africa, WO 33/154.
Night Actions in Manchuria, WO 106/180.
Organization and Equipment of Cavalry, WO 32/6781.
Preliminary and Further Reports (with Appendices) of the Royal Com-
missioners appointed to Enquire into the Civil and Professional
Administration of the Naval and Military Departments and the Re-
lation of the those Departments to each other and to the Treasury,
CAB 37/27/28.
Report on the Army Exercise 1913, WO 279/52.
Report on Foreign Manoeuvres 1912, WO 33/618.
Report on French Army Manoeuvres 1906, WO 27/507.
Reports from the Russian Army in Manchuria, WO 106/39.
Reports from South Africa on heavy artillery, WO 108/266.
Reports from South Africa on machine guns, WO 108/267.
Reports from South Africa on rifles, carbines, ammunition and bayonets,
WO 108/272.
Reports from South Africa on swords, lances and pistols, WO 108/273.
Reports on Foreign Militaries, WO 33/425.
Reports on Manchuria, WO 33/350.
Roberts, Lord, Papers. WO 105/29–45.
School of Musketry Reports, WO 140/8–13.
South Africa Despatches Nov. 1899–June 1900, WO 108/237.
Southern Command Training 1909, WO 279/524.
Training Reports 1903–1907, WO 279/516.
War Diary, I Corps, August–October 1914, WO 95/588.

National Army Museum, London, England
Roberts, Lord. Papers.

Royal Artillery Museum, London, England
School of Gunnery Reports 1905–1913.

BOOKS, ARTICLES, AND THESES

Adcock, A. St. John. *In the Firing Lines.* London: Hodder & Stroughton,
1914.
"After Mukden: A Russian Verdict on Russian Failures." *Journal of the*
Royal United Services Institute 49, no. 1 (1905): 557–60, 686–95.
Allenby, Major-General E.H.H. Comment on "The Proposed Changes
in Cavalry Tactics," by Captain C.W. Battine. *Journal of the Royal*
United Services Institute 54, no. 2 (1910): 1444.
Amery, Leo. *The Problem of the Army.* London: E. Arnold, 1903.
——, ed. *The Times History of the War in South Africa.* 7 vols. London:
Sampson Low, Marston and Company, 1900–1909.

Anglesey, Marquess of. *A History of the British Cavalry 1816–1919.* Vol. 4, *1899–1913.* London: Leo Cooper, 1986.

Anonymous. "The British Army and Modern Conceptions of War." *Edinburgh Review,* April 1911, 821–46.

Another Cavalryman. "The Squadron System." *United Service Magazine,* November 1904, 171–73.

Applin, Captain R. V. K. "Machine Guns with Cavalry." *Cavalry Journal* 2 (1907): 320–25.

———. "Machine Gun Tactics in Our Own and Other Armies." *Journal of the Royal United Services Institute* 54, no. 1 (1910): 34–64.

Arthur, Max. *Forgotten Voices of the Great War.* London: Ebury Press, 2002.

Ascoli, David. *The Mons Star.* Edinburgh, Scotland: Birlinn, 2001.

Atkinson, Captain B. "The Means to Ensure Co-Operation in Action between the Artillery and Infantry of the Field Army. How Are These Means Best Organised and Maintained?" *Minutes of the Proceedings of the Royal Artillery Institution* 35 (1908–1909): 329–43.

Baden-Powell, B. F. S. *War in Practice: Some Tactical and Other Lessons of the Campaign in South Africa 1899–1902.* London: Isbister & Company, 1903.

Baden-Powell, R. S. S. *Aids to Scouting for NCOs and Men.* London: Gale & Polden Ltd., 1899.

Badsey, Stephen. "The Boer War (1899–1902) and British Cavalry Doctrine: A Re-Evaluation." *The Journal of Military History* 71, no. 1 (2007): 75–97.

———. "Cavalry and the Development of Breakthrough Doctrine." In *British Fighting Methods in the Great War,* edited by Paddy Griffith, 138–166. London: Frank Cass, 1996.

———. *Doctrine and Reform in the British Cavalry 1880–1918.* Aldershot, U.K.: Ashgate, 2008.

———. "Mounted Combat in the Second Boer War." *Sandhurst Journal of Military Studies* 1, no. 2 (1992): 11–27.

Bailes, Howard. "Military Aspects of the War." In Warwick, *South African War,* 65–103.

———. "Patterns of Thought in the Late Victorian Army." *Journal of Strategic Studies* 4, no. 1 (1981): 28–45.

———. "Technology and Tactics in the British Army, 1866–1900." In Haycock & Neilson, *Men, Machines and War,* 21–49.

Bailey, J. B. A. *Field Artillery and Firepower.* Annapolis, Md.: Naval Institute Press, 2004.

Baillie-Grohman, W. A. "Marksmanship, Old and New." *Nineteenth Century,* May 1900, 750–59.

Balck, Major William. "Lessons of the Boer War and the Battle Workings of the Three Arms." *Journal of the Royal United Services Institute* 48, no. 2 (1904): 1271–78, 1393–1409.

Barnes, R. M. *The British Army of 1914.* London: Seely Service & Co., 1968.

Barret, Captain Ashley W. "Lessons to be Learned by Regimental Officers from the Russo-Japanese War." *Journal of the Royal United Services Institute* 51, no. 2 (1907): 797–823.

Battine, Captain C.W. "The Offensive versus the Defensive in the Tactics of To-day." *Journal of the Royal United Services Institute* 47, no. 1 (1903): 655–72.

———. "The Proposed Changes in Cavalry Tactics." *Journal of the Royal United Services Institute* 54, no. 2 (1910): 1416–45.

———. "The Use of the Horse Soldier in the 20th Century." *Journal of the Royal United Services Institute* 52, no. 1 (1908): 309–30.

Becke, A.F. *The Royal Regiment of Artillery at Le Cateau, 26 August, 1914.* Reprint, Uckfield, U.K.: Naval and Military Press, 2003.

Beckett, Ian. "The Historiography of Small Wars: Early Historians and the South African War." *Small Wars & Insurgencies* 2, no. 2 (1991): 276–98.

———. "The South African War and the Late Victorian Army." In *The Boer War: Army, Nation and Empire,* edited by Davis & Grey, 31–45. Canberra, Australia: Army History Unit, 2000.

———. *Ypres: The First Battle 1914.* Harlow, U.K.: Pearson/Longman, 2006.

Bedan, Lieutenant R.H. "How Can Moral Qualities Best be Developed During the Preparation of the Officer and the Man for the Duties Each Will Carry Out in War?" *Journal of the Royal United Services Institute* 59, no. 2 (1914): 113–154.

Beedos [pseud.]. "Military Training." *United Service Magazine,* October 1904, 75–81.

Belfield, General Herbert. Comment on "Employment of Heavy Artillery in the Field," by Colonel F.G. Stone. *Journal of the Royal Artillery* 35 (1908–1909): 16.

Bernhardi, Friedrich von. *Cavalry in Future Wars.* London: John Murray, 1906.

———. *Cavalry in War and Peace.* London: H. Rees, 1910.

Bethell, Major H.A. "Has the Experience of the War in South Africa Shown That Any Change Is Necessary in the System of Field Artillery Fire Tactics (In the Attack As Well As in Defence) in European Warfare?" *Minutes of the Proceedings of the Royal Artillery Institution* 29 (1902–1903): 136–46.

Bethune, Brigadier General E.C. "Uses of Cavalry and Mounted Infantry in Modern Warfare." *Journal of the Royal United Services Institute* 50, no. 1 (1906): 619–36.

Bidwell, Shelford, and Dominick Graham. *Firepower: The British Army Weapons and Theories of War 1904–1945.* Barnsley, U.K.: Pen & Sword, 2004.

Bird, Anthony. *Gentlemen, We Will Stand and Fight: Le Cateau 1914.* Ramsbury, U.K.: Crowood, 2008.

Bird, Brevet Major W.D. "Infantry Fire Tactics." *Journal of the Royal United Services Institute* 49, no. 2 (1905): 1175–82.

———. "Some Notes on Modern Tactics." *Journal of the Royal United Services Institute* 53, no. 1 (1909): 492–98.

Bird, Lieutenant Colonel W. D., trans. "A Company of Russian Machine Guns at the Battle of Liao-Yang." *Journal of the Royal United Services Institute* 50, no. 2 (1906): 1498–1503.

Bloem, Walter. *The Advance from Mons 1914: The Experiences of a German Infantry Officer.* 1916. Reprint, Solihull, U.K.: Hellion, 2004.

Bond, Brian. "Doctrine and Training in the British Cavalry, 1870–1914." In Howard, *Theory and Practice of War*, 95–125.

———, ed. *"Look to Your Front": Studies in the First World War.* Staplehurst, U.K.: Spellmount, 1999.

———. *The Victorian Army and the Staff College 1854–1914.* London: Eyre Methuen, 1972.

———, ed. *Victorian Military Campaigns.* London: Tom Donovan, 1967.

Bou, Jean. "Modern Cavalry: Mounted Rifles, the Boer War, and the Doctrinal Debates." In Dennis & Grey, *Boer War*, 99–115.

Bourne, John M. *Britain and the Great War 1914–1918.* London: Arnold, 1989.

Bourne, John, and Gary Sheffield, eds. *Douglas Haig: War Diaries and Letters 1914–1918.* London: Weidenfeld & Nicolson, 2005.

A British Officer [William Elliot Cairnes]. *An Absent Minded War.* London: John Milne, 1900.

Bryson, Richard. "The Once and Future Army." In Bond, *Look to Your Front*, 25–63.

Budworth, Major C. E. D. "British and French Q.F. Artillery." *Minutes of the Proceedings of the Royal Artillery Institution* 37 (1910–1911): 377–85.

———. "Training and Action Necessary to Further Co-operation between Artillery and Infantry." *Journal of the Royal United Services Institute* 57, no. 1 (1913): 67–86.

Burney, Major P. De. S. "The Role of Heavy Artillery: Its Employment in the Field and its Consequent Position on the March." *Journal of the Royal United Services Institute* 53, no. 1 (1909): 499–504.

Caddell, Major J. F. "Contrasts in the Conditions of Warfare at the Beginning of the Nineteenth and Twentieth Centuries and Some Deductions as to Possible Tactical Formations for the Future." *Minutes of the Proceedings of the Royal Artillery Institution* 28 (1901–1902): 351–64.

———. "Should We Re-Introduce Common Shell for Use with Our Field Artillery?" *Minutes of the Proceedings of the Royal Artillery Institution* 32 (1905–1906): 537–40.

———. "Theories as to the Best Position for Quick Firing Shield Field Artillery." *Journal of the Royal United Services Institute* 50, no. 2 (1906): 1477–89.

Callwell, Brevet Lieutenant Colonel C. E. "Looking Back." *Minutes of the Proceedings of the Royal Artillery Institution* 30 (1903–1904): 258–64.

———. "The Use of Heavy Guns in the Field in Europe." *Minutes of the Proceedings of the Royal Artillery Institution* 31 (1904–1905): 1–12.

Callwell, Colonel Charles. *Small Wars: Their Principles and Practice.* 3rd ed. London: H.M.S.O., 1906.

Callwell, Major C. E. "Artillery Notes from the Veld." *Minutes of the Proceedings of the Royal Artillery Institution* 28 (1901–1902): 281–88.

Campbell, Lieutenant Colonel J. "Infantry in Battle." *Journal of the Royal United Services Institute* 56, no. 1 (1912): 349–67.

Carr-Ellison, Lieutenant Colonel R.H. "The Interests of Officers and the Service." *United Service Magazine*, April 1904, 72–76.

Carrier, Captain P.A. "Correspondence Re: Theories as to the Best Position for Q.F. Shielded Artillery." *Journal of the Royal United Services Institute* 51, no. 1 (1907): 109.

Carter, Brigadier General F.C. "Our Failings in 'The Assault.'" *Army Review* 3 (1912): 90–104.

Carter, Major J.E. "From Enslin to Bloemfontein with the 6th Division." *Journal of the Royal United Services Institute* 44, no. 2 (1900): 1145–53.

Carver, Field Marshal Lord. *The National Army Museum Book of the Boer War*. London: Pan Books, 2000.

Cavalryman. "The Education of the Cavalry Officer." *United Service Magazine*, December 1904, 276–83.

———. "The Squadron System." *United Service Magazine*, October 1904, 82–86.

Cavalry Officer. "British Cavalry." *Journal of the Royal United Services Institute* 43, no. 1 (1899): 452–55.

Cave, Nigel, and Jack Sheldon. *Le Cateau*. Barnsley, U.K.: Pen & Sword, 2008.

Childers, Erskine. *German Influence on British Cavalry*. London: E. Arnold 1911.

———. *War and the Arme Blanche*. 1910. Reprint, Uckfield, U.K.: Naval and Military Press, n.d.

Churchill, Winston. *Ian Hamilton's March*. London: Longmans, Green & Co., 1900.

———. "Impressions of the War in South Africa." *Journal of the Royal United Services Institute* 45, no. 1 (1901): 835–48.

———. *London to Ladysmith via Pretoria*. London: Longmans, Green & Co., 1900.

Clarke, Captain R.G. "Machine Guns." *Army Review* 4 (1913): 95–117.

Clarke, Major J.L.J. "The Double Company System for British Infantry." *United Service Magazine*, June 1904, 267–72.

Colleton, Major Sir R. "The Training of a Battalion in the Attack." *Journal of the Royal United Services Institute* 43, no. 1 (1899): 129–47.

"Combination in the Attack." *Journal of the Royal United Services Institute* 54, no. 2 (1910): 1196–1201.

Congreve, Colonel Walter. Comment on "Machine Guns," by Captain R.V.K. Applin. *Journal of the Royal United Services Institute* 54, no. 1 (1910): 63.

"Communications on the Battlefield." *Journal of the Royal United Services Institute* 53, no. 1 (1909): 357–69.

Conan Doyle, Arthur. *The Great Boer War*. London: Smith & Elder, 1901.

Cooper, Duff. *Haig*. 2 vols. London: Faber and Faber, 1935.

"Correspondence—Artillery Support of Infantry." *Journal of the Royal United Service Institution* 54, no. 1 (1910): 665.

Cox, Gary P. "Of Aphorisms, Lessons, and Paradigms: Comparing the British and German Official Histories of the Russo-Japanese War." *The Journal of Military History* 56, no. 2 (1992): 389–401.

Craster, Captain J. E. E. "The Attack of Entrenched Positions." *Royal Engineers Journal* 3 (1906): 339–42.

Crookenden, Captain A. "Co-Operation between Infantry and Artillery in the Attack." *Army Review* 5 (1914): 118–126.

Crowe, Lieutenant Colonel J. H. V. "Artillery from an Infantry Point of View." *Minutes of the Proceedings of the Royal Artillery Institution* 36 (1909–1910): 74–81.

Crusader [pseud.]. "The Problem of Numbers." *United Service Magazine*, October 1904, 69–74.

Culmann, Captain F. "French and German Tendencies with Regard to the Preparation and Development of an Action." *Journal of the Royal United Services Institute* 52, no. 1 (1908): 690–703.

Darling, J. C. *20th Hussars in the Great War*. Hampshire, U.K.: Lyndhurst, 1923.

Dawnay, Captain H. "Artillery and Infantry in the Final Stages of the Attack: An Infantry View." *Minutes of the Proceedings of the Royal Artillery Institution* 35 (1908–1909): 49–56.

Dawson, Lieutenant A. T. "Modern Artillery." *Journal of the Royal United Services Institute* 45, no. 1 (1901): 462–65.

De Groot, Gerard. *Douglas Haig 1861–1928*. London: Unwin Hyman, 1988.

———. "Educated Soldier or Cavalry Officer? Contradictions in the Pre-1914 Career of Douglas Haig." *War and Society* 4, no. 2 (1986): 51–69.

De Lisle, Brigadier General H. De. B. "The Strategical Action of Cavalry." *Journal of the Royal United Services Institute* 56, no. 1 (1912): 787–806.

De Negrier, General François Oscar. "Some Lessons of the Russo-Japanese War." *Journal of the Royal United Services Institute* 50, no. 1 (1906): 687–98, 805–809.

Dennis, Peter, and Jeffrey Grey, eds. *The Boer War: Army, Nation and Empire*. Canberra, Australia: Army History Unit, 2000.

De Thomasson, Commandant. "The British Army Exercise of 1913." *Army Review* 5 (1914): 143–156.

De Wet, Christiaan Rudolf. *Three Years' War*. London, Archibald Constable & Co. Ltd., 1902.

Dilke, Charles. Comment on "The Use of the Horse Soldier," by Captain C. W. Battine. *Journal of the Royal United Services Institute* 52, no. 1 (1908): 320.

Dilke, Sir Charles. "The Report of the War Commission." *Journal of the Royal United Services Institute* 48, no. 1 (1904): 213–44.

Dooner, Captain J. G., transl. "Employment of Field Artillery with Small Detachments." *Minutes of the Proceedings of the Royal Artillery Institution* 37 (1910–1911): 107–110.

Du Cane, Brevet Lieutenant Colonel J. P. "Cover and Co-Operation." *Minutes of the Proceedings of the Royal Artillery Institution* 30 (1903–1904): 358–63.

———. "Some Problems Presented by the Introduction of Q. F. Guns for Field Artillery." *Minutes of the Proceedings of the Royal Artillery Institution* 30 (1903–1904): 249–57.

Du Cane, Brigadier General J. P. "The Co-Operation of Field Artillery with Infantry in the Attack." *Army Review* 1 (1911): 97–113.

Ducrot, Major L. H. "Guns in South Africa." *Minutes of the Proceedings of the Royal Artillery Institution* 28 (1901–1902): 203–208.

Dunlop, John. *The Development of the British Army 1899–1914.* London: Methuen, 1938.

Duxbury, G. R. *The Battle of Belmont, 23rd November 1899.* Johannesburg, South Africa: S.A National Museum of Military History, 1995.

———. *The Battle of Colenso 15th December 1899.* Johannesburg, South Africa: S.A National Museum of Military History, 1995.

———. *The Battle of Graspan/Enslin 25th November 1899.* Johannesburg, South Africa: S.A National Museum of Military History, 1995.

———. *The Battle of Magersfontein 11th December 1899.* Johannesburg, South Africa: S.A National Museum of Military History, 1995.

———. *The Battle of Modder River 28th November 1899.* Johannesburg, South Africa: S.A National Museum of Military History, 1995.

———. *The Battle of Spioenkop, 24th January 1899.* Johannesburg, South Africa: S.A National Museum of Military History, 1995.

———. *The Siege of Ladysmith, 2nd November 1899 to 28th February 1900.* Johannesburg, South Africa: S.A National Museum of Military History, 1995.

Editor. "Review of German Official History of War in South Africa." *United Service Magazine,* April 1904, 97–100.

Edmonds, Brigadier-General Sir James, ed. *Official History of the Great War: Military Operations France and Belgium 1914.* 2 vols. London, H.M.S.O, 1925.

Ellis, John. *The Social History of the Machine Gun.* London: Pimlico, 1993.

Ellison, Brigadier General G. F. "Our Army System, in Theory and Practice." *Army Review* 2 (1912): 382–96.

Evans, Nicholas. "From Drill to Doctrine: Forging the British Army's Tactics 1897–1909." PhD diss., King's College London, 2007.

Falls, Captain Cyril. *Official History of the Great War: Military Operations France and Belgium 1917.* 2 vols. London: H.M.S.O., 1940.

Falls, Cyril. "The Reconquest of the Sudan, 1896–1898." In Bond, *Victorian Military Campaigns,* 286–306.

Farndale, Martin. *History of the Royal Regiment of Artillery, Western Front 1914–18.* London: Royal Artillery Institution, 1986.

"The Fighting Value of Modern Cavalry." *Journal of the Royal United Services Institute* 55, no. 1 (1911): 352–56.

Footsoldier. "Some Thoughts on the War Organization of an Infantry Battalion." *Army Review* 3 (1912): 72–80.

Forbes, G. "Experiences in South Africa with a New Range Finder." *Journal of the Royal United Services Institute* 46, no. 2 (1902): 1381–94.

Forth, Captain Willoughby. "The Delhi Manoeuvres December 1902." *Journal of the Royal United Services Institute* 47, no. 1 (1903): 673–79.

Frankland, Lieutenant T.H.C. "Mounted Infantry Maxims—Being Notes Based on Active Service." *Journal of the Royal United Services Institute* 47, no. 1 (1903): 155–170.

French, Colonel J.D.P. "Cavalry Manoeuvres." *Journal of the Royal United Services Institute* 39, no. 1 (1895): 559–88.

French, Lieutenant-General Sir John. Comment on "Uses of Cavalry and Mounted Infantry," by Brigadier General E.C. Bethune. *Journal of the Royal United Services Institute* 50, no. 1 (1906): 633.

"Frontal Attack and Infantry Fire-Superiority." *Journal of the Royal United Services Institute* 51, no. 1 (1907): 80–82.

Gall, H.R. *Modern Tactics.* London: W.H. Allen, 1890.

Gardner, Nikolas. "Command Control in the Great Retreat of 1914: The Disintegration of the British Cavalry Division." *Journal of Military History* 63, no. 1 (1999): 29–54

———. *Trial by Fire: Command the British Expeditionary Force in 1914.* Westport, Conn.: Praeger, 2003.

Garwood, Lieutenant F.S. "Realistic Targets." *Journal of the Royal United Services Institute* 46, no. 2 (1902): 929–46.

Gatacre, Major-General Sir W.F. "A Few Notes on the Characteristics of Hill-Fighting in India." *Journal of the Royal United Services Institute* 43, no. 2 (1899): 1066–72.

G.C.W. [Graeme Chamley Wynne], trans. *Ypres 1914: An Official Account Published by Order of the German General Staff.* London: Constable and Company Ltd., 1919.

General Staff. *Report on Foreign Manoeuvres in 1912.* 1912. Reprint, Uckfield, U.K.: Naval and Military Press, n.d.

———. "The War and the Arme Blanche: The General Staff's Views on Mr. Childers's Book." *Journal of the Royal United Services Institute* 54, no. 2 (1910): 1059–67.

General Staff Translation. "The Employment of Machine Guns in the Field." *Journal of the Royal United Services Institute* 54, no. 1 (1910): 214–27.

———. "The Importance Attached to Movement in Japanese Tactics." *Journal of the Royal United Services Institute* 54, no. 1 (1910): 95–98.

———. "Lessons of the Russo-Japanese War Applied to the Training of Infantry." *Journal of the Royal United Services Institute* 53, no. 2 (1909): 1190–1201.

———. "Machine Gun Fire." *Journal of the Royal United Services Institute* 55, no. 2 (1911): 911–14.

———. "Opinions with Regard to the Attack of Entrenched Positions." *Journal of the Royal United Services Institute* 51, no. 2 (1907): 1005–15.

———. "The Russo-Japanese War: Opinions and Criticism by Those Who Took Part in It." *Journal of the Royal United Services Institute* 53, no. 1 (1909): 789–94.

"German Ideas on the Role and Employment of Cavalry." *Journal of the Royal United Services Institute* 48, no. 2 (1904): 825–31, 947–54.

Gillings, Ken. *The Battle of the Thukela Heights: 12–28 February 1900.* Randburg, South Africa: Ravan Press, 1999.

——. "Indirect Artillery Fire in the Anglo-Boer War 1899–1902." *Journal of the Society for Army Historical Research* 89 (2011): 182–83.

Godley, Colonel A. J. "Mounted Infantry." *Cavalry Journal* 4 (1909): 140–144.

Gooch, John, ed. *The Boer War: Direction, Image and Experience.* London: Frank Cass, 2000.

——. *The Plans of War: The General Staff and British Military Strategy c.1900–1914.* London: Routledge, 1974.

Gordon, Captain N. F. "The Future Training, Organization and Tactical Employment of Q.F. Field Artillery." *Minutes of the Proceedings of the Royal Artillery Institution* 31 (1904–1905): 177–190.

——. "Has the Experience of the War in South Africa Shown That Any Change Is Necessary in the System of Field Artillery Fire Tactics (In the Attack As Well As in Defence) in European Warfare?" *Minutes of the Proceedings of the Royal Artillery Institution* 29 (1902–1903): 247–65.

Gordon, General W. Comment on "Notes on Musketry Training of Troops," by Captain H. R. Mead. *Journal of the Royal United Services Institute* 42, no. 1 (1899): 254.

Gore-Browne, Lieutenant S. "The Best Methods to be Adopted to Secure Co-Operation Between Infantry and Artillery in the Attack." *Minutes of the Proceedings of the Royal Artillery Institution* 33 (1906–1907): 304–12.

Gough, Lieutenant Colonel H. De la P. "The Strategic Employment of Cavalry." *Journal of the Royal United Services Institute* 49, no. 2 (1905): 1117–37.

Graham, Dominick. "The British Expeditionary Force in 1914 and the Machine Gun." *Military Affairs* 46 (1982): 190–93.

Greenly, Lieutenant Colonel W. H. "Employment of Cavalry in a Retreat." *Army Review* 4 (1913): 379–90.

Grierson, J. M. *Scarlet into Khaki.* Reprint, London: Greenhill, 1988.

Gudmundsson, Bruce. *Stormtroop Tactics: Innovation in the German Army 1914–1918.* New York: Praeger, 1989.

Gunter, Lieutenant Colonel E., trans. "A German View of British Tactics in the Boer War." *Journal of the Royal United Services Institute* 46, no. 1 (1902): 801–806.

Haig, Major-General Douglas. "Army Training in India." *Army Review* 2 (1912): 55–78.

——. *Cavalry Studies.* London: H. Rees, 1907.

Hall, Darrell. *The Hall Handbook of the Anglo-Boer War 1899–1902.* Pietermaritzburg, South Africa: University of Natal Press, 1999.

Hamilton, General Sir Ian. "Remarks by General Sir Ian Hamilton K.C.B, D.S.O., C-in-C Southern Command, on the Training of the Troops during 1907." *Journal of the Royal United Services Institute* 52, no. 1 (1908): 83–96.

——. "Remarks by General Sir Ian Hamilton, K.C.B, D.S.O, C-in-C Southern Command, on the Training of Troops under His Command during 1908." *Journal of the Royal United Services Institute* 52, no. 2 (1908): 1550–61.

Hamilton, Ian. *The Fighting of the Future.* London: K. Paul, Trench & Co., 1885.

———. *A Staff Officer's Scrap Book during the Russo-Japanese War.* 2 vols. London: E. Arnold, 1908.

Hamilton, Lieutenant-General Sir Ian. "The Training of Troops during 1906." *Journal of the Royal United Services Institute* 50, no. 2 (1906): 1517–26.

Hamilton-Gordon, Major Alexander. "Fourteen Days' Howitzer Work on Service." *Minutes of the Proceedings of the Royal Artillery Institution* 27 (1900–1901): 347–64.

Hamilton-Grace, Captain R. S. "Cavalry in the Russo-Japanese War." *Cavalry Journal* 5 (1910): 213–19.

Hamley, E. B. *Operations of War.* 3rd ed. Edinburgh, Scotland: Blackwood, 1872.

Hartesveldt, van Fred R. *The Boer War: Historiography and Annotated Bibliography.* Westport, Conn.: Greenwood Press, 2000.

Haycock, R., and K. Neilson, eds. *Men, Machines and War.* Ontario, Canada: Wilfried Laurier University Press, 1988.

Head, Major C. O. "The Desirability of the Acquirement by Infantry Officers, Especially of High Ranks, of a More Intelligent Knowledge of the Use of Field Artillery Than They Generally Possess." *Journal of the Royal United Services Institute* 48, no. 2 (1904): 1172–78.

Headlam, John. *History of the Royal Artillery from the Indian Mutiny to the Great War.* 3 vols. Reprint, Uckfield, U.K.: Naval and Military Press, 2005.

Heath, Lieutenant Colonel G. M. "Field Engineering in the Light of Modern Warfare." *Journal of the Royal United Services Institute* 50, no. 1 (1906): 314–16.

"The Heavy Artillery of a Field Army at River Crossings." *United Service Magazine,* November 1904, 164–68.

Henderson, Colonel G. F. R. *The Science of War: A Collection of Essays and Lectures 1892–1903,* edited by N. Malcolm. London: Longmans, Green & Co., 1905.

Hepper, Captain L. L. "The Royal Artillery: A Plea for Common Sense Organisation." *United Service Magazine,* June 1904, 237–40.

Herwig, Holger. *The Marne, 1914: The Opening of World War 1 and the Battle That Changed the World.* New York: Random House, 2009.

Hezlet, Lieutenant R. K. "The Capabilities and Future Role of Field Howitzers." *Minutes of the Proceedings of the Royal Artillery Institution* 31 (1904–1905): 54–59.

Hogg, Ian V., and John Weeks. *Military Small Arms of the 20th Century.* 6th ed. London: Cassel, 1992.

Holmes, Richard. *The Little Field Marshal: A Life of Sir John French.* London: Weidenfeld and Nicolson, 2004.

———. *Riding the Retreat: Mons to the Marne 1914 Revisited.* London: Pimlico, 2007.

Holmes Wilson, Captain C. "Armoured Field Artillery." *United Service Magazine,* December 1904, 267–71.

——. "The Employment of QF Artillery in the Field." *United Service Magazine*, May 1904, 192–99.

Horne, Major J. M. "Reflections on the Tactics of the Attack." *Journal of the Royal United Services Institute* 52, no. 2 (1908): 1631–52.

Howard, Michael. "Men against Fire: Expectations of War in 1914." *International Security* 9, no. 1 (1984): 41–57.

——, ed. *The Theory and Practice of War: Essays Presented to Captain B. H. Liddell Hart on his 70th Birthday.* London: Cassell, 1965.

Howard-Gill, Captain D., trans. "Methods of Fire and Ranging of the French Artillery." *Minutes of the Proceedings of the Royal Artillery Institution* 30 (1903–1904): 334–51.

Ikona [pseudo]. "The Passing of the Old M.I." *Cavalry Journal* 9 (1914): 209–13.

Immanuel, Major. "The Importance of Fighting Dismounted for Cavalry, and the Place to be Assigned to it in Action and Instruction." *Journal of the Royal United Services Institute* 52, no. 2 (1908): 1273–80.

"Infantry Combat in the Russo-Japanese War: Observations and Personal Reminiscences of the Commandant of a Russian Company." *Journal of the Royal United Services Institute* 50, no. 2 (1906): 1048–53, 1169–77, 1273–80.

Infantry Officer. "A Short Plea in Favour of the Present Organization of the Infantry Battalion." *Journal of the Royal United Services Institute* 56, no. 2 (1912): 1579–82.

Inglefield, Lieutenant Colonel N. B. "Some Remarks on the Royal Artillery in the War in South Africa, Chiefly with Reference to Heavy Guns in the Field." *Minutes of the Proceedings of the Royal Artillery Institution* 39 (1902–1903): 499–526.

Jackman, Steven D. "Shoulder to Shoulder: Close Control and 'Old Prussian Drill' in German Offensive Infantry Tactics, 1871–1914." *Journal of Military History* 68, no. 1 (2004): 73–105.

Jackson, M. *The Record of a Regiment of the Line: Being a Regimental History of the 1st Battalion Devonshire Regiment During the Boer War 1899–1902.* London: Hutchinson Co., 1908.

Johnstone, H. M. *A History of Tactics.* Reprint, Uckfield, U.K.: Naval & Military Press, 2004.

Joll, James. *Europe Since 1870.* London: Penguin, 1990.

Judd, Denis, and Keith Surridge. *The Boer War.* New York: Palgrave Macmillan, 2002.

"K" [pseudo.]. "Suggestions for the Improvement of the Annual Course of Musketry." *United Service Magazine*, June 1904, 300–303.

Kearsey, Captain A. H. C. "Manner in Which the Infantry Attack Best Be Supported by Artillery Fire." *Journal of the Royal United Services Institute* 54, no. 1 (1910): 753–74.

Kenjiro, Major Ishiura. "The New Japanese Infantry Training (Provisional) December 1906." *Journal of the Royal United Services Institute* 51, no. 1 (1907): 715–19.

Kennedy, Paul M., ed. *The War Plans of the Great Powers, 1880–1914.* London: George Allen & Unwin, 1979.

Kentish, Captain R. J. "The Case for the Eight Company Battalion." *Journal of the Royal United Services Institute* 56, no. 2 (1912): 891–928.

Kirton, W. "With the Japanese on the Yalu." *Journal of the Royal United Services Institute* 49, no. 1 (1905): 269–86.

Klingelhoffer, General. "Artillery Support of the Infantry Attack." *Journal of the Royal United Services Institute* 59, no. 2 (1914): 518–19.

Knapp, Major K. K. "Pack Artillery and the Close Support of the Infantry Attack." *Journal of the Royal United Services Institute* 52, no. 2 (1908): 963–67.

———. "The Tactical Employment of Pack Artillery—The Influence of Armament on the Question." *Journal of the Royal United Services Institute* 51, no. 1 (1907): 720–28.

———. "The Tactical Employment of Pack Artillery." *Journal of the Royal United Services Institute* 50, no. 1 (1906): 200–206.

Kowner, Rotem. "Between a Colonial Clash and World War Zero: The Impact of the Russo-Japanese War in a Global Perspective." In Kowner, *Impact of the Russo-Japanese War*, 1–27.

———, ed. *The Impact of the Russo-Japanese War*. London: Routledge, 2007.

Kruger, Rayne. *Good-Bye Dolly Gray: The Story of the Boer War*. London: Cassell, 1967.

Kuropatkin, G. N. *The Russian Army and the Japanese War*. London: John Murray, 1909.

Langlois, General H. "The British Army in a European Conflict." *Journal of the Royal United Services Institute* 54, no. 2 (1910): 903–17.

Lascelles, Captain E. "The Influence of the Ground on Shock Action." *Cavalry Journal* 5 (1910): 492–98.

Lawson, Major A. "How Can Moral Qualities Best Be Developed During the Preparation of the Officer and the Man for the Duties Each Will Carry out in War?" *Journal of the Royal United Services Institute* 58, no. 1 (1914): 431–76.

Lee, John. *A Soldier's Life: General Sir Ian Hamilton 1853–1947*. Basingstoke: Macmillian, 2000.

Leeson, D. M. "Playing at War: The British Military Manoeuvres of 1898." *War in History* 15, no. 4 (2008): 432–61.

"Lessons of the South African and Chinese Wars." *Journal of the Royal United Services Institute* 45, no. 1 (1901): 291–93.

Levita, Major C. B. "A Plea for More Intimate Connection between Infantry and Field Howitzers." *Minutes of the Proceedings of the Royal Artillery Institution* 32 (1905–1906): 37–40.

Lloyd, Francis Thomas. *First or Grenadier Guards in South Africa 1899–1902*. London: J. J. Keliher, 1907.

Lucy, John. *There's a Devil in the Drum*. London: Faber & Faber, 1938.

Luvaas, Jay. *The Education of an Army: British Military Thought 1815–1940*. London: Cassell, 1965.

Lyttelton, Neville. *Eighty Years: Soldiering, Politics, Games*. London: Hodder & Stoughton, 1927.

MacDonald, Colonel Sir J. H. A. "Infantry in a New Century." *Journal of the Royal United Services Institute* 45, no. 1 (1901): 242–58.

Mahan, Alfred Thayer. *The War in South Africa: A Narrative of the Anglo-Boer War from the Beginning of Hostilities to the Conclusion of Peace.* New York: F.P. Collier & Son, 1902.

Marble, Sanders. "'The Infantry cannot do with a gun less': The Place of the Artillery in the B.E.F. 1914–1918." PhD diss., Kings College London, 2001.

Markham Rose, Captain J. "Lessons to be Derived from the Expedition to South Africa in Regard to the Best Organisation of the Land Forces of the Empire." *Journal of the Royal United Services Institute* 45, no. 1 (1901): 541–93.

Martin, Lieutenant-Colonel A.G. "Cavalry in the Great War: A Brief Retrospect." *Cavalry Journal* 24 (1934): 131–37, 437–48.

Maude, Captain F.N. *Military Letters and Essays.* Kansas City, Kans.: Hudson Kimberley, 1895.

Maude, Colonel F.N. "Mobility: Its Influence on Strategy." *Journal of the Royal United Services Institute* 52, no. 1 (1908): 196–207.

Maude, Lieutenant-Colonel F.N. *Cavalry: Its Past and Future.* London: Clowes, 1903.

———. "Continental versus South African Tactics: A Comparison and Reply to Some Critics." *Journal of the Royal United Services Institute* 46, no. 1 (1902): 318–54.

———. "Military Education." *Journal of the Royal United Services Institute* 48, no. 1 (1904): 1–29.

Maurice, Frederick, ed. *History of the War in South Africa.* 7 vols. Uckfield, U.K.: Naval & Military Press, 2007. First published 1906–1910 by Hurst & Blackett.

———. "Omdurman." *Nineteenth Century* 4 (1898): 1048–62.

Maurice, Major-General J.F. Comment on "Lessons of the War," by Colonel Sir C.E. Vincent. *Journal of the Royal United Services Institute* 44, no. 1 (1900): 658–59.

Maxse, Brigadier General F.I. "Battalion Organisation." *Journal of the Royal United Services Institute* 56, no. 1 (1912): 53–85.

May, Major-General M.D, "Freedom of Manoeuvre." *Army Review* 4 (1913): 440–49.

Mayne, Lieutenant Colonel C.B. "The Lance as a Cavalry Weapon." *Journal of the Royal United Services Institute* 49, no. 1 (1905): 118–139.

McHardy, Captain A.A. "On Heavy Artillery." *United Service Magazine,* April 1904, 54–61.

Mead, Captain H.R. "Notes on Musketry Training of Troops." *Journal of the Royal United Services Institute* 43, no. 1 (1899): 234–57.

Mead, Major H.R. "Notes on Night Attacks during the Early Part of the Boer War." *United Service Magazine,* May 1904, 200–10.

Meinertzhagen, R. *Army Diary 1899–1926.* Edinburgh, Scotland: Oliver & Boyd 1960.

"Military Observations of the War in South Africa." *Journal of the Royal United Services Institute* 46, no. 1 (1902): 355–63, 468–78.

Miller, Carman. *Painting the Map Red: Canada and the South African War 1899–1902.* Natal, South Africa: University of Natal Press, 1998.

Miller, Stephen M. *Lord Methuen and the British Army: Failure and Redemption in South Africa*. London: Frank Cass, 1999.

———. *Volunteers on the Veld: Britain's Citizen-Soldiers and the South African War, 1899–1902*. Norman: University of Oklahoma Press, 2007.

Miller Maguire, T. "The Metaphysical Manoeuvres of a Phantom Army." *United Service Magazine*, November 1904, 146–53.

———. "The Mounted Infantry Controversy." *United Service Magazine*, March 1904, 602–605.

Millin, Sarah. *General Smuts*. Boston: Little, Brown, and Co., 1936.

Mitake, Major. "The Infantry Battlefront." *Journal of the Royal United Services Institute* 51, no. 1 (1907): 327–31.

Molyneux, Captain E. M. J. "Cavalry Suggestions." *Journal of the Royal United Services Institute* 48, no. 2 (1904): 1164–71.

Molyneux, Major E. M. "Artillery Support of Infantry." *Journal of the Royal United Services Institute* 53, no. 2 (1909): 1454–70, 1607–17.

Monro, Major-General C. C. "Fire and Movement." *Army Review* 1 (1911): 92–96.

Moore, Major A. T. "The Defence of a Position upon Open Ground." *Royal Engineers Journal* 3 (1906): 185–87.

Moreman, Tim. "The British and Indian Armies and North West Frontier Warfare 1849–1914." *Journal of Imperial and Commonwealth History* 20, no. 1 (1992): 35–64.

Morris, A. J. A., ed. *The Letters of Lieutenant Colonel Charles à Court Repington*. Stroud, U.K.: Army Records Society, 1999.

Morrison, Lieutenant Colonel R. H. "Lessons to Be Derived from the Expedition to South Africa in Regard to the Best Organisation of the Land Forces of the Empire." *Journal of the Royal United Services Institute* 45, no. 2 (1901): 797–825.

Morton, Major R. O. "The Role of Heavy Artillery on the Modern Battlefield." *Royal Engineers Journal* 10 (1913): 23–32.

———. "Siege Artillery: Methods and Requirements from RE." *Royal Engineers Journal* 10 (1913): 355–63.

Murray, Captain Stewart. "Musketry and Tactics." *United Service Magazine*, August 1898, 653–60.

Nasson, Bill. *The South African War 1899–1902*. London: Arnold, 1999.

———. "Waging Total War in South Africa: Some Centenary Writings on the Anglo-Boer War, 1899–1902." *Journal of Military History* 66, no. 2 (2002): 813–28.

Neillands, Robin. *The Old Contemptibles: The British Expeditionary, 1914*. London: John Murray, 2004.

Neilson, Keith. "Watching the 'Steamroller': British Observers and the Russian Army before 1914." *Journal of Strategic Studies* 8, no. 2 (1985): 199–217.

———. "That Dangerous and Difficult Enterprise: British Military Thinking and the Russo-Japanese War." *War & Society* 9, no. 2 (1991): 17–37.

Newell, Clayton R. *The Framework of Operational Warfare*. London: Routledge, 1991.

Nicolls, Lieutenant Colonel E.G. Comment on "Some Remarks on the Royal Artillery in the War in South Africa," by Lieutenant Colonel N.B. Inglefield. *Minutes of the Proceedings of the Royal Artillery Institution* 39 (1902–1093): 521.

Nicolls, Major E.G. "The Training, Organisation and Equipment of Companies of the Royal Garrison Artillery with Medium Guns, and Howtizers, and their tactics in Future Field Operations." *Minutes of the Proceedings of the Royal Artillery Institution* 28 (1901–1902): 97–110.

———. "The Type of Guns That Should Be Employed with Artillery in the Field." *Minutes of the Proceedings of the Royal Artillery Institution* 28 (1901–1902): 225–33.

Not a Staff Officer. "Some Remarks on Recent Changes." *United Service Magazine*, October 1904, 46–48.

Notes from the Front. London: H.M.S.O., 1914.

Notes from the Front, Part II. London: H.M.S.O., 1915.

An Old Soldier. "Retrospect of a Successful Campaign." *United Service Magazine*, April 1904, 77–80.

Ormsby-Johnson, Major F.C. "Reconnaissance as a Fine Art under the Present Conditions of War." *Journal of the Royal United Services Institute* 46, no. 2 (1902): 1194–1215.

Outsider [pseudo.]. "Artillery Training." *Minutes of the Proceedings of the Royal Artillery Institution* 38 (1911–1912): 213–30.

Owen, Major-General C.H. Comment on "Lessons of the War," by Colonel Sir C.E. Vincent. *Journal of the Royal United Services Institute* 44, no. 1 (1900): 641–42.

Pakenham, Thomas. *The Boer War.* Reprint, London: Abacus, 1997.

Pearson, Captain C.C. "Light Infantry: A Suggestions." *Journal of the Royal United Services Institute* 45, no. 1 (1901): 60–72.

Peters, Colonel J. "Teach the Boys to Shoot." *United Service Magazine*, March 1904, 598–601.

Phillips, Gervase. "The Obsolescence of the *Arme Blanche* and Technological Determinism in British Military History." *War and Society* 9, no. 1 (2002): 39–59.

———. "Scapegoat Arm: Twentieth Century Cavalry in Anglophonic Historiography." *Journal of Military History* 71, no. 1 (2007): 37–74.

Phillips, L.M. *With Rimington.* London: Edward Arnold, 1902.

Philpott, William. *Bloody Victory: The Sacrifice on the Somme and the Making of the Twentieth Century.* London: Little Brown, 2009.

Pilcher, T.D. *Some Lessons from the Boer War, 1899–1902.* London: Ibister, 1903.

Poe, Bryce. "British Army Reforms 1902–1914." *Military Affairs* 31, no. 3 (1967): 131–38.

Pollock, Lieutenant Colonel A.W.A. "Smokeless Powder and Entrenchments." *Journal of the Royal United Services Institute* 47, no. 2 (1903): 805–808.

———. "The Tactical Inefficiency of the Regular Army: Its Causes and Remedy." *Fortnightly Review* 75 (1904): 831–39.

————. "The Training of the Army." *Journal of the Royal United Services Institute* 47, no. 1 (1903): 176–180.

Pollock, Major A. W. A. "The Battle Drill of Infantry." *Journal of the Royal United Services Institute* 42, no. 1 (1898): 540–56.

————. "Training Recruits at Regimental Depots." *Journal of the Royal United Services Institute* 46, no. 1 (1902): 676–83.

Porch, Douglas. *The March to the Marne: The French Army 1871–1914.* Cambridge: Cambridge University Press, 2003.

Powell, Geoffrey. *Buller: A Scapegoat? A Life of General Sir Redvers Buller 1839–1908.* London: Leo Cooper, 1994.

Pretorius, Fransjohan. *Life on Commando During the Anglo-Boer War, 1899–1902.* Cape Town, South Africa: Human & Rosseau, 1999.

Pridham, C. H. B. *Superiority of Fire: A Short History of Rifles and Machine Guns.* London: Hutchinson, 1945.

P. S. [pseudo.]. *Cavalry in Action in the Wars of the Future: Studies in Applied Tactics,* translated by J. Formby. London: H. Rees, 1905.

Ram, Captain Jonkheer J. H. "Observations of the War in South Africa." *Journal of the Royal United Services Institute* 47, no. 2 (1903): 1386–99.

Ramsay, M. A. *Command and Cohesion: The Citizen Soldier and Minor Tactics in the British Army 1870–1918.* Westport, Conn.: Praeger, 2002.

Ransford, Oliver. *The Battle of Spion Kop.* London: John Murray, 1969.

Ratzenhofer, Lieutenant Field Marshal Gustav. "A Retrospect of the War in South Africa." *Journal of the Royal United Services Institute* 45, no. 1 (1901): 40–50.

Red Coat [pseud.]. "Concerning Individuality." *United Service Magazine,* October 1903, 64–69.

————. "Recruiting." *United Service Magazine,* December 1904, 272–75.

Report of His Majesty's Commissioners Appointed to Inquire into the Military Preparations and Other Matters Connected with the War in South Africa. 4 vols., including Report, Command No. 1789–1792. London: H.M.S.O., 1903.

Richardson, Major-General J. B. "Protection for Infantry in Action: A Means of Restoring the Power of Frontal Attack." *Minutes of the Proceedings of the Royal Artillery Institution* 32 (1905–1906): 138–44.

Rimington, Brigadier General M. F. "The Spirit of Cavalry under Napoleon." *Journal of the Royal United Services Institute* 50, no. 2 (1906): 1209–36.

Rimington, Major-General M. F. *Our Cavalry.* London: Macmillan, 1912.

Ripperger, Robert M. "The Development of French Artillery for the Offensive, 1890–1914." *Journal of Military History* 59, no. 4 (1995): 599–618.

Robertson, William. *From Private to Field Marshal.* London: Constable, 1921.

Robinson, Peter. "The Search for Mobility During the Second Boer War." *Journal of the Society for Army Historical Research* 86, no. 346 (2008): 140–58.

Rogers, Captain E. "Siege Warfare." *Royal Engineers Journal* 10 (1913): 281–87.

Rogers, Lieutenant Colonel E. "Machine Guns Up-to-Date." *Journal of the Royal United Services Institute* 48, no. 2 (1904): 1032–49.

Rohne, Lieutenant-General Heinrich. "How Is Fire Superiority to Be Attained in the Infantry Attack?" *Journal of the Royal United Services Institute* 44, no. 1 (1900): 258–61.

———. "Optimism in the German Field Artillery." *Journal of the Royal United Services Institute* 49, no. 1 (1905): 547–56.

———. "The Problem of Fire Superiority." *Journal of the Royal United Services Institute* 50, no. 2 (1906): 1036–42.

Rooke, Major G.H.J. "Shielded Infantry and the Decisive Frontal Attack." *Journal of the Royal United Services Institute* 58, no. 1 (1914): 771–84.

Ross, Captain C. "Departments in War." *Journal of the Royal United Services Institute* 47, no. 2 (1903): 977–1011.

Rowan-Robinson, Major H. "More Accurate Methods with Field Artillery." *Journal of the Royal United Services Institute* 58, no. 1 (1914): 111–15.

Samuels, Martin. *Command or Control? Command, Training and Tactics in British and German Armies 1888–1918.* London: Frank Cass, 1995.

Sankey, Captain C.E.P. "The Campaign of the Future: A Possible Development." *Royal Engineers Journal* 4 (1907): 4–6.

Scales, Robert. "Artillery in Small Wars: The Evolution of British Artillery Doctrine 1860–1914." PhD diss., Duke University, 1976.

Scott, Douglas, ed. *Douglas Haig: The Preparatory Prologue 1861–1914: Diaries and Letters.* Barnsley, U.K.: Pen & Sword Military, 2006.

Scovell, Captain G.J. "The Organization of a Battalion in War and Peace." *Journal of the Royal United Services Institute* 55, no. 2 (1911): 1293–1317.

Searle, G.R. *The Quest for National Efficiency: A Study in British Politics and Political Thought 1899–1914.* Oxford, England: Basil Blackwell, 1971.

Seki, Captain T. "The Value of the Arme Blanche, with Illustrations from the Recent Campaigns." *Journal of the Royal United Services Institute* 55, no. 2 (1911): 885–906, 1017–34, 1147–56.

A Sergeant. "The Evolution of the Short Service System: Its Effect on Personnel." *United Service Magazine*, November 1904, 137–40.

Sheffy, Yigal. "A Model Not to Follow: The European Armies and the Lessons of the War." In Kowner, *Impact of the Russo-Japanese War*, 257–72.

Sheldon, Jack. *The German Army at Ypres 1914.* Barnsley, U.K.: Pen & Sword, 2010.

"Shooting after Long Distance Marches." *Journal of the Royal United Services Institute* 54, no. 1 (1910): 775–80.

Simpson, Colonel H.C.C.D. "The Education of the Soldier." *Journal of the Royal United Services Institute* 51, no. 1 (1907): 206–212.

Smith, Frederick. *A Veterinary History of the War in South Africa.* London: H.W. Brown, 1919.

Smith-Dorrien, Horace. *Memories of Forty-Eight Years' Service.* London: John Murray, 1925.

Snyder, Jack. *The Ideology of the Offensive: Military Decision Making and the Disasters of 1914.* Ithaca, N.Y.: Cornell University Press, 1984.

Solando [pseudo.]. "The Decisive Range." *United Service Magazine,* June 1904, 295–99.

Spears, Edward. *Liaison 1914: A Narrative of the Great Retreat.* London: Eyre and Spottiswoode, 1968.

Special Correspondent [Charles Repington]. "Cavalry Lessons of the War." *Cavalry Journal* 1 (1906): 56–59.

Spiers, Edward. "The British Cavalry 1902–1914." *Journal of the Society for Army Historical Research* 57, no. 230 (1979): 71–79.

———. "Intelligence and Command in Britain's Small Colonial Wars of the 1890s." *Intelligence and National Security* 22, no. 5 (2007): 644–60.

———. *The Late Victorian Army 1868–1902.* Manchester, England: Manchester University Press, 1999.

———. "Rearming the Edwardian Artillery." *Journal of the Society for Army Historical Research* 57, no. 231 (1979): 167–76.

———. "The Reform of the Front-Line Forces of the U.K., 1895–1914." PhD diss., University of Edinburgh, 1974.

———. "Reforming the Infantry of the Line 1900–1914." *Journal of the Society for Army Historical Research* 59, no. 238 (1981): 82–94.

Stewart, Leslie. "Hythe and Its School of Musketry." *Cassel's Magazine* 27 (1904): 479–84.

Stirling, John. *Our Regiments in South Africa.* London: Blackwood, 1903.

Stone, Colonel F. G. "The Employment of Heavy Artillery in the Field." *Journal of the Royal Artillery* 35 (1908–1909): 1–27.

———. "The Heavy Artillery of a Field Army: A Comparison." *Journal of the Royal United Services Institute* 52, no. 2 (1908): 925–35.

Stone, Jay, and Erwin A. Schmidl. *The Boer War and Military Reforms.* Lanham, Md.: University Press of America, 1988.

Stone, Lieutenant Colonel F. G. "Army Training for Officers of the R.G.A." *Minutes of the Proceedings of the Royal Artillery Institution* 32 (1905–1906): 392–401.

Strachan, Hew. *European Armies and the Conduct of War.* London: George Allen, 1983.

Surridge, Keith. "'All you soldiers are what we call pro-Boer': The Military Critique of the South African War, 1899–1902." *History* 82, no. 268 (1997): 583–600.

Swanton, Major J.H. "Collective Practices." *Journal of the Royal United Services Institute* 44, no. 2 (1900): 922–27.

Swinton, E. *The Defence of Duffer's Drift: A Few Experiences in Field Defence for Detached Posts Which May Prove Useful in Our Next War.* London: Clowes, 1909.

Symons, Julian. *Buller's Campaign.* London: Cressent Press, 1963.

Takenouchii, Captain F. "The Tactical Employment of Machine Guns with Infantry in Attack and Defence." *Journal of the Royal United Services Institute* 51, no. 1 (1907): 450–57.

Teagarden, Ernest. *Haldane at the War Office: A Study in Organization and Management.* New York: Gordon Press, 1976.

Terraine, John. *Mons: The Retreat to Victory.* Reprint, Ware, U.K.: Wordsworth Editions, 2000.

Towle, Phillip. "The Influence of the Russo-Japanese War on British Military and Naval Thought 1904–1914." PhD diss., University of London, 1973.

Townshead, Major-General C. V. F. "The Strategical Employment of Cavalry." *Journal of the Royal United Services Institute* 56, no. 2 (1912): 1171–78.

Travers, Tim. "The Hidden Army: Structural Problems in the British Officer Corps, 1900–1918." *Journal of Contemporary History* 17 (1982): 522–44.

———. *The Killing Ground: The British Army, the Western Front and the Emergence of Modern War 1900–1918.* Barnsley, U.K.: Pen & Sword, 2003.

———. "The Offensive and the Problem of Innovation in British Military Thought 1870–1915." *Journal of Contemporary History* 13 (1978): 530–53.

———. "Technology, Tactics and Morale: Jean De Bloch, the Boer War and British Military Thought 1900–1914." *Journal of Military History* 51, no. 2 (1979): 264–86.

Trew, Peter. *The Boer War Generals.* Stroud, U.K.: Sutton, 1999.

Trimmel, Captain R. "South African Campaign." *Journal of the Royal United Services Institute* 45, no. 1 (1901): 182–190.

Tudor, Captain L. H. "Collective Fire." *Journal of the Royal United Services Institute* 56, no. 2 (1912): 1021–25.

Turner, Major-General Sir A. E. "Corps Manoeuvres of the German XIV. Army Corps 1903." *United Service Magazine,* March 1904, 606–36.

Tyler, J. E. *The British Army and the Continent 1904–1914.* London: Edward Arnold & Co., 1938.

United States War Department. "Strength and Organisation of the Armies of France, Germany and Japan." *Journal of the Royal United Services Institute* 56, no. 1 (1912): 193–208.

Van Creveld, M. *Technology and War: From 2000 B.C to the Present.* London: Collier Macmillian, 1989.

Van Emden, Richard, ed. *Tickled to Death to Go: Memoirs of a Cavalryman in the First World War.* Staplehurst, U.K.: Spellmount, 1996.

Van Heister, Carl. "The Orange Free State Artillery." *Journal of the Royal United Services Institute* 45, no. 1 (1901): 188–92.

Vaughan, Captain J. "Cavalry Notes–South Africa 1899–1900." *Journal of the Royal United Services Institute* 45, no. 1 (1901): 448–55.

Viljoen, Ben. *My Reminiscences of the Anglo-Boer War.* London: Douglas & Howard, 1903.

Vincent, Captain B. "Artillery in the Manchuria Campaign." *Journal of the Royal United Services Institute* 52, no. 1 (1908): 28–52.

Vincent, Colonel Sir C. E. Howard. "Lessons of the War: Personal Observations and Impressions of the Forces and Military Establishments Now in South Africa." *Journal of the Royal United Services Institute* 44, no. 1 (1900), 608–59.

———. "The Situation in South Africa: Further Personal Observations and Impressions." *Journal of the Royal United Services Institute* 46, no. 1 (1902): 141–204.

von Czerlieu, Major-General M. "The Lance as the Weapon of Cavalry." *Journal of the Royal United Services Institute* 47, no. 1 (1903): 39–47.

von der Goltz, General Baron Colmar. "What Can We Learn from the Boer War?" *Journal of the Royal United Services Institute* 46, no. 2 (1902): 1533–39.

von Kluck, Alexander. *The March on Paris and the Battle of the Marne 1914.* London: Edward Arnold, 1920.

von Lindeau, Lieutenant Colonel. "What Has the Boer War to Teach Us as Regards Infantry Attack?" *Journal of the Royal United Services Institute* 47, no. 1 (1903): 48–56, 186–95, 314–25, 443–49.

von Pelet-Narbonne, Lieutenant-General. "Primary Conditions for Success of Cavalry in the Next European War." *Journal of the Royal United Services Institute* 50, no. 1 (1906): 220–24, 326–34.

———. "The Roles of Cavalry in Modern War." *Journal of the Royal United Services Institute* 49, no. 1 (1905): 287–92.

von Swartz, A. B. "Some Field Fortifications Deductions from Port Arthur." *Royal Engineers Journal* 3 (1906): 32–49.

Wade, Captain H. A. L. H. "The Tactical Role of the Field Howitzer." *Minutes of the Proceedings of the Royal Artillery Institution* 31 (1904–1905): 409–420.

Wake, Brevet Major Hereward. "The Four Company Battalion in Battle." *Journal of the Royal United Services Institute* 59, no. 2 (1914): 362–77.

Walter, W. H. H., trans. *The German Official Account of the War in South Africa.* 2 vols. London: J. Murray, 1904–1906.

War Office. *Cavalry Training 1904 (Provisional).* London: H.M.S.O., 1904.

———. *Cavalry Training 1907.* London: H.M.S.O., 1907.

———. *Cavalry Training 1912.* London: H.M.S.O., 1912.

———. *Combined Training 1902.* London: H.M.S.O., 1902.

———. *Combined Training 1905.* London: H.M.S.O., 1905.

———. *Field Artillery Training 1904.* London: H.M.S.O., 1904.

———. *Field Artillery Training 1914.* London: H.M.S.O., 1914.

———. *Field Service Regulations Part 1: Operations 1909.* London: H.M.S.O., 1909.

———. *Infantry Training 1902.* London: H.M.S.O., 1902.

———. *Infantry Training 1905.* London: H.M.S.O., 1905.

———. *Infantry Training 1911.* London: H.M.S.O., 1911.

———. *Musketry Regulations 1909.* London: H.M.S.O., 1909.

Warwick, Peter, ed. *The South African War: The Anglo-Boer War 1899–1902.* Harlow, U.K.: Longman, 1980.

Webber, Major-General C. E. "Army Reform Based on Some 19th Century Lessons in Warfare." *Journal of the Royal United Services Institute* 45, no. 1 (1901): 388–414.

Weber, Captain W. H. F. "The Employment of Divisional Artillery." *Journal of the Royal United Services Institute* 54, no. 1 (1910): 355–63.

Weber, Major W. H. F. "A Plea for the Better Representation of the Artillery Arm at Manoeuvres." *Journal of the Royal United Services Institute* 59, no. 2 (1914): 248–52.

Wessels, Andre, ed. *Lord Roberts and the War in South Africa 1899–1902.* Stroud, U.K.: Army Records Society, 2000.

———. *The Phases of the Anglo-Boer War 1899–1902.* Bloemfontein, South Africa: War Museum of the Boer Republics, 1998.

Wing, Colonel F. D. V. "Cavalry and Horse Artillery." *Cavalry Journal* 3 (1908): 33–38.

———. "The Distribution and Supply of Ammunition on the Battlefield." *Journal of the Royal United Services Institute* 52, no. 2 (1908): 895–924.

Wood, Evelyn. *From Midshipman to Field Marshall* [*sic*]. Reprint, Uckfield, U.K.: Naval and Military Press, 2005.

Wynter, 2nd Lieutenant H. W. "Has the Experience of the War in South Africa Shown That Any Change Is Necessary in the System of Field Artillery Fire Tactics (In the Attack as Well as in Defence) in European Warfare?" *Minutes of the Proceedings of the Royal Artillery Institution* 29 (1902–1903): 266–78.

Wynter, Captain H. W. "Comparisons of British, French and German Methods of the Employment of Artillery in the Field." *Minutes of the Proceedings of the Royal Artillery Institution* 39 (1912–1913): 81–107.

Yale, Captain C. A. L. "Our Present Infantry Organisation: A Suggestion." *Journal of the Royal United Services Institute* 50, no. 2 (1906): 1043–47.

Zuber, Terrence. *The Mons Myth: A Reassessment of the Battle.* Stroud, U.K.: The History Press, 2010.

INDEX

CPSIA information can be obtained at www.ICGtesting.com
Printed in the USA
LVOW10s0408110913

351806LV00006B/14/P